Praise for *Career Match*

"This is the indispensable guide we've all been looking for. It takes all the guesswork out of trying to find the career path and job that's the best match for you. 'Bloom where you're planted' takes on a whole new meaning when you can choose your best soil!"

—Cynthia Shapiro, Job Search Consultant and author of
*Corporate Confidential: 50 Secrets Your Company Doesn't
Want You to Know—And What to Do About Them*

"People rise to leadership roles who work from their inner core strengths. I have seen this time and again in my Leadership Institute—this can make or break careers. *Career Match* is a great way to hone in on your own strengths, and start to focus on where they can take you."

—Dr. Yasmin Davidds, CEO, Latina Global
Executive Leadership Institute

"Fitness as a leader starts with fitness in one's career. *Career Match* is a terrific resource for tomorrow's leaders . . . and today's mentors."

—Carol J. Geffner, Ph.D., Professor and Director, Executive Master of
Leadership, Sol Price School of Public Policy, University of
Southern California; President, Newpoint Healthcare Advisors

"Shoya's assessment and book make 'climbing a ladder of success' easy and fun. Like a laser beam she goes to the heart of the issue—providing deep and insightful feedback, and tools that enable people to move forward."

—Marianna Lead, MCC, Master Certified Coach
with the International Coach Federation, and
Founder/Executive Director of the Goal Imagery® Institute

"The right career path will bring passion to your job and your life. Look inside yourself and discover the best fit for your unique personality type."

—Jim Donald, former President and
CEO, Starbucks Coffee Company

Career Match

Connecting Who You Are with What You'll Love to Do

Second Edition

SHOYA ZICHY

WITH ANN BIDOU

AMACOM AMERICAN MANAGEMENT ASSOCIATION

New York • Atlanta • Brussels • Chicago • Mexico City
San Francisco • Shanghai • Tokyo • Toronto • Washington, DC

Bulk discounts available. For details visit:
www.amacombooks.org/go/specialsales
Or contact special sales: Phone: 800-250-5308
Email: specialsls@amanet.org
View all the AMACOM titles at: www.amacombooks.org
American Management Association: www.amanet.org

Library of Congress data available upon request.

ISBN: 978-0-8144-3815-2
EISBN: 978-0-8144-3816-9

© 2017 Shoya Zichy
All rights reserved.
Printed in the United States of America.

About AMA
American Management Association (www.amanet.org) is a world leader in talent development, advancing the skills of individuals to drive business success. Our mission is to support the goals of individuals and organizations through a complete range of products and services, including classroom and virtual seminars, webcasts, webinars, podcasts, conferences, corporate and government solutions, business books, and research. AMA's approach to improving performance combines experiential learning—learning through doing—with opportunities for ongoing professional growth at every step of one's career journey.

10 9 8 7 6 5 4 3 2 1

CONTENTS

INTRODUCTION

Where It All Began

On a muggy night in May, I sat stranded in an Asian airport. It was the end of a long, overscheduled business trip—one of the many I took each year in the search for new banking clients. In the midst of a large pile of waiting room debris, I noticed a book. Dog eared and well used, it caught my attention. I picked it up, and my view of the world was altered forever.

"If a man does not keep pace with others, perhaps it is because he hears a different drummer," it began, with the oft-quoted Henry David Thoreau. The book, an obscure and since-discontinued interpretation of Swiss psychologist Carl Jung's theories, outlined the seemingly obvious differences in the way people take in information and make decisions. Some of this I knew intuitively. Yet the information hinted at a new way to deal with my clients and associates.

On returning to my Hong Kong office, I set out to color code each of my customers based on their Jungian behavioral profiles. Each client file contained brief instructions for support staff to follow in the event of my absence. "When a Gold comes in, make sure all statements are up to date and organized in date-sequential order. If a Blue makes an appointment, call our investment guys in New York and get three new ideas." And so it continued, outlining a strategy for each of four color groups.

It proved uncannily effective. Almost overnight, our new business increased by 60 percent. But there was more. I began to enjoy my clients more, my stress level went down, and, in time, my relationships with others outside of work began to improve.

For some ten years, I continued to use this technique. The bank sent me back to the United States, and the clients grew more diverse: white-robed sheiks in Abu Dhabi, shipping magnates in Athens, aristocratic landowners in Spain. But the same color-coding instructions dotted their files. What's more, they worked: for men, for women, old and young, widely varying ethnicities, the results were universal.

In that decade, I never met another individual who spoke of Jung, at least not in terms of applying his concepts to marketing. Then, in 1995, I joined some friends in Maine to escape from burnout and institutional reorganization. I needed to rethink my career.

The small Port Clyde Inn sparkled in the crisp October sunlight, and on the front porch sat a man reading a book. We began to chat and he spoke of the author Isabel Myers and her new applications for the work of Jung, a system called the Myers-Briggs Type Indicator.® It was the conversation I had been looking for.

Over the next few years, I discovered a hidden universe of books, seminars, and associations involving hundreds of people around the world. I had a new, strong sense of internal direction. Suddenly, things just began to happen; the right people and events began to materialize. Jung would have called it synchronicity.

It was a couple of years before I could undertake my own research, but eventually my life became focused on the business applications for personality styles. The material that follows sums up the information provided by the over 60,000 people who have attended Color Q seminars around the world and the personality-type experts who have laid the intellectual groundwork that serves as the basis of this book.

Evaluating people was key to survival during my unusual childhood. I was born a countess in Hungary. When my family fled the communists, we landed in the court of King Farouk of Egypt, where I played with his daughters in his 550-room palace. Seven years later, we fled the horrifying bloodshed of Gamal Abdel Nasser's revolution and were fortunate to find a new home in the United States.

I've turned what I learned through these many stages of my life into a system that helps all of us define our unique strengths, pursue the best career, and reduce conflicts in key areas of our lives.

For the sake of simplicity, I have adopted my own color-coding system of earlier times, which I call Color Q ("When you meet a Gold, make sure that . . ."). It served me well for many years, and it will serve you well, too. For further information, check out my website www.ColorQPersonalities.com.

The Purpose of This Book

Many of us share the fantasy that we can do anything and be anyone with just a little more effort. This is an illusion that blocks real development. Growth does not require significant change or that we emulate role models because we are somehow innately inadequate. It does require that we understand and accept the dynamics of our own genuine style—its unique strengths and weaknesses. It also means that in time, we tone down some of our blind spots.

There are many systems for understanding people. This is the one I have found that probes most deeply into the core of human behavior. It confirms that each personality style is natural, equal, observable, and predictable, and that each can be equally effective at work.

Truly exceptional people always do so much more than is required. The only way to do that without severe burnout is from passion born of confidence. You are the right person doing the right thing in the right place and enjoying it. Sound impossible? Not at all, for those who are true to themselves in spite of naysayers, parental expectations, and societal pressures. Use this book to reveal your road to being exceptional.

What Color Q Is Not

Color Q is not the answer to all career problems. It is not a painless shortcut to maturity and wisdom. Most of all, it does not measure the impact of education, intelligence, mental health, special talents, economic status, motivation, drive, or environmental influences on the core personality type. There are billions of unique people on our planet and only four Color groups. If you wonder what that leaves, I say only the deepest, most important part of you— the part that always knows what it really wants and won't be happy until it gets respect.

The framework is not gender specific. It works equally well for males and females. Men and women are found in each personality style, though in some groups the percentages differ.

Finally, Color Q is not a complete, in-depth Myers-Briggs evaluation. It is a ten-minute self assessment designed to acquaint you with concepts that are applicable to your career and personal life.

What Color Q Is

Color Q is about coding people—ourselves and others. We do it all the time. "He is shrewd and entrepreneurial." "She is energetic and artistic." This helps us to group our impressions mentally and store them in the appropriate synapse of our brain for future use.

Color Q is also a tool for understanding the sometimes incomprehensible behaviors of bosses and coworkers (and even friends, dates, and mates). Since so much career advancement depends on your people skills, you'll find your increased ability to read people perhaps the most valuable outcome of reading this book.

Enjoy this journey.

ACKNOWLEDGMENTS

I've been blessed to connect with so many people who share my passion for the study of personality differences. I am particularly grateful to the following:

- Peter and Katharine Myers, for continuing to support new applications of personality type.

- David Keirsey, whose book *Please Understand Me* started me on my journey, and Linda Berens, whose ongoing research continues to enrich our understanding of temperaments.

- Career development specialists who have focused on the connection between personality and careers, in particular Paula Cohen, Allen Hammer, Laura Hill, Donna Dunning, Charles Martin, and Hile Rutledge. My international licensees, Dr. Mobarak Aldosari of Saudi Arabia along with Andrea Fuks Ribeiro and Maria Tereza Vargas of Brazil, have provided valuable contributions in this area as well.

- The individuals profiled in the book and the thousands who have participated in my seminars. Your life stories have brought my model to life.

- Linda Konner, our agent, for seeing the potential of the manuscript and providing steadfast focus, support, and wisdom.

- The vibrant AMACOM team of Andrew Ambraziejus, Ellen Kadin, Barry Richardson, Ron Silverman, Irene Majuk, and Miranda Pennington for their professionalism and dedication to the publishing and marketing of this book.

- Our interns Emily Hennessey, Adiba Khan, and Kseniya Kosmina, for taking time out of their work and graduate studies to check resources and find new jobs of the future and marketing technologies.

- Russ Cohen (*russ@russcohen.com*) for his innovative cartoons.

- And last, but certainly not least, thanks to my family, Charles, Sheila, and Fiona, for always being the cheerleaders.

From Ann Bidou:

Premier thanks to Shoya Zichy for undertaking this effort once again, and for being such a brilliant expert and guide.

Deepest thanks to Emily Hennessey, Sabrina O'Brien, Daisy Torres, and Olivia Wadsworth, who did the grunt work in Toymakers Café so I could write.

And to our focus group members who helped us identify important trends, Paul Silverman and Anna Swarz.

Premier thanks to Ellen Kadin and Linda Konner, who kept a polite but persistent fire burning under us to undertake this task of updating.

And always, to Greg, my husband, thank you for your invaluable support, encouragement, and belief, for sure, for sure.

PEOPLE PROFILED

In Order of Appearance

GREENS: Carolyn Maloney, Democratic congresswoman from New York City; **Diane Sawyer**, television journalist; **Frank McCourt**, Pulitzer Prize-winning author; **Angelina Jolie**, actress and humanitarian; **Alexandra Lebenthal**, CEO, Lebenthal and Company; **Fiona Thompson**, human resources business partner, First Midwest Bank; **Adam Ozmer**, marketing executive, finance, New York Stock Exchange; **Lonnie Carter**, award-winning playwright; **Maggie Hoffman**, healthcare senior vice president of public relations; **Dr. Mobarak Aldosari**, owner, Almaarefa Educational Consulting; **Gloria Parker**, model, actress, and author; **Dan Shaw**, author and editor; **Anne Thayer**, conference planner.

REDS: Donald Trump, 45th president of the United States; **Christie Todd Whitman**, consultant and former governor of New Jersey; **Peter Tanous**, author and owner/investment consulting firm; **Laura Hill**, career coach/entrepreneur; **Bunny Williams**, high-end interior designer; **Alex Lee**, deputy chief, educational support team; **Gregory Bidou**, entrepreneur/restaurant and mail-order businesses; **Ria Davis**, Esq., general counsel chief compliance officer and newly appointed executive director, Financial Women's Association; **Howard Platt**, TV/film actor and producer; **Christopher L. Dutton**, president and CEO, Green Mountain Power.

BLUES: Hillary Rodham Clinton, former U.S. senator, secretary of state and Democratic presidential nominee in 2016; **Elon Musk**, innovator and entrepreneur; **Charles Schwab**, founder/chairman, Charles Schwab Corporation; **Rehana Farrell**, executive director, Youth INC.; **Michael Isaacs**, CEO, U.S. Balloon Company; **Kat Burke**, associate, major law firm; **Jeannette Hobson**, group chair and business advisor, Vistage International; **Larry**

Spencer, vice president, application development, ScerIS; **Joshua Stone**, music composer; **Deborah Finley-Troup**, vice president, human resources, Children's Village; **Charles M. "Chuck" Sheaff**, surgeon; **Chuck Wardell**, managing director, executive recruiting; **Jack Rubinstein**, small business advisor; **Bruce Terman**, Ph.D., medical research scientist; **Ari Levy**, hedge fund manager.

GOLDS: **Joan Shapiro Green**, board member; **Monica Lakhmana**, beauty queen, business owner, and philanthropist; **Betsy Howie**, author and playwright; **Mellody Hobson**, president, Ariel Capital Management; **Max Calder**, owner, Anytime Fitness Villanova; **Linda Konner**, literary agent; **Kathleen Waldron**, Ph.D., president, William Paterson University; **Sergio I. de Araujo**, investment and real estate advisor; **Martin Deeg**, chemical engineer and manufacturing company owner; **Frankie Lucostic**, corporate event planning executive; **Princess Fazilé Ibrahim**, philanthropist; **Laura Van Wie McGrory**, energy efficiency executive, Alliance to Save Energy; **Dr. Elizabeth Lucal**, obstetrician/gynecologist; **Martha Miller**, tax lawyer.

ENTREPRENEURS: **Trisha Rooney Alden and Phillip Rooney**, father/daughter entrepreneurial team, R4 Services; **Dianne Morris**, serial entrepreneur; **Nordahl Brue**, Bruegger's Bagels; **Sasha Fitzroy**, restaurant owner.

PART 1

THE JUMP START

Defining Yourself and Others

CHAPTER 1

Don't Read the Whole Book

THIS IS NOT YOUR typical career book. The Color Q system doesn't change people, but it does change how they view themselves. You will not be told to be more organized, to assert yourself, imitate your boss, or emulate some celebrity CEO. You will not even have to change how you dress. Instead, every word will move you to operate from your deepest, most natural talents, fueling the passion that separates good workers from great achievers. You just need to recognize your strengths and use them on a daily basis.

Sound easy? It's not. Most of us come loaded down with guilt and parental/societal expectations that push us in unnatural directions. Did pressures like money, prestige, educational opportunity, or family desires force you into making more "practical" choices? If doing so hasn't made you happy, then what will?

You need to get back to your core and make it work in the workplace. Define this core by taking the Color Q self assessment in chapter 2 and being bluntly honest. For many of you it will be career altering, if you answer as you really are. Please note that a preference is not "I generally work with piles, but I'd prefer if I kept my desk clean." What you actually *do* is what you prefer.

You do not need to read the whole book, unless you want to explore all sixteen Color Q personality types. Learning a little about other people's styles, however, will help you in:

» Job or promotion interviews

» Team projects

» Salary/contract negotiations

» Sales

» Boss/coworker conflicts

» Dates

» Family relations

The theory behind the Color Q system has been tested for decades on millions of people worldwide. It has changed lives and altered careers, including those of both authors of this book. If it changes your life, as we think it will, we'd like to know. Your story is as significant as the ones included in this book. Email me at *Zichy@earthlink.net* and check out my website at www.ColorQPersonalities.com.

CHAPTER 2

The Color Q Personality Style Self Assessment

Instructions: Part I

IN THE COLOR Q personality profiling system, you have a primary personality Color. This is who you are at your core. You also have a backup Color—a strong secondary influence. Finally, you have an Introvert or Extrovert tendency. Color Q describes people, for example, as Green/Red Introverts. This ten-minute either/or self assessment will reveal all three aspects of your personality.

Select one of the two choices in each line according to your first impulse, which is usually correct; but choose as you *are*, not as you would *like* to be. Don't overanalyze your choice. There are no right or wrong answers. Think of this like your left or right hand. While you can use both, you have a preference for one over the other, and you use that hand with less effort and better results. If you are truly torn between the two choices, it may mean you either feel guilty about your honest answer or feel pressured to function in a certain way.

First, fill out Section I, choosing what you (not your boss, mate, parents, or anyone else) prefer. Choose from column A or column B. Each A or B choice must be filled in by choosing the statement that describes you at least 51 percent of the time. **You should wind up with nine checkmarks total in this section.**

Section I

Be sure to answer every question. Total each column, and then follow the instructions to Sections II or III.

At least 51 percent of the time I tend to:

Column A		Column B
○ value accuracy more	**OR**	○ value insights more ✓
○ be interested in concrete issues	**OR**	○ be interested in abstract ideas ✓
○ prefer people who speak ✓ plainly	**OR**	○ prefer unusual ways of expression
○ remember many details ✓	**OR**	○ be vague about details
○ be down to earth	**OR**	○ be complex ✓
○ focus on the present	**OR**	○ focus on future ✓ possibilities
○ be valued for my ✓ common sense	**OR**	○ be valued for seeing new trends
○ be realistic and ✓ pragmatic	**OR**	○ be theoretical and imaginative
○ be trusting of facts ✓	**OR**	○ be trusting of my intuition

If you have chosen more items in Column A, please **go directly to Section III**.
If you have chosen more items in Column B, please **go directly to Section II**.

Section II

At least 51 percent of the time I tend to be more:

Column 1		Column 2
○ frank and direct	OR	○ tactful and diplomatic ✓
○ skeptical at first ✓	OR	○ accepting at first
○ won over by logic ✓	OR	○ won over by appeals to values
○ analytical ✓	OR	○ empathetic
○ apt to meet conflict head on	OR	○ apt to avoid conflict where possible ✓
○ interested in fairness	OR	○ sympathetic ✓
○ objective when criticized	OR	○ apt to take things personally ✓
○ impartial	OR	○ compassionate ✓
○ competitive	OR	○ supportive ✓

If you have chosen more items in Column 1, **you are a Blue.**

If you answered more items in Column 2, **you are a Green.**

Section III

At least 51 percent of the time I tend to:

Column @		Column #
○ meet deadlines early ✓	OR	◉ meet deadlines at the last minute
○ make detailed plans before ✓ I start	OR	◉ handle problems as they arise
○ be punctual and sometimes ✓ early	OR	◉ be leisurely, sometimes late
○ like to be scheduled	OR	◉ prefer to be ✓ spontaneous
◉ like clear guidelines ✓	OR	○ like flexibility
○ feel settled	OR	◉ feel restless ✓
○ have a tidy workplace	OR	◉ have a workplace with many piles/papers ✓
○ be deliberate ✓	OR	◉ be carefree
◉ like to make plans ✓	OR	○ like to wait and see

If you have chosen more items in Column @, **you are a Gold.**

If you answered more items in Column #, **you are a Red.**

Instructions: Part II

Now read the short overview of your primary Color below. Does it ring true? If yes, continue to part III to determine your backup style. If not, skip down to part V, "What to Do If This Doesn't Ring True for You."

Golds (46% of population)

Grounded, realistic, and accountable, Golds are the backbone of institutions of all kinds—corporate and public. They are society's protectors and administrators who value procedures, respect the chain of command, and have finely tuned systems for everything. From raising children to running large divisions, Golds get involved in details and are known for following through and mobilizing others to achieve concrete goals. They are most interested in making lists, planning in advance, and dealing with what has worked in the past.

Blues (10% of the population)

Theoretical, competitive, and always driven to acquire more knowledge and competence, Blues are unequaled when it comes to dealing with complex, theoretical issues and designing new systems. As natural skeptics, their first reaction is to criticize and set their benchmarks against which they measure everyone and everything. They are highly precise in thought and language, trusting only logic, not the rules or procedures of the past. Blues are future-oriented visionaries who do best in positions requiring strategic thinking. Then they move on with little interest in maintenance.

Reds (27% of the population)

Action-oriented, spontaneous, and focused on "now," Reds need freedom to follow their impulses, which they trust over the judgment of others. Cool headed and ever courageous, they get things done and handle a crisis better than most. Found in careers that provide freedom, action, variety, and the unexpected, they bring excitement and a sense of expediency. Work must be fun and the environment collegial for them. Reds resist schedules and hierarchies. Long-term planning is a low priority for them, as each day brings its own agenda.

Greens (17% of the population)

Creative, empathetic, and humanistic, Greens need an environment that is idea oriented and egalitarian and that provides the chance to impact the lives of others. Gifted in their understanding of people's motivations, they have an unusual ability to influence and draw the best out of others. They also excel in verbal and written communications and in the ability to position ideas. Greens are enthusiastic spokespersons for the organizations of their choice, and have a unique, charismatic quality that sweeps others into their causes.

Instructions: Part III

Now that you have determined your primary style, go back to the assessment and fill out the section you originally left out (Section II or III). This will provide you with your backup style. You should share about 40 to 50 percent of the characteristics of your backup style. The backup style refines your primary style.

If your primary is Gold or Red, your backup is either Blue or Green.

If your primary is Blue or Green, your backup is either Gold or Red.

My primary style is ___Red___. My backup style is ___Blue___.

Instructions: Part IV

From each pair of statements, choose one from the left or right column. You should wind up with seven checkmarks in this section.

At least 51 percent of the time I tend to:

Column (e)		Column (i)
✓ like to talk	**OR**	○ prefer to listen
✓ become bored when alone too much	**OR**	◉ need time alone to recharge batteries
✓ prefer to work in a group	**OR**	○ prefer to work alone or with one other person
◉ speak first—then reflect	**OR**	✓ reflect first—then speak
◉ be more interactive and and energetic	**OR**	○ be more reflective and thoughtful
✓ know a little about many topics	**OR**	◉ know a few topics in depth
◉ initiate conversations at social gatherings	**OR**	○ wait to be approached at social gatherings

If you answered more items on the left, **you are an Extrovert** (drawing energy from group activity).

If you answered more items on the right, **you are an Introvert** (drawing energy from your own inner resources).

Note your full style here:

Primary: _____Red_____

Backup: _____Blue_____

Extrovert or Introvert: _____Extrovert_____

Gold Green Introvert

More About the Extrovert and Introvert

Since the Extrovert/Introvert dimension is often misunderstood, it is worth explaining further. First of all, it appears to be biologically based and has nothing to do with liking people or being socially adept.

Extroverts (which Jung and the Myers-Briggs community spells "extraverts") get their energy from being with people and doing group activities. If they have to spend too much time alone or doing tasks that require solitude, they quickly become tired, bored, and dispirited. Introverts get energized from their inner resources, that is, spending time alone to recharge their internal batteries. Even if they like being with people, which most Introverts do, interacting too much can drain their energy.

The population divides fairly equally between Extroverts and Introverts, and many hide their natural preference well. An Introvert who needs to socialize for business can appear Extroverted to casual acquaintances. We all use both dimensions, but not at the same time. Also, as your score will indicate, you may be mild or pronounced in this dimension. Relationships between the two are often tense until this dimension is understood and valued.

Next Step

If your overview sounds right, read about your primary Color first: Greens in chapter 4, Reds in chapter 9, Blues in chapter 14, and Golds in chapter 19. Then read your individual chapter, which is one of the four immediately following your primary Color.

If you want to delve deeper, read about your backup Color. For skeptical Blues, reading chapter 3, "A Quick History of Personality Typing," might be your first stop so you don't feel you're wasting your time on an unproven methodology. Greens may want to skip straight to their individual chapter, and then into chapter 24, "Before I Do Something Stupid: Adjusting to Other Styles," to learn about other Colors. Golds will prefer to follow the recommendations above, and reading one chapter a day will allow you to absorb and review this material. Reds, we know the self assessment wasn't all that much fun, but your individual chapter will be. Go there now and skim it; you'll see it can be quite entertaining.

What to Do If This Doesn't Ring True for You: Part V

Your personality Color is simply who you really are when not pressured by family, friends, or work life. But if the majority of characteristics do not ring true, it is likely that you belong to another group.

Go back to the self assessment and check the section where you had close scores. Did you answer the way *others* need you to be? Or as you feel you *ought* (instead of prefer) to be? That creates false results. Choose the opposite column choice and follow instructions to a new Color. If that fits better, go up to Section III and continue.

Or, see if a family member or friend who knows you well agrees with your self assessment. You might be very surprised, as one lawyer was when her friend of thirty years corrected her answers to most of her self assessment. The lawyer didn't want to admit to her real preferences for piles on her desk and last-minute deadline rushes. Remember, we're not judging you here, or even suggesting that you need to change. And what you categorize as a weakness actually might be a strength—for example, the tendency to focus primarily on short rather than long term goals.

People are multifaceted. Though everyone has a predominant type, people may be one of several shades of that style. A person may be a strong Gold with a Blue backup. Another might be a light Gold and hence not as pronounced a Gold. Also, as you get older, you develop the nonpreferred parts of your personality and may appear less Gold than in younger years.

If you are going through catastrophic life changes or have been dissatisfied with your life for some time, scores can reflect your survival skills and not your real preferences. You may have "forgotten" your real preferences, although unhappiness is a signal that they're being denied. Try answering as if, right now, you lived in the world of your choice. If your personality Color still seems wrong, wait until things have stabilized and retest yourself.

CHAPTER 3

A Quick History of Personality Typing

CATEGORIZING PERSONALITIES into types—an activity called typology—has been embraced by major civilizations since ancient times. For more than twenty centuries, scientists and scholars have recognized that while individual people are unique, there are predictable patterns of human behavior. Around 400 BC, the Greeks, most notably Aristotle, Hippocrates, and Galen, believed human behaviors fell into four groups, or "humors": sanguine, melancholic, phlegmatic, and choleric.[1]

In the 1920s, the pioneering Swiss psychologist Carl Gustav Jung, who had been a favorite student of Sigmund Freud's, split away and developed his own typology.[2] According to Jung, human beings' four ways of intersecting with reality were thinking, feeling, sensation, and intuition, which he outlined in his book *Psychological Types*, published in 1921. He called these the four "functions."

Jung spent most of his life studying how people are similar and different. He concluded that certain inborn or early emerging preferences become the steadfast core of our likes and dislikes about other humans and the physical world. He further described each of these functions as being used in either the outer or inner world and hence in different ways, concluding that each person has one of eight mental processes as the most preferred or dominant.

Jung's theories were abstract. Fortunately, in the 1940s, a mother and daughter team began to provide a practical key to unlocking his work. These two U.S. women, Isabel Myers and her mother, Katharine Briggs, individually and together spent the next forty years testing Jung's ideas by observing the people around them. They quantified their observations, then rigorously tested and validated them. They created the most extensively tested personality typing system ever developed, the Myers-Briggs Type Indicator® (MBTI®) inventory,[3] which to date has been administered to millions of people around the world.

In the 1950s, another typology enthusiast, David Keirsey, did work that overlaid the Greek humors onto the Jungian/Myers-Briggs types. In his book *Please Understand Me*, he outlined four temperament groups, which serve as the basis of the Color Q model in this book. Since then, his work has been expanded by his longtime student Linda Berens, who continues to provide a rich array of new insights.

Today, work on the MBTI is continued by the next generation, Peter and Katharine Myers, co-owners of the MBTI copyrights.

"The Jungian model is an excellent nonthreatening tool for developing career goals," said Katharine Myers in a recent interview. "Extensive research shows that certain types more than others are drawn to each career. However, since every type is found in every field, no one should be told not to go into any specific career. If an individual is strongly drawn to a profession, he or she needs to be clear on the tasks inherent in the job and then evaluate what their skills will contribute." It is not uncommon for people to create special niches in areas dominated by other types.

Myers is a Green, as defined in chapter 4. And like many in her group, she excels at fostering the growth of others.

Meanwhile, modern brain imaging technology has validated many of the MBTI's theories by showing how chemicals and activity in different parts of the brain impact behavior. Most importantly, it has been demonstrated that Jung was indeed correct. While each person is unique, a part of that person— a core, if you will—is solid and steady. It is that core that the MBTI, and the Color Q system, define and apply to a multitude of life issues.

I developed Color Q as a quick introduction to the concepts of personality typing. When running team-building and leadership seminars for my corporate clients like the U.S. Treasury, Bank of America, Northern Trust, Merrill Lynch, the Government of Pennsylvania Leadership Institute, UBS, and Prudential Insurance, among others, I also asked participants to fill out an investment questionnaire. From this pool of knowledge emerged the Money Q profiles, which explain how different personality types approach money and compensation. Several results of this proprietary research are presented in chapter 26, which sheds light on how individuals approach the financial negotiation aspects of their job search.

PART 2

GREENS

"Let's Humanize It"

Greens thrive in a work environment that supports personal development and feels like an extended family.

CHAPTER 4

Greens Overall

GREENS REPRESENT approximately 17 percent of the overall world population. If you are not a Green but would like to learn how to identify and communicate with one, go to figure 4–1.

FIGURE 4–1 **How to Recognize a Green**

- ○ Big-picture thinker
- ○ Informal and warm
- ○ Unusual ability to influence by persuasion
- ○ Bridge builder; resolves conflicting views
- ○ Draws the best out of people
- ○ Verbally fluent and metaphoric
- ○ Intent listener
- ○ Sensitive to criticism
- ○ Avoids confrontation
- ○ Chic, flamboyant, or careless dress

How to Communicate with a Green

○ Pick a harmonious environment for meetings

○ Personalize the relationship—ask about family, hobbies, and pets

○ Listen empathetically

○ Encourage creative freedom and input

○ Expect nonsequential discussions that eventually return to the main point

○ Stress any opportunity for personal growth

○ Stress solutions that are innovative and future oriented

○ Use inspiring and positive phrases

○ Limit mundane support facts

○ Eliminate conflict and competitiveness; be collaborative

○ Give all feedback diplomatically

Congresswoman Carolyn Maloney

Congresswoman Carolyn Maloney understands that leadership and success come from first mastering the issues, cultivating alliances, and then mustering all your resources. For nine terms she has represented the 12th district of New York City in the U.S. House of Representatives. In 2015, the nonpartisan website Govtrack.us ranked her as the number one Democrat in the House for leadership and the number two member in Congress for the number of cosponsors her bills and resolutions attracted. She was the first woman to chair the Joint Economic Committee and is a nationally recognized leader in the fields of economic policy, financial services, national security, and women's issues. She was the powerhouse behind the landmark credit card reform legislation that an independent study found saves consumers $12 billion annually.[1]

"I have learned how to pull together bipartisan support, and that has really been the key in passing many important bills that people thought could never overcome the opposition of special interests," says Maloney, demonstrating the Green/Red's dynamic initiation and ability to persuade. Her alliance with Republican Marcia Blackburn of Tennessee to pass a bill aimed at establishing a National Women's History Museum is one good example of her ability to reach across the aisle, find areas of agreement, and build alliances. In one session alone, she introduced over seventy pieces of legislation, tying the record for the most from any legislator.

Her tireless efforts over the course of a decade led to the passage of a bill that provided badly needed healthcare for New York's ailing 9/11 first responders. Her dogged perseverance won her plaudits and admiration around the world. "If you believe passionately in and understand fully the importance of the goal," says Maloney, "it's not work. And no obstacle can withstand the unwavering determination of a united people committed to a just cause." She is also proud of having helped draft the Anti-Terrorism Intelligence Report Act, which changed the structure of the U.S. intelligence system.

Along with being a national leader on many issues, she is primarily driven by her deep concern for her New York constituents. Maloney secured critical federal funding for the badly needed Second Avenue subway, the largest infrastructure project in the country. And she recently prevented the closing of a veteran's hospital on Twenty-Third Street. "Sometimes, it's not what you do, it's what you stop," she said in 2012.[2] Her efforts to keep post offices open and fund schools in her district have been decidedly Green endeavors. She is currently leading an effort to secure two giant pandas from China for a New York City zoo, to not only bring delight to millions of children but to engage people in thoughtful conversations on a wide variety of environmental issues.

She also has a feisty Red side, and her opponents know she is no easy target. A strong proponent of women's rights, she was a chief sponsor of the Equal Rights Amendment and author of the Debbie Smith Act that funds the processing of DNA evidence in sexual assault cases. She has stood firm against right-wing efforts to roll back the historic gains of women. And when Rep. Darrell Issa, a Republican from California, chaired a religious-freedom and birth-control panel with no female witnesses, Maloney rocked the hearing with her simple question: "Where are the women?" A picture of the all-male panel of witnesses along with her question appeared in news outlets all over the country the next day. Her response to conflict is typical of a Green/Red Extrovert: "I deal with it in steps. A lot of it is educating people, and listening to all points of view, to see if there is a way to move forward together. I encourage people to try more listening. It really works."

News Personality Diane Sawyer

Before stepping down from her anchor position to spend time with her husband, Mike Nichols, in his final days, ABC News television journalist Diane

Sawyer was one the best-known Greens in the United States. She epitomizes many of the group's artistic and interpersonal skills.

In high school she won the U.S. Junior Miss pageant and after college moved to Washington, DC, to serve as assistant to Richard Nixon's White House press secretary, Ron Ziegler.

In 1978, she took a job with CBS, but Dan Rather and other senior figures were vocal about the presence of someone tainted by Watergate. She ultimately won over her colleagues with her incredible stamina, spending a week at the State Department during the Iranian hostage crisis, sleeping no more than an hour a day. They also were disarmed by her typical Green charm and ability to let her ego go for the sake of the story.

Working with, instead of against, her natural Green core traits led to a string of successes. In 1981, she was promoted to the *CBS Morning News Show*; in 1984 she became the first female correspondent on the prestigious *60 Minutes*. Greens are among the most intuitive of all the Color types. In 1989, Sawyer jumped to ABC to coanchor the news magazine *Prime Time Live*, which became *20/20*. As of this writing, she has begun to make special appearances, such as hosting the live broadcast of *The Sound of Music* and doing the last interview with Caitlyn Jenner prior to her transition in April 2016.

Diane Sawyer evinces the typical polarities of the Green personality: the ability to be earnest and irreverent, intense and funny, authoritative and vulnerable. True to her type, she is both intensely private and genuinely interested in people.

The people in Sawyer's group, the Greens, need opportunities to use their creativity and to impact the lives of others. They excel in verbal and written communications and are heavily represented among writers, TV anchors, and biographers. In corporate settings, they excel in sales, marketing, and public relations. Whatever the work setting, they thrive when their uniqueness is recognized. Harmony and authenticity bring out a Green's best.

Pulitzer Prize winner Frank McCourt, author of *Angela's Ashes*, *'Tis*, and *Teacher Man*, expressed Green characteristics through his teaching and writings. For thirty years he taught high school English in New York City. Defying established guidelines, he turned his own poverty-soaked background in the slums of Ireland into a valuable lesson plan. Without losing his humor or sense of compassion, he described the fleas in his mattress; the smell of one toilet shared by an entire street; and the foibles of his alcoholic father and depressed mother. In so doing, he formed a powerful bond with his students.

Greens often are found at the forefront of human-interest causes. Actress Angelina Jolie is special envoy to the United Nations High Commissioner for Refugees. She has traveled worldwide in her role as spokesperson for war-traumatized children and refugees. While it is not unusual for celebrities to adopt humanitarian causes, the kind of fervor and commitment Jolie brings to hers is.

She is known for her work on the ground, making some forty field missions for her refugee work alone in addition to multimillion-dollar relief donations.[3] She was recognized in 2005 with the United Nations Global Humanitarian Action Award. She has received an honorary damehood from the Order of St. Michael and St. George, as well as the 2013 Jean Hersholt Humanitarian Award, given by the Academy of Motion Picture Arts and Sciences. Jolie made repeated headlines with her three adoptions of children from impoverished overseas circumstances. In a 2016 visit to a refugee camp in Jordan during which she noticed the large percentage of children in residence, Jolie said that "like any other parent, it would be impossible for me to imagine what it would be like for my own children in this situation. And it breaks my heart."[4] Jolie's numerous causes and the large amount of time she devotes to them are excellent examples of the Green personality's focus on the needs and feelings of others. Whether in her personal or public life, her empathetic efforts to help others are notable for their consistency and authenticity.

Making a difference in the world is paramount for the Green personality.

Other famous Greens in the news and entertainment world are singer Adele, Oprah Winfrey, Jennifer Aniston, Sandra Bullock, Katie Couric, and Jane Fonda. Barack Obama, Mahatma Gandhi, Mikhail Gorbachev, and Eleanor Roosevelt illustrate the Green leadership style in politics; Arianna Huffington, co-founder of The Huffington Post, she is also a Green. Ralph Waldo Emerson was a well-known Green writer and so is J. K. Rowling. Abraham Maslow was a Green psychologist. Pope John Paul XXIII and Mother Teresa were prominent Greens in the religious field, as is Pope Francis.

This chapter will help you determine if you've tested your primary and backup personality Colors correctly. It also will help you identify Greens among people you know, as will chapter 24, "Before I Do Something Stupid: Adjusting to Other Styles."

If the self assessment at the beginning of the book has scored you as a Green, you are brilliant with people and communications issues. More than the other three Colors, you will enjoy this book because it will help you learn even more about people. You are likely to Color code everyone you know and test the tips supplied here for communicating with them.

Of all the Colors, your skills are more often (unfairly) considered "soft." This book will show how they can be put to economic advantage. Your highly developed marketing abilities make you a top choice for creating lasting product brands. Your people skills calm turbulent teams and departments in record time. Staff turnover can be staunched by putting a Green in charge; productivity spikes when a Green is in charge of a team.

Go to your specific profile now to discover your most natural path to professional satisfaction and success.

CHAPTER 5

Green/Gold Extroverts

YOU'RE NOT ONLY a Green, you also have strong secondary characteristics of the Gold personality. And you have tested as a Color Q Extrovert, which means you recharge your batteries by being with others, rather than being alone. You are compassionate, persuasive, loyal, and have a talent for predicting future trends.

You Overall

You are outgoing, sociable, warm, and articulate. Green/Gold Extroverts are gifted communicators with an unusual ability to influence. Those you admire receive your deep loyalty. In return, you expect equal appreciation. This can lead to frustration and disappointment.

You have an abundance of innate emotional intelligence and interact well with most Color types. You operate best in harmonious groups. Driven by intuition, foresight, and compassion, you excel at leading others to achieve their potential. You are exceptionally skilled at projecting the trends and pitfalls of the future.

People who are rude or bully others are a major irritant. You respond well to praise but are easily hurt by criticism. This makes you appear touchy, as even the most well-intentioned criticism may fluster you. Actual conflict disturbs you (except when standing up to rude bullies, which you do with steely strength).

You are enthusiastic, with the energy to work on several projects at once. Decisive and often in a hurry, you can be more than a little impatient with anyone who slows you down. While it is your nature to be supportive, you can be both critical and confrontational when your standards are not being met.

Your interest in others is so strong that you run the risk of not giving enough time to yourself. In both personal and professional relationships, you make others feel valued and liked.

CASE STUDY ONE

Financial Executive

Alexandra Lebenthal, CEO of Lebenthal and Company, comes from a storied Wall Street family. Her grandparents, Louis and Sayra Lebenthal, founded Lebenthal & Co., Inc., in 1925. Alexandra joined Lebenthal in 1988 and became president and CEO in 1995—at age 31, the youngest-ever female president of a brokerage firm.

Despite an earlier interest in becoming an actress (a career attractive to Greens), Alexandra allowed herself to be groomed by her grandmother to take over the family business. Upon doing so, she received high marks from her Wall Street peers, particularly for the quality of her advertising and brand positioning. Green/Golds are creative abstract thinkers and gifted at positioning products and ideas. Alexandra says, "We came up with a commercial line that announced, 'I have a mission to make you a customer for life, and all I have to do is put your needs first.'" Treating clients like members of the family differentiated her firm's client service and satisfied Alexandra's Green side.

Her natural Green/Gold ability to predict future trends alerted Alexandra to new product offerings that kept Lebenthal and Company strong, profitable, and ultimately marketable. It sold to Advest Group in 2001 for $25 million. In 2005, Merrill Lynch acquired Advest and laid the Lebenthal name to rest. Alexandra's noncompete clause expired in mid-2006, and she resurrected the family firm in 2007.

When heading a firm, she embodies the typical democratic management style of her Color. "I want the people who report to me to feel that they are a meaningful part of shaping the company," she says, "and shaping me as a leader." A passionate supporter of women in business, she was named one of the top fifty Women in Wealth Management by *Wealth Manager Magazine*.[1] She has also been named to *Crain's* New York Top Women Owned Businesses[2] and *Crain's* Fastest 50 Growing Businesses[3] in New York.

Greens are often drawn to writing, and Alexandra published her first novel, *Recessionistas*, in August 2010, which sold to Sony Television. As one of the most recognizable women on Wall Street, she is an official CNBC contributor and frequent commentator in the media.

CASE STUDY TWO

Human Resources Business Partner

Fiona Thompson is an approachable young woman whose intelligent eyes communicate her interest in you almost immediately. She is also an excellent example of how a Green's supposedly "soft" interpersonal skills can save a company a lot of money. Fiona is a human resources business partner for First Midwest Bank, a fast-growing, Chicago-based, community-focused bank with over one hundred branches in three states.

One of the biggest assets a company possesses (particularly a larger, publicly traded one like First Midwest) is its workforce. It also can be one of its most economically draining if mishandled. Fiona partners with senior management to develop and deploy all aspects of effective workforce planning, including employee development and handling complex employee relations investigations. Fiona says, "I especially enjoy advising and coaching managers on employee relations matters such as succession planning, performance concerns, and engagement issues."

While her high emotional intelligence benefits her company by minimizing employee turnover and reducing, Fiona also sees a downside. "Sometimes I am too empathetic and struggle when balancing the needs of the business and employees," she says. The added value of her unique interpersonal skills really offsets this, however. "I love engaging with people—listening to employee feedback and acting as quarterback in pulling people from different departments to collaborate on new solutions to problems." This keeps her motivated to handle her role's many intricacies.

When employee interactions involve conflict or having to give constructive feedback, Fiona has learned to wall off her natural Green sensitivity. "I alter my communication style to be more in tune with the other's personality," she says. (Greens do this naturally and easily.) It's the walling-off effort that requires more energy and discipline on her part, as it goes against a Green's nature (but would be easy for a Blue).

At her previous job with the Urban Land Institute in Washington, DC, Fiona "helped open up offices in foreign countries, which required learning about human resources practices that differed significantly from those in the United States." She hopes to continue traveling the world for business advancement and pleasure. Extroverted Green Fiona thrives on meeting and interacting with new people.

She likes to throttle down in her private time, however. "I read or listen to music to provide some quiet time to balance all the human interaction of my day."

Overall, Fiona is in a position that suits her very well. "I like feeling that my job matters," she says. "That I have, in a small way, made the lives of our employees better, so they are more productive in advancing our company's mission."

CASE STUDY THREE

Marketing Executive, Finance

Adam Ozmer is an effective Green in a corporate America predominantly run by Golds and Blues. He has turned his innate visionary ability into a career as head of marketing for the New York Stock Exchange, governance services.

"I work with a team to devise strategy and execution plans to market products to compliance officers and boards of directors," Adam explains. "We develop messaging, advertising, strategic partnerships, campaigns, and sales enablement with the intent of driving significant growth in our business."

In college, Adam aspired to be a magazine editor but diverted from that course during his senior year. "I interned at Christie's Auction House in New York, and they placed me in the marketing department," he says. "I really loved it, and the experience started me down a different road."

His first job was in the advertising department of Circuit City Corporate as an assistant media buyer. Advertising-agency, corporate-marketing, and branding stints followed. "I have experience across both business-to-business marketing and business-to-consumer marketing . . . with the heaviest concentration in marketing professional and financial services products," Adam says. Here his Green visionary capabilities work well. "I'm very strong on looking at the big picture and devising a plan forward. Ideating what something might look like in its end state is a joy for me," Adam says.

Although he can effectively venture into the Red's technology territory, he is less comfortable. "I tend to involve myself in the early stages of figuring out technology needs and specifications but remove myself from the middle stages of working through the gritty stuff," he says. "In sorting out the minute details, I can either become completely absorbed and obsessed with working through each one . . . or I can gloss over details in my drive to get to the end state." This is a classic Green/Gold conflict; he values colleagues who help him stay on track.

Adam hits his stride when projects demand imagination and innovation. "I love the creative side of my job; starting with a blank page and figuring out what to do." When he starts new departments, "There's tremendous freedom in creating your own process and establishing something new."

Adam recharges by doing simple physical activities that provide a mental break from technology and routine, like walking his dog or working around his 1830s Connecticut weekend house.

But the Green artistic soul in Adam yearns for greater expression than the corporate milieu provides. "I have always had a strong desire to work in a more creative field . . . outside of corporate America," he says. "I can't articulate what that job looks like or sounds like, but it's simpler and more artistically focused. I think (hope) I'll know it when I see it . . . one day."

You on the Job

AS A LEADER

A people-centered, idealistic vision drives your enthusiastic style. You respect the needs and opinions of staff at all levels, influencing with persuasion rather than control. Consensus and cooperation are your goals. You provide your people sensitive and appropriate support through personal difficulties.

Your Gold side introduces structure and organization and initiates action. You are usually upbeat, accepting setbacks as new challenges rather than defeats.

AS A TEAM PLAYER

If a team is stalled by interpersonal conflict, you are the bridge builder. Others understand that you merely want to achieve stated objectives. Rather than being dictatorial, you energize the team with enthusiasm and a warm sense of humor. You inspire former combatants to their best combined efforts. Because you are focused and results oriented, it's rare that your team misses a deadline.

Look at figure 5–1 for a list of your natural work-related strengths.

FIGURE 5–1 *Natural Work-Related Strengths*

Approximately 80 percent of these attributes will apply to you. Check off those that do, and use them in your resume and interviews. This will set you apart from the canned responses of others. You:

- ○ Excite others with high-quality ideas and enthusiasm

- ○ Organize people and resources

- ○ Build morale, loyalty, and productivity

- ○ Mentor others well, exponentially increasing your value to the firm

- ○ Create harmonious teams; turn around troubled departments

- ○ Think creatively; see future trends

Now see how another Green/Gold Extrovert uses his strengths in a very different field.

Ideal Work Environment

Alexandra and Fiona each gravitated to environments where they have control of products or services that contribute in some way to the well-being of society. These are key elements of Green/Gold Extrovert satisfaction.

When a job offer is made, leverage as much as you can from the list in figure 5–2.

FIGURE 5–2 *The Ideal Green/Gold Extrovert Work Environment*

Compare your current work environment to the descriptions below. If these descriptions seem obvious, that confirms you've tested your Color correctly. Other Colors, especially Golds, would find this environment uncomfortable and unproductive. The optimal Green/Gold Extrovert work environment:

- ○ Is harmonious, with people who can be trusted. Backbiting and internal competition are discouraged and viewed as unproductive.

○ Has strong values that align with your own. Its mission is to produce products and services that contribute to the well-being of society.

○ Makes good use of your well-developed organizational skills. Your projects draw on your people, communications, and organizational skills simultaneously.

○ Allows responsibility for one's own projects. You see a big picture and possess the ability to excite others about it. When you work too long on someone else's project, his or her constraints may leave you feeling frustrated and unfulfilled.

○ Provides ongoing new learning experiences. You're enthused by assignments that publicize new products or services, learn or teach new technologies, create promotional strategies, discover new markets, or require continuing education.

The worst type of work culture for an Extroverted Green/Gold is tense, overly competitive, and highly political. It is secretive about critical information, rewarding power plays over productivity. The atmosphere is impersonal among management, staff, and coworkers. The company compromises your core values; it exploits its workers and its customers.

While Green/Gold Extroverts can progress in such corporate cultures, your interpersonal talents usually must remain low-key in order to survive. Productivity and accomplishment are stunted, and career achievements become an uphill climb.

The Extroverted Green/Gold's Ideal Boss

Even a great job can be frustrating under the wrong boss; a mediocre job under a great boss is pretty hard to leave. Green/Golds get on especially well with other Greens. But bosses of the Color types who possess the skills in figure 5–3 also can be good mentors.

FIGURE 5-3 *The Green/Gold Extrovert's Ideal Boss*

Check off if your boss:

○ Is insightful

○ Asks you about your vision for the project, the company, or your career

○ Gives positive feedback and stresses areas where he or she agrees with you

○ Is organized and delivers on commitments—a good role model

○ Shares the same values of improving the world

Careers That Attract Green/Gold Extroverts

As our case studies illustrate, you have deep personal values and care about the needs of others (on the Green side) and value organization (on the Gold side).

Please note that not all the following careers will appeal to you, but recognize that each, in some way, draws on the strengths of your style and appeals to a significant number of your Color group. This is not a comprehensive list, but it will show underlying patterns of preference. If unlisted careers offer similar patterns, your chances of success increase. Text in parentheses at the end of each section highlights the Color-style characteristics that create success in that broad area.

According to our research, jobs italicized in the lists below are predicted to benefit from an above-average growth rate over the next several years. This information is based on the continuously revised data provided by the U.S. Department of Labor and Bureau of Labor Statistics on their websites O*NET OnLine (www.onetonline.org) and http://www.bls.gov/CAREER-OUTLOOK/. There you will find in-depth information about job requirements and salary ranges.

There are successful people of all Color styles in all occupations. In non-ideal jobs, you can still shine by creating your own niche.

ARTS/COMMUNICATIONS/PROMOTION

art director ▸ book and magazine editor ▸ *curator* ▸ digital media planner ▸ fine artist ▸ graphic artist/designer/animator ▸ interior decorator ▸ journalist/writer ▸ librarian ▸ literary agent ▸ merchandise displayer ▸ *multimedia specialist* ▸ museum director ▸ *public relations director/specialist* ▸ set/costume/exhibit designer ▸ TV and film director/producer ▸ TV/stage producer/newscaster ▸ *website editor/graphic designer* (involvement with media, superior language skills, communication through graphic presentation, abililty to manage the corporate image)

BUSINESS/MANAGEMENT

advertising account executive/sales manager ▶ *communications director* ▶ *corporate outplacement consultant* ▶ *corporate trainer* ▶ *customer sales representative* ▶ *development specialist* ▶ family business owner/executive ▶ *group sales manager* ▶ *hotel manager* ▶ *human resources specialist/trainer* ▶ industrial psychologist ▶ labor relations manager ▶ *marketing specialist/manager* (ideas and services) ▶ *meeting/event planner* ▶ recruiter/employment interviewer ▶ *translator* ▶ *urban/regional planner* (foster relationships essential for company productivity, develop colleagues, use communication and facilitation skills)

EDUCATION

bilingual education teacher ▶ career/guidance counselor ▶ *college professor (humanities)* ▶ *curriculum developer* ▶ *educational administrator* ▶ *online educator* ▶ *school psychologist* ▶ *social worker* ▶ *teacher* (all levels: *art, drama, English, humanities, languages, special education*) (helping others reach their potential, patient one-on-one influencing)

HEALTH SCIENCE/PSYCHOLOGY

alternative (holistic) healthcare practitioner ▶ *assisted living facilities manager* ▶ *audiologist* ▶ *clinical psychologist/psychiatrist* ▶ dental hygienist ▶ *dietician/nutritionist* ▶ *elder care specialist* ▶ *general practitioner* ▶ *genetic counselor* ▶ *hearing aid specialist* ▶ home health aide ▶ *internist/medical researcher* ▶ *mental health counselor (marriage, occupational, substance abuse)* ▶ *nurse practitioner* ▶ *optometrist* ▶ *pediatrician* ▶ *physical therapist* ▶ *physician assistant* ▶ *public health educator* ▶ *speech pathologist* ▶ *veterinarian* (environment congruent with values, insights into others, see new ways to solve problems, patient one-on-one influencing)

LAW

lawyer (children, communication and media, domestic relations, environmental, intellectual property, trust and estates) ▶ *mediator* (understanding of human motivation)

SOCIAL SERVICES

child care specialist ▶ child welfare specialist ▶ *coach* (business, life) ▶ *counselor* (career, child welfare, outplacement, pastoral, substance abuse) ▶ *director child care center* ▶ fund-raiser/institutional solicitor ▶ philanthropic director/consultant ▶ *religious leader/educator* ▶ *senior care director/specialist* ▶ social worker/community services manager (need for good organizational skills, goal setting, using all resources, helping people who need it, work congruent with your values, improving the world)

DIGITAL/HIGH TECH

customer relations manager ▸ *human resources recruiter* ▸ *social media manager* ▸ technology consultant to internal staff (excel at connecting technology people with staff and clients)

CASE STUDY FOUR

When a Career Isn't Working

Buddy Coleman (a composite of the author's clients) sold insurance for fifteen years for a leading company. He really enjoyed dealing with customers and took pride that he was helping them shape their futures in positive ways.

After fifteen years, this was no longer enough. The amount of paperwork had increased over the years, something that Green/Gold Extroverts find suffocating. Dealing with concrete events and practical rules-based questions had burned him out. He craved something (anything!) that would engage his Green/Gold's preferred focus on the big picture.

At a meeting of his professional insurance sales organization, he was intrigued to hear that the long-time director was retiring and a search was on to replace her. Buddy immediately expressed his interest to an attending board member and was strongly encouraged to submit a resume. Today, he directs the efforts of twelve volunteers and flexes his Green/Gold creativity writing a monthly "Future Trends" column for the organization's glossy newsletter. He has increased the number of membership events by 50 percent and attends each one, providing the people contact that this Green/Gold always enjoyed.

Your Personality's Challenges

Green/Gold Extroverts have a unique set of potential work-related blind spots. Some listed below you have, others you don't. Tone down a blind spot by focusing on it, then choose more-productive actions and make them habits. (Suggestions for doing so are in parentheses below.) You:

▸ Avoid conflicts and confrontations. (You take conflict and criticism very personally and protect yourself by avoidance. Instead, face it. Build a thicker skin by repeated exposure, on your terms.)

‣ Tend not to recognize underperforming workers or manipulative friends/relatives. (Don't shove aside that little alarm bell inside. Memorize this phrase and speak up immediately: "I see you [are/are not] doing X. I want to say something now so you don't think I'm OK with this going forward.")

‣ Base important decisions too much on likes and dislikes and not enough on facts, figures, and research. (Guide yourself by your likes and dislikes, but force yourself to assemble a few facts and figures. See what happens when you consider this new input.)

‣ Can irritate others by being moralistic. (Practice saying: "And now, I'll get off my soapbox! But do you agree? How would you handle it?")

Your Job Search—the Good, the Bad, and the Ugly

Green/Gold Extroverts have outstanding people skills. Many interviewers are Greens, with whom you'll feel an immediate rapport. But with interviewers of other Colors, you need to rehearse different communications styles.

Your natural strengths easily allow you to:

‣ Organize and execute a comprehensive job-search campaign

‣ Network widely to get leads

‣ Impress your interviewer with your verbal skills and confidence

‣ Project your past experience into new fields or functions

In order to avoid your blind spots, you need to:

‣ Thoroughly check out the facts about a position rather than rely on intuition

‣ Slow down in making decisions until there has been sufficient reflection

‣ Not take rejection personally

‣ Not be too accommodating in discussing your compensation package. Treat the process as a chess game to increase respect and compensation

The Green/Gold Extrovert's Interviewing Style

You'll feel immediate rapport with an interviewer whose Color is close to your own. However, if your interviewer seems to have a significantly different style, use the suggestions in the parentheses below.

In following your natural style, you will:

- Express yourself with warmth and passion. (Tone it down with a cooler type of interviewer.)

- Stress the big picture first and place less emphasis on the details of your experience and goals. (Some interviewers prefer sequential or chronological presentations. If so, avoid brainstorming and metaphoric language.)

- Try to personalize the relationship as quickly as possible. (If you are greeted coolly and the interviewer seems analyzing and detached, be formal. Focus only on answering the questions succinctly.)

- Avoid subjects that cause conflict. (Rehearse difficult questions ahead of time, such as: Why did you leave your last job? What are your weaknesses? What would your former boss say about you? Do you have budgeting skills?)

- Have trouble negotiating salary and other financial issues. (Research comparable pay and standard benefits. If you have a strong resume, don't hesitate to ask for more, saying, "With my qualifications, I'm expecting X." If they still lowball you, leave. You'll respect yourself, and you may get a counteroffer.)

- Think on your feet and respond quickly; talk more than listen. (Active listening is essential to understand the interviewer's priorities. Prepare a list of questions important to you, and listen closely to the answers.)

Okay, go do something with friends or family now. Later, check out chapter 19, "Golds Overall," to learn about the strengths of your secondary Color. Read chapter 24, "Before I Do Something Stupid: Adjusting to Other Styles," to learn how to recognize the Colors who can best assist you.

CHAPTER 6

Green/Gold Introverts

YOU'RE NOT ONLY a Green, you also have strong secondary characteristics of the Gold personality. And you have tested as a Color Q Introvert, which means you recharge your batteries by being alone rather than being with people. Your Color group's members are a curious combination of warmth and reserve. Sharing primarily with those closest to you, you don't reveal much to others until trust is established. You have deep insights into people and enjoy helping them grow. Although an idealist, you also are good at organizing and following through on projects.

You Overall

Intuition, foresight, and compassion drive Green/Gold Introverts, who excel at understanding and motivating others to achieve their greatest potential. You have a deep need for empathetic relationships, but your intimate group is small. Appearing cool and detached outwardly, you harbor strong feelings about your loved ones and your values. When those values are violated or those people threatened, you surprise others by shedding your easygoing nature and becoming tough, demanding, and aggressive.

Because you are a keen and penetrating observer, you know what motivates others. You have a good handle on the cosmic drama around you. Routine stifles you, but you take life as it comes and do what you must.

A harmonious environment, where your originality and interpersonal skills are used to organize and inspire, is a necessity. You enjoy exercising your considerable emotional intelligence in circumstances where it is appreciated. Very loyal to individuals, causes, and institutions you admire, you expect a high degree of loyalty and support in return.

Others see you as patient, creative, committed, stubborn, and somewhat enigmatic. In relationships, you are supportive and affirming, making people you care about feel valued and liked. Conflicts at home and work are problematic and will be ignored as long as possible.

Green/Gold Introverts are tactful, complex, and articulate. Some of the words that describe your work ethic are *conscientious, goal-oriented, orderly, serious, hardworking,* and *ambitious.* You are decisive and often in a hurry, impatient with anyone who slows you down in achieving objectives. You can be so ambitious that you'll actually do more than the task requires.

Creative and full of penetrating insights, you are gifted at predicting trends. This also allows you to solve problems in new ways.

As an Introvert, you get fatigued and cranky working in open office settings or when your privacy is not respected. Yet your interest in others is so strong that you run the risk of not giving yourself that all-important time alone to recharge.

The people who irritate you most are superficial or rude, or invade your privacy. When angered, you become critical and confrontational. In the second half of your life, you handle these folks better, using your superior verbal abilities to extricate yourself from the web of their agendas. You realize that you are not obligated to help everyone who needs it.

You on the Job

AS A LEADER

"Work hard to convert ideals into reality" is your mantra. You see an idealized vision of the future (usually farther out than most can envision) and strive to make it happen. Building consensus and cooperation through persuasion rather than control is the Green/Gold Introvert's hallmark. You give all opinions an airing, bringing out people's best through appreciation and support.

Naturally and almost fiercely committed to your work, you have integrity about what you do. You are an outstanding role model, inspiring others to great heights. But you don't just sit in your office and dream; you get out there, putting real-world structures and organization into place to achieve your goals. Accepting setbacks as simply new challenges, you sometimes find startlingly new and better ways to meet goals. When staffers have professional or personal difficulties, you are there for them in appropriate ways.

AS A TEAM PLAYER

Since your goal is harmony, you build bridges (often with humor) between conflicting factions. The focus is on results and providing the structure to achieve them. You brainstorm multiple ideas, get people laughing about the one that really will work, and inspire their best efforts before they finish chuckling.

Although you navigate emotional territory well, you have your practical side. You meet deadlines and ensure that human and material resources are not wasted.

You may irritate teammates by sticking to ideas not shared by the rest of the team.

Look at figure 6–1 for a list of your natural work-related strengths.

Now see how some Green/Gold Introverts use these strengths in very different fields.

FIGURE 6–1 *Natural Work-Related Strengths*

Approximately 80 percent of these attributes will apply to you. Check off those that do, and use them in your resume and interviews. This will set you apart from the canned responses of others. You:

○ Are visionary; you can see trends and far-reaching potentials of situations.

○ Coach and mentor others well, giving diplomatic feedback.

○ Organize projects well and ensure timely follow-through.

○ Recognize the right people for the right task.

○ See new ways to solve problems and express solutions in a clear way.

CASE STUDY ONE

Award-Winning Playwright

Lonnie Carter has been a professional playwright since 1969, when he graduated from the Yale School of Drama in New Haven, Connecticut. He saw his first live play at age 19, a Tennessee Williams work that formed a lasting impression of the theater. "I liked what language did in plays," he recalls. "I felt I could do something, if not similar, then complementary, with the use of language. It makes me feel good; I have fun doing it."

Lonnie has taught at Columbia and New York Universities, an occupation that has energized and inspired him. "Students will suck you dry," Lonnie admits. "But I like my students; some I like enormously. I love hearing from a student five years down the road saying, 'I'm in a play in San Diego that's a great success; thank you.' That's thrilling. Two students, both Latinos, were about to kill each other in my class. That was seven or eight years ago. Now they make films, really good ones, together. Christopher Gabriel Nunez and Saila Reyes. Look out for them."

Although he never experienced overnight success as a playwright, he recently won a *Village Voice* OBIE Award (off-Broadway theater's highest honor) for his work *The Romance of Magno Rubio*. He attributes his success to persistence. "Each year was just another step in the process," Lonnie says. "Then it was forty years of steps." Now he is so busy going from one production to another that "I seem to write in moving vehicles more than anything else!"

Lonnie does not like the air travel that cuts into his creative time or the bureaucracy of working within a large university structure. "Bureaucrats everywhere and nary a brain in sight," he complains. Out of the university system once and for all, he devotes his time to his own writing and the raising of his children, even though three of the four are now grown. "There will always be raising to do," he sighs, happily.

CASE STUDY TWO

Senior Vice President, Public Relations, Healthcare

Maggie Hoffman is a master in the management of perception. Her public relations savvy is brought into play every day as she assesses and manages the opinions of important groups and individuals for her clients. Though her job is to make her clients look good, Maggie didn't mention one of the measures of her own success—we had to hear it from her subordinates. They call themselves MITs—"Maggies in Training."

In keeping with her Green/Gold personality, Maggie does three things very well. She discerns future trends and does quality research to back up her predictions. She is a superior communicator with clients and staff. Finally, she stays focused on maximizing billable hours and productivity while avoiding costly staff burnout.

She is very structured in how she produces work and how she thinks things through, note those who work with her. These are the qualities of her Gold component. Of her Green side, Maggie says, "Most satisfying to me is knowing people on my teams are engaged, challenged, and happy."

Her associates say Maggie is the go-to person on their team for clients seeking business advice and resources. This is unusual in the public relations industry and speaks to her professional credibility.

Maggie stresses out when involved in group activities that are not well-orchestrated. Cold calling and prospecting, functioning under huge time crunches and managing people during crisis phases are her least favorite work situations. But when she nails the right strategy for a particular client or brand, she feels deeply energized.

Ideal Work Environment

Your ideal work environment allows you to contribute in some way to the well-being of society. Other than that, you're flexible.

When a job offer is made, leverage as much as you can from the list in figure 6–2.

FIGURE 6-2 *The Ideal Green/Gold Introvert Work Environment*

Compare your current work environment to the descriptions below. Check all that ring true for you. If these descriptions seem obvious, that confirms you've tested your individual color correctly. Other Colors, especially Blues, would find this environment uncomfortable and unproductive. The optimal Green/Gold Introvert work environment:

○ Has people who can be trusted.

○ Rewards creativity.

○ Is an egalitarian culture with strong values and a willingness to invest in staff development.

○ Produces products and services that contribute to the well-being of society.

○ Provides opportunity to work on a variety of activities.

○ Offers control of and responsibility for your own projects.

○ Rewards your well-developed organizational skills.

○ Allows for quiet time, reflection, minimal paperwork, and private work space.

The worst type of work culture for a Green/Gold Introvert is tense, overly competitive, and highly political. Here the creative drive is crushed, and Green/Gold Introverts become critical and defensive. Any work culture where products or services exploit both staff efforts and customer vulnerabilities is intolerable to the Green/Gold Introvert. You desire deeply to contribute positively to the world. Requiring focus on too many details or being too hierarchical and status conscious also are work cultures that destroy your creativity and productivity.

When Green/Gold Introverts work in such nonideal corporate cultures, productivity is stunted and career achievements become an uphill climb.

The Introverted Green/Gold's Ideal Boss

Even a great job can be frustrating under the wrong boss; a mediocre job under a wonderful boss is pretty hard to leave. Green/Golds get along especially well with other Greens. But bosses of other Color types who possess the characteristics in figure 6–3 also can be good mentors.

FIGURE 6–3 *The Green/Gold Introvert's Ideal Boss*

Check off if your boss:

○ Has high integrity

○ Shares your values

○ Personalizes your relationship

○ Supports staff through obstacles

○ Protects you from office politics

Careers That Attract Green/Gold Introverts

Like Lonnie and Maggie, you are most attracted to careers that provide recognition for your creativity or that help others grow and develop. Green/Gold Introverts need to work with people who can be trusted. Working alone or in small groups is best, ideally allowing for private space and quiet time.

Please note that not all the following careers will appeal to you, but recognize that each, in some way, draws on the strengths of your style and appeals to a significant number of your Color group. This is not a comprehensive list, but it will show underlying patterns of preference. If unlisted careers offer similar patterns, your chances of success increase. Text in parentheses at the end of each section highlights the Color style characteristics that create success in that broad area.

According to our research, jobs italicized in the lists below are predicted to benefit from an above-average growth rate over the next several years. This information is based on the continuously revised data provided by the U.S. Department of Labor and Bureau of Labor Statistics on their websites O*NET OnLine (www.onetonline.org) and http://www.bls.gov/CAREEROUTLOOK/. There you will find in-depth information about job requirements and salary ranges.

There are successful people of all Color styles in all occupations. In non-ideal jobs, you can still shine by creating your own niche.

ARTS/COMMUNICATIONS/COMPUTER

advertising/promotion/marketing manager ▶ art/graphic designer/director, animator ▶ artist ▶ exhibit designer ▶ film editor ▶ *interior designer* ▶ *Internet marketing manager/customer relations* ▶ librarian ▶ *literary agent/book publishing professional* ▶ magazine/book editor ▶ media planner ▶ *merchandise displayer* ▶ *multimedia specialist/producer* ▶ museum director/curator ▶ music composer/director ▶ *public relations director/specialist* ▶ *set/costume designer* ▶ translator ▶ TV producer ▶ *website editor* ▶ writer/playwright/journalist (involvement with media, often work alone, creativity rewarded, superior language skills needed)

BUSINESS/MANAGEMENT

communications director ▶ consultative salesperson (ideas more than tangible products) ▶ ebook publisher ▶ employee assistance program director ▶ employment interviewer ▶ *human resources/diversity manager* ▶ industrial psychologist ▶ job analyst ▶ marketer (ideas/services) ▶ merchandise planner ▶ *organizational development consultant* ▶ *outplacement consultant* ▶ philanthropic officer/consultant ▶ public relations professional ▶ *training and development specialist* ▶ *translator/interpreter* (help others achieve their potential, need for tact)

EDUCATION
educational administrator ▸ educational consultant ▸ *educational software developer* ▸ instructional coordinator ▸ *online educator* ▸ school counselor ▸ *teacher* (all levels: art, drama, English, humanities, languages, social studies, special education, *bilingual education*) ▸ university professor (helping others reach their potential, patient one-on-one influencing)

HEALTH SCIENCE/PSYCHOLOGY
alternative healthcare practitioner ▸ *child care worker* ▸ *chiropractor* ▸ *clinical psychologist/psychiatrist* ▸ *dietician/nutritionist* ▸ *elder care specialist* ▸ *general practitioner* ▸ healthcare administrator ▸ *holistic health practitioner* ▸ *mental health counselor/therapist (marriage, occupational, substance abuse)* ▸ *occupational therapist* ▸ *optometrist* ▸ *pediatrician* ▸ physical/massage therapist ▸ *physician assistant* ▸ public relations specialist ▸ senior day care coordinator ▸ *speech pathologist* ▸ therapist (environment congruent with values, insights into others, see new ways to solve problems, patient one-on-one influencing)

LAW/SCIENCE
animal/food and environmental scientist ▸ genealogist (look for intellectual challenge and scientific careers that relate to their values) ▸ *lawyer* (children, communication and media, environmental, estate, intellectual property, poverty law) ▸ mediator (organizational abilities, helping others, making the world a better place)

SOCIAL SERVICES
coach (business, life) ▸ *counselor* (career, child welfare, outplacement, pastoral, occupational therapist) ▸ fund-raiser/institutional solicitor, grant coordinator ▸ philanthropic consultant/director ▸ religious leader/educator ▸ social scientist ▸ *social worker/community services director/manager* (need for good organizational skills, goal setting, and using all resources, helping people who need it, work congruent with your values, improving the world)

TECHNOLOGY
customer relations manager ▸ project manager ▸ recruiter ▸ staff technology consultant (excel at connecting technology people with staff and clients)

CASE STUDY THREE

The Successful Green/Gold Introvert

Dr. Mobarak Abdulhadi Aldosari has been at the forefront of the career guidance and counseling field in Saudi Arabia for the past twenty-five years. He helped establish the first Guidance Center in the kingdom's Eastern Province in 1998. His Ph.D. in guidance and counseling "matches my personality type," he says.

Dr. Aldosari's work with Color Q demonstrates the method's applicability across cultures. He owns the Rowad Almaarefa Educational Consulting Firm in Saudi Arabia and is a Color Q licensee. "I have conducted the Color Q Personality System on more than 70,000 students (boys and girls), teachers, and counselors in the Arab Gulf Countries. This is really what our people want," he says.

Dr. Aldosari is a highly intuitive Green/Gold Introvert who describes his professional strengths as wanting to help others, motivate them, and see them succeed. He says that career guidance isn't available yet in many of his kingdom's schools. "I was most frustrated when one day I asked a grade 12 high school student about his dream. He answered, 'I am not thinking about it yet.' That shocked me and led me to work and concentrate on the career guidance field."

Today, he focuses on helping students find their career paths and works with the private sector for employees and leaders.

Your Personality's Challenges

Green/Gold Introverts have a unique set of potential work-related blind spots. Some listed below you have, others you don't. Tone down a blind spot by focusing on it, then choose more productive actions and make them habits. (Suggestions for doing so are in parentheses below.) You:

▸ Can be too idealistic and ignore bottom-line consequences. (There is a practical side to making an ideal real. The benefits you envision may be prohibitively expensive. Consult Golds and Blues about processes and costs.)

▸ Don't have a talent for politics. (Find a boss or other superior who can shield you from such things. If you become embroiled, just refuse to play—walk away. Strangely, that works most of the time.)

- Avoid conflicts, confrontations, and underlying problems. (These bring up strong emotions that you would rather not reveal. Don't wait until things boil over; it's easier—and quicker—to address these problems when everyone is calm.)

- Overpersonalize criticism. (You see criticism as a seismic rift in a relationship. Next time a friend criticizes you, ask if he or she still likes you. Will you be surprised if they say, "Of course"? Much criticism is well-meaning.)

- Go off on unrealistic tangents. (What's possible in five years excites you. But it won't tell a Red what to do today, a Gold how to administer today, or a Blue how to strategize the way there. Ask them, "What should I do now to achieve this later?" You'll get a lot more buy-in.)

Your Job Search—the Good, the Bad, and the Ugly

Green/Gold Introverts need to be recognized for their unique creative ideas, even during their job search. You find fun ways to rise to the top of the resume pile. With some interviewers, particularly Greens and Golds, you will feel a comfortable rapport. But for other Colors, you need to prepare responses.

Your natural strengths easily allow you to:

- Cull leads from a small but trusted network of friends and former associates

- Create a master plan using facts and intuition

- Open yourself to new fields and unusual opportunities

- Brainstorm trends and creative solutions, which can lead to new positions created for you

- Follow through on calls and leads

- Keep paperwork organized

- Present yourself as committed and competent

- Read the interviewer well

In order to tone down your blind spots, you need to:

- Network with friends first; work up to contacting people you don't know

- Research and understand a job's compensation range (find a willing Gold to help)

- Talk more; sell your accomplishments

- Stay practical about costs and the bottom line

- De-emphasize the needs of others; prioritize your own

- Practice your salary negotiation with a willing Red

- Take rejection less personally (find another Green for encouragement)

The Green/Gold Introvert's Interviewing Style

If your interviewer seems to have a significantly different personality style, use the suggestions in parentheses. Mercilessly exploit these natural abilities of yours and get more job offers.

In following your natural style, you:

- See the big picture and typically present that first. (Great if you're interviewing for a senior level position, irritating if for a junior slot. No boss wants a subordinate who sees more on the horizon than he or she does. Share only if asked, do not volunteer.)

- Listen well with an unusual capacity to understand the viewpoints of others. (This impresses many interviewers. Some, though, want to see the tough professional. Focus on your viability for the job.)

- Present in an orderly way. (Be prepared to show the pros and cons of your background and goals. Use practical language; downplay metaphors or abstractions with interviewers who speak concretely.)

- Use personal experiences to make your points. (If your interviewer seems uncomfortable or breaks eye contact, cut it short.)

Okay, go do something cultural now. Later, check out chapter 19, "Golds Overall." Like all Colors, your blind spots can be complemented by the strengths of others if you know where to look and how to ask. Invest time learning how to recognize the Colors who can best assist you; it honestly will make your life a whole lot easier. If you are actively engaging in a job search, jot notes in the Roadmap in chapter 27. Recording your strengths and strategies will keep you organized and on track, and provide a creative springboard for your networking.

CHAPTER 7

Green/Red Extroverts

YOU'RE NOT ONLY a Green, you also have strong secondary characteristics of the Red personality. And you have tested as a Color Q Extrovert, which means you recharge your batteries by being with people rather than being alone. Green/Red Extroverts are warm, free spirits who often feel forced to conform to norms of practicality set by other Colors. You'll likely have more career changes than other Colors, not because you're unfocused but because you are gifted, curious, and flexible.

You Overall

Energized by new ideas, you're intrigued by the unusual. Your deepest satisfaction is to be acknowledged for your originality and unique contributions. A free spirit, you are unconventional and admire the bravely creative.

A keen and penetrating observer, you know what motivates others. You're aware of what's going on at any moment in the cosmic drama around you. You love challenges that require you to be ingenious. Routine is a drag, but you take life as it comes and do what you must.

If you're not changing careers frequently, you definitely are changing projects and goals more often than other Colors. While you fear others may see you as a flake, in reality they think of you as dynamic and highly skilled at juggling lots of people and events, often simultaneously.

Have you taken up writing or public speaking yet? If not, you probably want to. Your verbal and written skills are superior. You can convince employers that you can do the job, even if you've never done it before, and by the way, do it better and more innovatively than anyone else.

You are a gleeful warrior against bureaucracy. It is imperative that you be allowed creative freedom, or you wither.

A need for empathetic relationships is another driving force. Warm and insightful, you establish rapport quickly by being genuine and nonjudgmental.

The trends and pitfalls of the future spread themselves out like a feast on the banquet table of your intuition. Intuition drives you into many areas of interest, almost against your will. Most areas have an impact on people or are of global concern.

The people who irritate you most are manipulative or controlling. In the second half of your life, you'll move toward a more objective and logical approach to these people. You'll use your superior verbal abilities to extricate yourself from the web of their agendas.

CASE STUDY ONE

Business Consultant

Greg is a typical Green/Red Extrovert who has carved out a niche in an atypical field. In senior management of a leading strategy consulting firm he has found success emphasizing the creative and relationship-building aspects of the work.

Not surprisingly, Greg says, "It's always been the hardest job for me to be an analyst relentlessly focusing on detailed facts. I prefer the 80/20 rule," he says. "Find the key facts but don't overdwell, then move on trusting your intuition."

Greg is in charge of managing a team whose goal he describes as "leading the client through change, which requires a strong point of view, persuasive skills, and building trust."

His biggest stress is having to act as an expert when he doesn't feel like one, since Green/Reds revere authenticity. He prefers long-term assignments; it takes him about twelve months to really talk his clients' talk with ease.

Building relationships with staff and clients energizes him most, as it does for most Green/Reds. He especially enjoys seeing ads and products from clients he has helped. "I want to actually touch the products on the shelf and bring them home and say, 'I was part of this.'"

Greg describes his top three strengths as "motivating others, coaching, and building relationships." These are core Green/Red Extrovert strengths.

Also typical are his dreams for the future. He'd like to be a published poet (most Green/Red Extroverts turn to writing at some point in their lives), a small business owner, a photographer, or a nonprofit manager. Drawn to artistic and socially relevant endeavors, Green/Red Extroverts also love working in groups small enough to know everyone well.

You on the Job

AS A LEADER

Bringing out the best in people is your real gift. During the startup phase of a company or project, you are a strong leader (particularly if conditions are chaotic). You inspire confidence and support, and are able to rally others to achieve difficult goals. Your understanding of what motivates people allows you to create unwavering loyalty from your staff. Inviting everyone from all levels to make suggestions brings forth unique ways to solve problems. You then motivate with positive and constructive feedback during implementation.

AS A TEAM PLAYER

Brainstorming is your bread and butter, and you're better at it than almost anyone. Contributing idea after idea, no matter how outrageous, you eventually find those tremendously creative ideas that put your company on the cutting edge.

Others are at ease around your warmth, humor, and empowering can-do attitude. They then generate ideas and offer resources that otherwise would have been left dormant.

You may irritate teammates by talking too much and going off on tangents. Look at figure 7–1 for a list of your natural work-related strengths.

FIGURE 7-1 *Natural Work-Related Strengths*

Approximately 80 percent of these attributes will apply to you. Check off those that do, and use them in your resume and interviews. This will set you apart from the canned responses of others. You:

○ Inspire others

○ Express yourself in interesting and colorful ways

○ Have ideas ahead of their time and can predict future trends by making unusual connections

○ Establish rapport quickly

○ Build effective and loyal teams by respecting different points of view

○ Network well within the organization

Now see how some Green/Red Extroverts use their strengths in very different fields.

CASE STUDY TWO

Model, Actress, Interior Designer, Script Writer, Author

Gloria Parker's face may be familiar to you—she was Oleg Cassini's top model and has appeared in numerous movies, television shows, and commercials. If not her face, you may know her name as writer for television series like *Murphy's Law* and *Tour of Duty*. Perhaps you bought high-end furniture from her upscale store on Montana Avenue in Los Angeles. If you were lucky enough, you hired her to decorate your house, as movie stars Meg Ryan, Tom Hanks, Pierce Brosnan, and Arnold Schwarzenegger did.

"I loved being on stage, making people laugh and cry," says Gloria of her acting career. "It opened a world to me I might not ever have walked into."

When her acting career wound down, Gloria, in typical Green/Red Extrovert fashion, followed her heart and opened a furniture store, leveraging her show business contacts to sell and create a custom-interior-design clientele. "I enjoyed the artistic part, and I am really good at sales," she says.

Green/Red Extroverts build extensive personal networks, and Gloria's helped her crack open the screenwriting world. "The first play I did [*Women's Gym*] got produced and sold to television!" she recalls, with her natural enthusiasm.

Green/Red Extroverts love to be in the middle of things. Gloria is an especially good example. "It's really exciting when TV shows are interviewing you, you're in the public eye, you're young, and the world is at your feet," she says. "My store—the hottest people in California were coming to see me. And when my first play was produced, there was so much attention—the reviews were calling me brilliant and genius!"

When Green/Red Extroverts have done as much as they can enthusiastically and interest wanes in one career, they move on to the next exciting thing. They are merely following their artistic core, which leads them like a beacon to the next hot thing.

Gloria eventually burned out on the Los Angeles scene and, once again, followed her heart. It led her to write a cutting-edge book about her son's transgender journey. *Meeting Robyn* was published in 2013, three years before Caitlyn Jenner's transition garnered media attention.

Although Gloria's many careers bewilder other Colors, for her they were a natural progression. "My deepest satisfaction is when something is completed and beautiful and it gives pleasure to other people."

CASE STUDY THREE

Fine Artist, Commercial Artist, Art Teacher

Oldrich Teply is one of the envied men who make art their living. His corporate graphic work, fine art, and teaching fulfill him on many levels. Most energizing to Oldrich is his teaching work at the renowned Art Students League in New York City. Handling classes of fifty painting students, he gently and diplomatically corrects errors in proportion, drawing, composition, or color. Green/Red Extrovert teachers are known for their inspiring ways, and they love the contact they have with their students. Oldrich can respond to different ages, backgrounds, and skill levels with equal ease. He has the Green/Red core desire to develop potential in others and is most pleased when a student begins to show his or her own style.

For corporations, for example, he creates watercolors showcasing new high-rise condominiums. Such assignments can involve studying blueprints and conferring with architects and designers. Greens are particularly skilled at pulling together diverse data to create one compelling visual that communicates the spirit of a project.

At the request of Lou Gerstner, then-CEO of Nabisco, Oldrich drew twenty-eight caricature portraits of the company's new management team to ease their transition. At the annual meeting, as the pictures flashed onscreen, the humor Oldrich captured broke the tension surrounding the impending changes. Humor is one tool Green/Reds use to create harmony.

The variety and creative freedom of his work are deeply fulfilling to Oldrich, as is his minimal exposure to rules and bureaucracy.

Ideal Work Environment

For Greg, it's important that his clients know his heart is in the right place and he truly wants to be of service. Wherever Green/Red Extroverts work, if high value is placed on human well-being, they are happy. Green/Reds like Gloria crave creativity and idea generation in a lively, fast-paced world.

When a job offer is made, leverage as much as you can from the list in figure 7–2.

FIGURE 7–2 **The Ideal Green/Red Extrovert Work Environment**

Compare your current work environment to the descriptions below. Check all that ring true for you. If these descriptions seem obvious, that confirms you've tested your individual Color correctly. Other Colors, especially Golds, would find this environment uncomfortable and unproductive. The optimal Green/Red Extrovert work environment:

○ Is democratic and informal. Your title is less important than your ideas and contributions.

○ Encourages creativity and idea generation. It rewards you for your core talents rather than labeling you as "free spirit" or "too far out."

○ Provides freedom to work at your own pace. The more you are controlled, the less productive you become.

○ Is lively and fast moving. You are energized by the new.

○ Rewards humor and fun. A good laugh relaxes you and makes you want to contribute more.

○ Places high value on the well-being of staff and clients. Companies that disrespect the human side make you fight rather than contribute productively.

○ Focuses on the startup stage rather than maintenance. You will find ingenious ways to divest yourself of administrative details.

○ Fosters cooperation and trust. Backstabbing and politics drain so much energy from the task at hand. You have no patience for these.

○ Provides good training and development opportunities. Self-improvement is a lifelong pursuit.

The worst type of work culture for an Extroverted Green/Red emphasizes routine and details, like the paperwork and accounting tasks Gloria hates. Rules and procedures dominate, against which Green/Reds can't help but rebel. Highly political atmospheres destroy the creative freedom and trust necessary for Green/Reds to contribute their best.

When Extroverted Green/Reds work in nonideal corporate cultures, productivity is stunted and career achievements become an uphill climb.

The Extroverted Green/Red's Ideal Boss

Even a great job can be frustrating under the wrong boss; a mediocre job under a wonderful boss is pretty hard to leave. Green/Reds get along especially well with other Greens. But bosses of other Color types who possess the characteristics in figure 7–3 also can be good mentors.

FIGURE 7-3 *The Green/Red Extrovert's Ideal Boss*

Check off if your boss:

○ Is flexible

○ Appreciates your authenticity and energy

○ Has a sense of humor

○ Personalizes your relationship

○ Likes brainstorming new ideas and exploring new areas

○ Provides frequent feedback

○ Does not micromanage you

Careers That Attract Green/Red Extroverts

Like Gloria and Greg, you are most attracted to careers that provide recognition for your creativity and versatility. Or you may be attracted to professions that involve teaching and helping others. Others will include those listed later in this section.

Please note that not all the following careers will appeal to you, but recognize that each, in some way, draws on the strengths of your style and appeals to a significant number of your Color group. This is not a comprehensive list, but it will show underlying patterns of preference. If unlisted careers offer similar patterns, your chances of success increase. Text in parentheses at the end of each section highlights the Color style characteristics that create success in that broad area.

According to our research, jobs italicized in the lists below are predicted to benefit from an above-average growth rate over the next several years. This information is based on the continuously revised data provided by the U.S. Department of Labor and Bureau of Labor Statistics on their websites O*NET OnLine (www.onetonline.org) and http://www.bls.gov/CAREEROUTLOOK/. There you will find in-depth information about job requirements and salary ranges.

There are successful people of all Color styles in all occupations. In nonideal jobs, you can still shine by creating your own niche.

ARTS/DESIGN

art director ▶ *creative director, multimedia artist/animator* ▶ commercial artist ▶ desktop publisher ▶ designer (floral, interior decor, set, wardrobe) ▶ fine artist ▶ graphic designer ▶ landscape architect (encourages originality and uniqueness)

BUSINESS/COMMUNICATIONS/HUMAN RESOURCES

consultant/relationship manager ▶ *consultative salesperson* ▶ *convention/event planner* ▶ corporate communications director ▶ *corporate trainer* ▶ *diversity manager* ▶ *employment interviewer* ▶ *human resources manager/generalist/specialist* ▶ industrial psychologist ▶ *insurance agent* ▶ *market research analyst* ▶ *marketing consultant* ▶ organization development consultant ▶ *outplacement consultant* ▶ personnel recruiter ▶ philanthropic consultant ▶ planned giving officer ▶ publicity writer ▶ *real estate agent* ▶ sales manager ▶ *strategic partnership developer* (brainstorming ability and relationship building, strong verbal and written skills, good mediator)

COMMUNICATIONS/ENTERTAINMENT/MEDIA

actor ▶ *agent/manager* (artists, performers) ▶ author ▶ columnist/reporter ▶ editor (book, film) ▶ *film producer* ▶ journalist ▶ *literary agent* ▶ model ▶ motivational speaker ▶ playwright/screenwriter/TV script writer ▶ *social media manager* ▶ translator ▶ TV anchor/newscaster ▶ TV producer (superior verbal and written skills, going from one glamorous project to the next)

EDUCATION

adult literacy specialist ▶ *bilingual educator* ▶ educational consultant/psychologist (enjoy continuing education, establishing rapport) ▶ *guidance/child welfare counselor* ▶ high school guidance counselor ▶ *instructional coordinator* ▶ *teachers at all levels* (plus art, drama, music, special education)

HEALTH SCIENCE/PSYCHOLOGY

alternative healthcare practitioner ▶ *audiologist* ▶ conservation scientist (relationship building, empathy, juggling lots of people) ▶ *dietitian/nutritionist* ▶ *family practitioner* ▶ *marriage and family therapist* ▶ *nurse* ▶ *pediatrician* ▶ *psychologists/psychiatrist* (of all types) ▶ *public health educator* ▶ social psychologist ▶ *speech pathologist* ▶ *therapist* (physical, massage, speech, occupational)

LAW/HUMAN SERVICES

counselor of all sorts (career, crisis, high school guidance, substance abuse, etc.) ▶ fund-raiser/institutional solicitor ▶ labor relations specialist ▶ *lawyer* (intellectual property, environment, nonprofit) ▶ legal mediator ▶ religious leader ▶ *school psychologist* ▶ *social or community service manager* (child, family, school) ▶ social scientist ▶ *social worker* (understanding human motivation, relationship building, good people-/project-juggling skills)

MARKETING/PUBLIC RELATIONS

advertising account executive/manager ▶ *advertising creative director* ▶ *marketing specialist/consultant* ▶ media planner ▶ publicist ▶ public relations director/specialist (product positioning and understanding human motivation)

TECHNOLOGY

project manager ▶ *staff technology consultant* ▶ *technology recruiter* ▶ *web developer* (combining technology and communication skills to explain technology to staff)

CASE STUDY FOUR

When a Career Isn't Working

At age 52, Glen, a New York attorney, had just about achieved all his major goals. Partner of a prestigious Wall Street law firm, Glen was respected and lavishly compensated. His cases were high profile, the envy of his peers. Yet for some reason he could not understand, Glen was finding it increasingly difficult to get up in the morning. He visited a therapist three times a week, seeking answers without knowing the questions.

It turned out Glen had a classic case of burnout—a condition that results when the job does not fit the needs of the personality. Glen had sailed through law school on his smarts, fueled with the idealism that a law career could make big differences in the world (something important to Green/Reds).

In his early years at the firm, he worked long hours, energized by the camaraderie with his colleagues, as often is the case with this Color. Extroverted Green/Reds recharge their batteries through supportive interaction at work. This kept Glen going through the tough cases of his junior years. His outstanding ability to make clients feel special and well served (another Green/Red core aptitude) earned him an early partnership. This put him in high demand; ample and excellent word-of-mouth recommendations attracted career-making cases.

Yet, at the top of his game, his reward was loss of interest and constant fatigue. A brief introduction to his Color style brought several things to light. As a Green, he disliked confrontation, the basis of most prominent cases. The relentless drive for high-stakes settlements and the pressure of outwitting opponents was draining rather than satisfying, as it would be to a Blue.

Glen resigned, much to the surprise of family, friends, and colleagues. He enrolled in a university to earn a Ph.D. in psychology. Now, several years later and brimming with energy, Glen is hanging up his shingle as a therapist for lawyers.

Your Personality's Challenges

Green/Red Extroverts have a unique set of potential work-related blind spots. Some listed below you have, others you don't. Tone down a blind spot by focusing on it, then choose more-productive actions and make them habits. (Suggestions for doing so are in parentheses below.) You:

- Pay too little attention to rules you feel are obstacles to creativity. (Try to understand whose anxiety a rule addresses. Remember, genuine creativity can work around, and through, the rules.)

- Can go off on tangents during group discussions. (You think holistically; hence, all topics addressed in any order are relevant. Be considerate of your fellow Colors who need linear thought and get jangled when the lines aren't straight!)

▶ Are too sensitive to criticism. (Because relationships are top priority to you, criticism feels like condemnation when it's not. Dare to ask your critics if they still like you. Most likely, they do.)

▶ Avoid conflict, often delaying dealing with the issue. (Enjoy the realization that conflict worked through to conclusion actually strengthens relationships. If you are a young Green/Red, this is a very hard lesson to learn. A thicker skin will bring you more and deeper relationships in the long run.)

▶ Get excited by new projects and then don't complete old ones. (Most projects get "old" before they're complete, leaving unfinished business. Just finish or delegate so your energy can flow to the new.)

▶ Make errors of fact. (Gut feelings have always gotten you to the right place at the right time; decisions based on facts often have led you astray. Start intuitively, then prove yourself right. Other Colors need facts and will devalue your ideas if they contain errors.)

Your Job Search—the Good, the Bad, and the Ugly

Green/Red Extroverts love making a splash and impressing others. With some interviewers, particularly Greens and Reds, you blow away all competitors. With other Colors, you need a different strategy.

Your natural strengths easily allow you to:

▶ Actively network through a broad range of people for referrals.

▶ Enjoy exploring new options.

▶ Interview with enthusiasm.

▶ Establish quick rapport.

▶ Convince an employer to create a new job for you.

▶ Come across as adaptable, a quick learner, and a team player.

In order to tone down your blind spots, you need to:

▶ Role play negotiating salary and financial issues (find a willing Gold or Blue to help).

▶ Do more research on prospective companies.

- Subdue wardrobe, hairstyle, and manner in interviews to counterbalance seeming lack of seriousness.

- Talk less in interviews and ask more questions.

- Hold back ideas on which you have not done cost research.

- Require yourself to make a minimum number of contacts each day of your job search.

- Do a realistic budget for your job-search time.

- Ask for a couple of days to give it further consideration; don't jump at a job offer.

The Green/Red Extrovert's Interviewing Style

With an interviewer whose Color is close to your own, you will feel immediate rapport. However, if your interviewer seems to have a significantly different style, use the suggestions in parentheses. Mercilessly exploit these natural abilities of yours and get more job offers.

In following your natural style, you:

- Speak with geniality, fluency, and energy. (You can overwhelm more subdued interviewers. Try to match their energy.)

- Think on your feet and reply quickly. (It's possible to be too peppy. Mix it up—make some replies slow and thoughtful.)

- Make your points through lively and vivid imagery, personal stories, and humor. (With an interviewer who keeps his or her distance, replace imagery with facts—role play with a willing Gold, if possible. Use personal stories only when interviewers maintain eye contact. If humor falls flat the first time, don't keep trying. Let the interviewer set the tone.)

- See the big picture and typically present that first. (Great if you're interviewing for a senior level position, irritating if for a junior slot. No boss wants a subordinate who sees more on the horizon than he or she does. Share only if asked.)

Okay, go do something new now. Or continue reading chapter 9, "Reds Overall." Then learn how to Color code bosses and coworkers by checking out figure 24-1 in chapter 24, "Before I Do Something Stupid: Adjusting to Other Styles." The greatest value of this book really is learning how to interact with, appreciate, and use the strengths of other Colors. If you're doing a job search, jot notes in the Roadmap in chapter 27—it will keep you focused.

CHAPTER 8

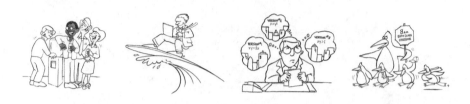

Green/Red Introverts

YOU'RE NOT ONLY a Green, you also have strong secondary characteristics of the Red personality. And you have tested as a Color Q Introvert, which means you recharge your batteries by being alone rather than being with people. Your Color group has warm, free spirits who typically feel forced to conform to norms of practicality and seriousness. You may have more career changes than other Colors, not because you are flawed but because you are multitalented, curious, and flexible. The drive to write is more intense in you than in most other Colors and is a part of most of your jobs.

You Overall

Thoughtful, insightful, intuitive, and complex, you do not usually impose your ideas on others. You prefer a small, intimate group of friends, even though you have a deep need for empathetic relationships. Outwardly cool and detached, you inwardly harbor strong feelings about people and values. When your values are violated or those people threatened, you surprise others by shedding your easygoing nature and becoming tough, demanding, and aggressive.

Your deepest satisfaction is to be acknowledged for your originality and unique contributions. You are unconventional and admire other nonconformists.

Because you are a keen and penetrating observer, you have a good handle on what's going on in the cosmic drama around you. You enjoy helping others, not out of guilt but a desire to assist. Life's challenges find you optimistic, adaptable, and ingenious. Routine saps your energy, but your adaptability helps you do what you must.

Projecting the trends and pitfalls of the future is one of your greatest gifts. A big-picture thinker, you take in everything, focusing on what impacts people and has global ramifications.

You are a gleeful warrior against bureaucracy. It is imperative that you be allowed creative freedom or you become a saboteur. While you are flexible and accommodating to work with, you get fatigued and cranky working in open office settings or when your privacy is not respected.

Others see you as insightful and an excellent listener. In relationships, you establish rapport by being genuine and nonjudgmental. But the true intensity of your feelings is revealed only to those who know you well.

The people who irritate you most are intrusive, controlling, and overly critical of others. In the second half of your life, as you move toward a more objective and logical approach to others, you will handle these folks better. Your superior verbal abilities extricate you from the web of their agendas.

CASE STUDY ONE

Author and Editor

Dan Shaw is a talented author with a long, well-credentialed resume mostly in the home design field. He has written and/or edited for the *New York Times, House and Garden,* and *O at Home,* among many other publications. The majority of the time he lived and worked in New York City.

Today, he calls a very small New England town home. "I went to an office for twenty years," says Dan. "I like not going to an office right now. The type of life change I wanted was spiritually oriented." Dan created that opportunity for himself on a deeply forested piece of land by a river. Green/Red Introverts enjoy working at home more than most.

He describes working at magazines as being "all about the social interactions," normally a stressor to Introverts. But Dan liked this part of his job. "It was easy for me because it was part of the work structure, and I did not have to initiate social interactions," Dan says.

He brought many Green gifts to his work. "I see things very well—the unfamiliar in the familiar," he says. "I am confident in what I do, and I am a good writer who's done serious journalism. So I have very high standards." Green/Reds are perfectionists, an advantage in writers.

Typically for a Green, money and success are only two of many equal motivators. When asked about them, Dan replied, "I wouldn't mind having money, but it doesn't pull me." He explained his choice to freelance, saying, "I attained the number two position at a couple of magazines and realized I did not have the ambition in me to be number one."

Today, Dan is developing two coffee-table books, both of which he expects to publish within a year or two. He's in his home office five to ten hours a day researching, writing, or arranging new, exciting projects such as the online magazine *Rural Intelligence,* which he founded. This allowed him to meet new people when he reported stories while maintaining his independence and ability to work from home. "When I am writing, I get lost in it—not looking at the clock," he says. Working at home, sometimes he chooses to chop firewood or make stew. "That's the nice part of it," this Introvert admits.

You on the Job

AS A LEADER

"Dogged consensus builder" describes the Green/Red Introvert leadership style. You work doggedly to achieve what is important to you, especially treating colleagues and staff well. *Ethical, supportive, motivating, creatively encouraging, sensitive,* and *patient* are words your people would use to describe you at the helm. A keen observer of people, you understand what motivates others, and you use that to draw the best out of them.

You build consensus by encouraging openness, giving positive feedback, being generous with time and resources, and being patient with process issues. Personalizing your relationships with staff and colleagues ensures support. You build extremely loyal teams by encouraging rather than commanding.

AS A TEAM PLAYER

You have deep and accurate insights into your team members because you hear what is really being said. Warmth and acceptance put them at ease.

Defining common goals is your gift to the team, drawing people together. Matching people to appropriate tasks is another talent; you may find yourself suggesting who should do what even if you're not the leader.

Your forward thinking and provocative ideas frequently get the juices flowing in others. The team often credits you with breaking them out of creative logjams.

You may irritate teammates by becoming too attached to a value not shared by the rest of the team.

Look at figure 8–1 for a list of your natural work-related strengths.

FIGURE 8–1 *Natural Work-Related Strengths*

Approximately 80 percent of these attributes will apply to you. Check off those that do, and use them in your resume and interviews. This will set you apart from the canned responses of others. You:

- ○ Like to explore new possibilities, solving problems in an original way

- ○ Support the development of others

- ○ Understand how underlying emotions impact productivity

- ○ Get right to the guts of an issue

- ○ Can concentrate and work for long periods alone

Now see how one Green/Red Introvert uses these strengths in a very different field.

CASE STUDY TWO
Business Conference Planner

Anne Thayer is one of the 5 percent of Greens who work in the Wall Street community. She has carved out a niche in relationship-building financial conferences. Seemingly going against her artistic, Introverted nature, Anne nonetheless enjoys the creative aspects of the planning process. She writes the program, gets the speakers, and produces the program brochure. On conference days, she brings her acting skills to the conference podium.

As an Introvert, Anne is challenged by the fifty-plus cold calls she makes each day. Fortunately, she has a private office. When she needs a break, she closes her door and does the Five Tibetan Rites of yoga for a quick recharge. Afterward, she eats a simple bowl of bean soup, and she's ready to rock and roll. Her colleagues, who enjoy her warmth and empathy, discreetly hold her calls.

A theater major in college, Anne drifted into popular culture event planning to support her studies. She found she was more skilled and better paid behind the scenes than onstage, and a career in conference planning blossomed.

Conference planning offers Anne the opportunity to use her relationship-building and writing skills and get well paid for them. The financial concepts she must master, though, can be onerous for her; Greens rarely choose financial careers.

Conference planning involves three very Green areas: relationship building, writing, and showcasing the leading ideas of the field. Anne loves to see people engaged in enthusiastic shop talk. She feels proud that her programs have paved the way for multimillion-dollar deals.

She also enjoys writing the programs and event brochures. Many Green/Red Introverts take up writing at some point, and Anne is fortunate that's part of her job. She enjoys being onstage emceeing her programs.

Cold calls, constant networking, and after-hours socializing leave her exhausted. If forced to work a weekend she would normally spend recharging, she frequently runs down her immune system and catches a cold. When she can get enough alone time, however, she enjoys her work.

Ideal Work Environment

Green/Red Introverts do best when not bombarded by the demands of an office; they make excellent telecommuters. You need reflective time and the control of a home environment, like Dan Shaw has.

When a job offer is made, leverage as much as you can from the list in figure 8–2.

FIGURE 8-2 *The Ideal Green/Red Introvert Work Environment*

Compare your current work environment to the descriptions below. If these descriptions seem obvious, that confirms you've tested your individual color correctly. Other Colors, especially Golds, would find this environment uncomfortable and unproductive. The optimal Green/Red Introvert work environment:

○ Is democratic and informal. You function best with a minimum of rules, paperwork, and supervision. Rank and status are fluid.

○ Is supportive and harmonious, fostering cooperation and trust. Backstabbing, confrontation, and malicious gossip irritate and distract you from the task at hand.

○ Encourages creativity and idea generation.

○ Recognizes individual needs of staff and clients. Seek companies that encourage work/life balance and high levels of customer service.

○ Is in sync with personal values. Companies that violate your values will soon see you gone.

○ Allows for private space. As an Introvert, your batteries get drained when dealing with people, even if your people skills are superb. You think, perform, and recharge best in a private space. Insist on one as a condition of employment if possible.

A corporate culture integrating the above elements is fertile soil for your career advancement.

The worst type of work culture for a Green/Red Introvert emphasizes routine and details. Highly political atmospheres and power struggles destroy the creative freedom and trust necessary for Green/Reds to flourish. Tight deadlines impose pressure that is anything but motivating to them.

When Introverted Green/Reds work in nonideal corporate cultures, productivity is stunted and career achievements become an uphill climb.

The Introverted Green/Red's Ideal Boss

Even a great job can be frustrating under the wrong boss; a mediocre job under a wonderful boss is pretty hard to leave. Green/Reds get along especially well with other Greens. But bosses of other Color types who possess the characteristics in figure 8–3 also can be good mentors.

FIGURE 8–3 *The Green/Red Introvert's Ideal Boss*

Check off if your boss:

○ Is flexible

○ Does not micromanage you

○ Takes a personal interest in you and your development

○ Protects you from professional intrigue and politics

○ Values innovation

○ Has a high level of integrity

Careers That Attract Green/Red Introverts

Like Anne, you are most attracted to careers that provide recognition for your creativity in writing and the visual and performing arts or your interest in helping others grow and develop. Green/Red Introverts need to work with people who have a personal interest in them and express appreciation. Working alone or in small groups is best for their productivity, especially if they are focusing on solutions that enhance the lives of others. The atmosphere ideally is casual and informal, like Dan's home office. Often Green/Red Introverts will change careers many times before finding something in which they believe.

Please note that not all the following careers will appeal to you, but recognize that each, in some way, draws on the strengths of your style and appeals to a significant number of your Color group. This is not a comprehensive list, but it will show underlying patterns of preference. If unlisted careers offer similar patterns, your chances of success increase. Text in parentheses at the end of each section highlights the Color style characteristics that create success in that broad area.

According to our research, jobs italicized in the lists below are predicted to benefit from an above-average growth rate over the next several years. This information is based on the continuously revised data provided by the U.S. Department of Labor and Bureau of Labor Statistics on their websites O*NET OnLine (www.onetonline.org) and http://www.bls.gov/CAREEROUTLOOK/. There you will find in-depth information about job requirements and salary ranges.

There are successful people of all Color styles in all occupations. In non-ideal jobs, you can still shine by creating your own niche.

ARTS/DESIGN

art director ▶ designer (interior decoration, fashion) ▶ fine artist ▶ graphic designer ▶ *landscape architect* ▶ multimedia animator/artist ▶ musician ▶ set/exhibit designer ▶ *video game designer* ▶ *website art director* (originality and uniqueness, work alone or in small teams)

BUSINESS/PROMOTION/HUMAN RESOURCES

advertising and promotion manager ▶ *human resources generalist/specialist* ▶ industrial/organizational psychologist ▶ *labor relations specialist* ▶ *meeting*

and event planner ▸ *public relations specialist* ▸ *team building/conflict reso-
lution trainer* ▸ *training and development specialist/manager* (good listening, understanding of human motivation, relationship building, strong
written skills)

COMMUNICATIONS/ENTERTAINMENT/MEDIA

actor and performing artist ▸ *advertising* ▸ author ▸ columnist ▸ curator ▸ editor
▸ film editor/producer ▸ literary agent ▸ photographer ▸ *producer/director* ▸ translator ▸ writers of all types (biographer, journalist, novelist, playwright, poet,
screenwriter) (involvement with media, often work alone, language skills,
creativity and written skills rewarded)

EDUCATION

adult literacy specialist ▸ *bilingual education* ▸ *college professor (humanities,
arts)* ▸ educational consultant ▸ guidance counselor ▸ instructional coordinator
▸ librarian ▸ *online educator* ▸ *school psychologist* ▸ *teachers* (at all levels, plus
art, drama, foreign language, music, special education) (enjoy continuing
education, helping others reach potential)

HEALTH SCIENCE/PSYCHOLOGY

audiologist ▸ *dermatologist* ▸ *dietician/nutritionist* ▸ *family practitioner* ▸ *geneticist*
▸ *holistic health practitioner* ▸ *home healthcare specialist* ▸ *personal trainer* ▸ *psy-
chiatrist/psychologist of all types* ▸ *speech/language pathologist* ▸ *therapist
(art/occupational, behavioral disorder, massage, physical, and substance abuse)*
▸ *veterinarian/veterinarian technician* (empathetic, excellent listener, keen
observer of others)

LAW/HUMAN SERVICES/SCIENCE

anthropologist ▸ *lawyer* (environment, intellectual property, nonprofit) ▸ legal
mediator ▸ philanthropic consultant ▸ religious leader/educator/worker ▸ *social
worker* (deeply held values, intuitive understanding of human motivation,
relationship building, explore/analyze human culture)

DIGITAL/HIGH TECH

customer relations manager ▸ *human resources recruiter* ▸ *social media manager*
▸ technology consultant to internal staff (excel at connecting technology professionals with staff and clients)

CASE STUDY THREE

When a Career Isn't Working

Financial trading desks are notorious for their frat-house culture. Those who thrive enjoy the adrenaline rush of making instant multimillion-dollar decisions. In the process they also scream, hurl obscenities at each other, and occasionally throw food across the room. And for the most part, colleagues do not take offense. Later they will all go out, share a few drinks, and wipe the slate clean.

Enter Phyllis Rosen. Riding the wave of the women's rights movement, she landed a plum job on the trading desk of a giant Wall Street brokerage firm when the company came under pressure to bring women into management.

"The trading desk was the center of everything," Phyllis says. "Whatever happened somewhere in the world had an immediate reaction on Wall Street. I became an information junkie." She also became an adrenaline junkie, her Red side loving the fast pace and the exhilaration of making good trades.

The rushes came at the expense of her Green side. Few Greens enter Wall Street, an arena that rewards risk taking and virtually ignores the emotional component. Her male coworkers were her biggest source of stress. "In those days, they treated each other crudely," she says, "and went for blood when they smelled a weakness."

Not all trades go well, and Phyllis found it very stressful when she lost money for her clients. After a while, the pressures became greater than the adrenaline rushes, and Phyllis had to make some hard decisions about what else to do. After twenty years on Wall Street, she became a career counselor based in New York City. Although she still has some stress in having to replenish clients constantly, she says, "I'm energized by this work because I feel I make a difference, I'm good at it, and I satisfy my curiosity about people and the choices they make."

Your Personality's Challenges

Green/Red Introverts have a unique set of potential work-related blind spots. Some listed below you have, others you don't. Tone down a blind spot by focusing on it, then choose more productive actions and make them habits. (Suggestions for doing so are in parentheses below.) You:

▶ Can be too idealistic and ignore bottom-line consequences. (Making an ideal real can be prohibitively expensive. Consult Golds and Blues about processes and costs.)

▶ Don't speak up enough and appear disengaged. (Few know how much energy it takes to listen, and you listen intently. Your concentration, however, comes across as aloofness. Just throw in a few comments to let others know you're present—humor counts.)

▶ Don't prioritize and appear disorganized. (You have only one priority a day—sit down and prioritize that day's activities. You can handle that, right?)

▶ Consider your own values superior. (Others may compromise or be more realistic, but your ideals are ideal. Once you recognize the strengths of other Colors, though, this tendency will mellow.)

▶ May miss deadlines because you are a perfectionist. (Being perfect means meeting the deadline. Your boss feels that way, so prioritize that career-important deadline over less important details.)

▶ Can be too reserved to be effective. (The more cautious you are about speaking up, the more valuable your insight is likely to be. Give yourself the opportunity for positive reinforcement.)

Your Job Search—the Good, the Bad, and the Ugly

Green/Red Introverts need to process information. With some interviewers, particularly Greens and Reds, you will feel a comfortable rapport. But with those of other Colors, you need a response strategy.

Your natural strengths easily allow you to:

▶ Get excited by new fields and unusual opportunities

▶ Brainstorm creatively

▶ Present yourself as adaptable, committed, easy to work with, and a quick study

▶ Create a master plan for your search with hard research and soul searching

In order to tone down your blind spots, you need to:

▶ Network a little more, even if it feels phony to you

▶ Stick with your objectives; don't change course on a whim

▶ Role play compensation negotiations (find a willing Gold or Red to help)

▸ Talk more and sell your accomplishments

▸ Hold back ideas on which you have not done cost research

The Green/Red Introvert's Interviewing Style

With an interviewer whose Color is close to your own, you will feel immediate rapport. However, if your interviewer seems to have a significantly different style, use the suggestions in parentheses.

In following your natural style, you:

▸ Are quiet and calm. (This can look like disinterest—most interviewers expect a certain amount of nervousness. Make sure to speak more than you normally do, especially at first.)

▸ Listen well. (This impresses many interviewers. But you may miss opportunities to sell your accomplishments. Role play with a willing Red.)

▸ Share values and feelings with only a few people. (You may be able to open up to a Green interviewer who puts you at ease. With others, pre-pared statements about yourself will keep you looking confident.)

▸ Are global and metaphoric in speech. (With interviewers who look skeptical or confused, read straight off your resume for a while.)

▸ Present information and schedules as tentative and adaptable. (But don't be vague about when you can start a job—give an exact date.)

▸ See the big picture and present that first. (Great if you're interviewing for a senior level position, irritating if for a junior slot. No boss wants a subordinate who sees more on the horizon than he or she does. Share only if asked; do not volunteer.)

Okay, go do something fun but nonfattening now. Later, read chapter 9, "Reds Overall." Chapter 24, "Before I Do Something Stupid: Adjusting to Other Styles," will help you identify different Colors and use their strengths collaboratively; you just have to know where to look and how to ask. If you are actively engaging in a job search, jot notes in the Roadmap in chapter 27. Recording your strengths and strategies feels supportive and encouraging.

PART 3

REDS

"Let's Do It Now"

Reds do best in fields that provide variety, change, and the opportunity to rise to the challenge of a crisis.

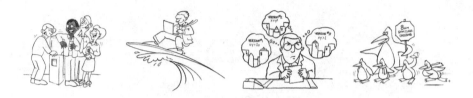

CHAPTER 9

Reds Overall

REDS REPRESENT approximately 27 percent of the overall world population. If you are not a Red but would like to learn how to identify and communicate with one, go to figure 9–1.

FIGURE 9–1 **How to Recognize a Red**

○ Interested in the external world: sports, tools, architecture, motorized vehicles of all kinds

○ Concrete vocabulary

○ Desk has many piles

○ Casual manner

○ Constantly in motion

○ Spontaneous

○ Often late

○ Great sense of humor

○ Seeks excitement and adventure, preferring activity to conversation

○ Knows food and wine

How to Communicate with a Red

○ Be stimulating

○ Avoid meetings, or schedule them in fun places

○ Make presentations brief; use action verbs like *attack, challenge, stimulate,* and *enjoy*

○ Use hands-on demonstrations

○ Avoid theories, get to the point, stay in the concrete here and now

○ Be very flexible and open-ended in conversation and plans

○ Stress immediacy of solutions—this will help "right now, today"

○ Acknowledge and appreciate their crisis-calming skills

○ Allow them to follow their instincts, give them freedom to do so

○ Make it fun, they respond

○ Accept that "timing" is everything

○ Be ready to go with fly-by-the-seat-of-your-pants decisions

Reds are among the most adventurous and entertaining people in the universe. Perhaps the best-known Red in the United States is President Donald Trump, who follows in the footsteps of other Reds such as George W. Bush, Bill Clinton, Lyndon Johnson, John F. Kennedy, Ronald Reagan, and Franklin D. Roosevelt. The former real-estate deal maker, frequently referred to merely as "the Donald," starred in his own reality television show, *The Apprentice,* which first appeared in 2004. (Donald has not taken the Color Q test, but his personality style has been determined by the Myers-Briggs community.)

"Deals are my art form," Trump said in his 1988 best-seller, *Trump: The Art of the Deal.* "Other people paint beautiful pictures on canvas or write wonderful poetry. I like making deals, preferably big deals; that's how I get my kicks."[1] Kicks are a prime motivator for Reds, who will scan the universe twenty-four hours a day to find the next exciting thing. "Money was never a big motivation for me except as a way to keep score," Trump added in his book. "The real excitement is playing the game."[2] In his 2016 presidential campaign Trump was frequently criticized for offering a platform low on details. This is in keeping with his Red nature, as Reds typically prefer to focus on crisis management and activities that generate immediate results.

Time magazine described then-presidential candidate Trump as a "gleeful provocateur" and "breaking every rule in the book."[3] Through his compelling energy as a speaker and unique charisma, "a party supposedly pledged to conservative values has elected a radical president who promises to tear up treaties, overturn laws, jail his opponent, and sue his critics."[4]

Donald graduated from Wharton Business School and quickly gravitated to his father's real-estate business. There he could get out in the field and apply his natural Red problem-solving skills in a hands-on way. But his superior Red negotiation abilities won out, and his real estate deals soon defined the trajectory of his career. Starting with a $1 million loan from his father,[5] Donald today is self-described as a billionaire, although there exists no certain public measure of his true net worth. Reds, more than any other Color, enjoy life's sensual pleasure such as great food and fine wines. Trump's wealth affords him the finest of everything the world has to offer, thus attracting the spotlight. Thrice-married, he spoke on video about his relationship with women.[6] Controversial events like this tainted his presidential bid. However, it's possible this may have actually attracted some voters. "No doubt there were many Trump voters who looked at the skyscrapers and jets and helicopters with his name emblazoned on them and figured any man who could do that could do anything."[7] Based solely on personality type, his presidential administration likely will be characterized by sudden reversals of policy, tough foreign policy negotiations, de-emphasis on long-term planning, and active crisis management.

These Red traits are shared by Christine "Christie" Todd Whitman, management consultant and former governor of New Jersey. Christie was born into a politically active family, so it was probably inevitable that she would achieve political noteworthiness. But it helped immensely that she was a Red. Those attributes catapulted her from an unknown county board member in 1982 to New Jersey governor a mere decade later.

Christie's father, Webster B. Todd, was a contractor whose family firm built Rockefeller Center in New York City and restored Williamsburg in Virginia. At age 50, he retired and turned to his true passion, Republican politics. His wife, Eleanor, joined him, attending every Republican national convention from 1940 to 1976 in an official capacity. Christie had experiences of which few children could boast: at age 6, presenting dolls to Richard Nixon's wife, Patricia, for their daughters, Julie and Tricia; and at age 9, attending her first national convention and presenting Dwight Eisenhower with a leather pouch she had made for his golf balls.

In 1990, Christie made a move that lower-risk personality types would have dismissed as sheer folly. She plunged into the limelight by running against incumbent U.S. Senator Bill Bradley. Many in her own party did not support her, figuring she was sure to lose to Bradley, an All-American Rhodes scholar, a former star forward of the New York Knicks, and formidable fundraiser. He spent $12 million, she spent $1 million. She lost, but only by just under 3 percent. The gamble had worked; people took notice. "I knew it was a long shot," Christie says today, "but I saw an opportunity to gain statewide exposure." She did so, in typical Red calculated-risk-taking fashion.

Reds enjoy camaraderie. To position herself in three years' time as a viable gubernatorial candidate, Christie hosted a talk show, wrote a newsletter, formed a political action committee, and spearheaded the Neighborhood Leadership Initiative, designed to identify and train grass-roots leaders. But what got her the most attention was an extended bus tour designed to meet as many New Jersey citizens as possible. She beat her opponent, incumbent Jim Florio, in 1993 by one percent of the vote.

Reds overflow with physical and mental energy, as well as competitiveness. It was said during Christie's tenure that the state troopers assigned to follow her around and guard her ended up in better physical shape than they ever were before.[8] She set aside several days a week as road days, talking to people around the state. Politics did not blunt her love of animals. Her position allowed her to join park rangers in freezing midwinter weather to observe as they placed ear tags on newly born bear cubs. Christie cuddled the cubs in her jacket as rangers tranquilized the mothers.

Reds are bold and not afraid of controversy, an asset in the political arena.

Their shirtsleeve management style is easygoing, down-to-earth, and expedient. Reds are flexible and, spontaneous, and they have the ability to relate to and persuade other people. Politics is high on the list of most satisfying occupations for a Red personality. More than any other type, Reds love risk and thrive in chaotic situations, moving in to bring order and focus. Christie, like Reds in the corporate world, leads by keeping close to the grass-roots, encouraging personal responsibility, seeking quick results, and focusing on personal goals. She is informal, action oriented, and collaborative, viewing emergencies as interesting challenges rather than intrusions.

Today, Christie Todd Whitman keeps herself visible by running the Whitman Strategy Group, an environmentally oriented management consulting and strategic planning firm with offices in New Jersey and Washington, DC.

Christie Todd Whitman embodies the typical traits of the Red personality—a let's-do-it-now, can-do, live-and-let-live super-realist who thrives from daring and an ability to handle a crisis better than any other Color.

Reds do not respond well to theories or abstract concepts, preferring instead to focus on today's reality. Their view of the world is what they can see, touch, taste, smell, and hear for themselves. Reds need freedom and independence and hate to feel trapped in either work or relationships. Guilt, obligation, and duty rarely motivate them. They are loyal to friends and family, but loathe being tied down to schedules and routines not of their own choosing. The pursuit of action drives many Reds to try new experiences, adventures, activities, or foods. They work in order to spend, rather than to save or invest. The saying "He who dies having worn out the most toys wins" is typical of the Red mentality.

Another famous Red in the political arena was Winston Churchill. J. Paul Getty represented Reds in the corporate world. Michael Jordan illustrates the Red style in sports, Amelia Earhart in adventuring, George Patton in the military, and Justin Bieber, Leonardo DiCaprio, Scarlett Johansson, Nicole Kidman, Ashton Kutcher, Jennifer Lawrence, Lady Gaga, Madonna, Katy Perry, and Barbra Streisand in the field of entertainment.

This chapter will help you determine if you've tested your primary color correctly. It also will help you identify Reds among people you know, as will figure 24–1 in chapter 24, "Before I Do Something Stupid: Adjusting to Other Styles."

If the self assessment at the beginning of the book scored you as a Red, congratulations. You are one of the most fun people in the known universe. You will also be impatient about reading a book like this, preferring instead to get on with things more real and less abstract. However, if you are interested in reading more about yourself, or you want to impress someone who thinks this is a great book and you should read it, go to your specific Color's chapter. We know you're going to skim it. Just be sure to read the section about your most satisfying careers, or you'll miss the most practical part.

CHAPTER 10

Red/Blue Extroverts

YOU'RE NOT ONLY a Red, you also have strong secondary characteristics of the Blue personality. And you have tested as a Color Q Extrovert, which means you recharge your batteries by being with people rather than being alone. It's likely you have little patience for this book and are just reading it to please someone. So we'll keep this realistic, or we know you're out of here.

You Overall

High energy, good humor, and optimism are hallmarks of Red/Blue Extroverts. Unusually effective in times of crisis and change, you seek and revel in the unexpected. Active and independent, you function best in small collegial teams where hierarchy is secondary to getting the job done. Variety makes you happy, as does operating outside the norms followed by others.

Realistic and pragmatic, you trust only what you have personally observed. A particularly acute visual memory makes you exceptional at recalling details. You want the facts but enjoy humorous anecdotes.

Your communication style is blunt and direct, which you find efficient. Others, however, may be put off by your style, and this confuses you. Though very attentive in the moment, you have a short attention span.

You resist making decisions under pressure. You like to keep all options open as long as possible. When ready, however, you decide with the speed of light.

Unusually adept at sizing up problems, you move in quickly for solutions. You trust your own instincts first, bureaucracy last, and often bypass rules and procedures. While adept at handling immediate problems, you have a hard time staying focused on long-term challenges.

Others see you as a gifted negotiator who can make logical and difficult decisions. Although you are tolerant of most folks, you get annoyed by bossy people who insist on "doing things the right way," or whose emotionalism clouds the issue.

In the second half of life, Red/Blue Extroverts continue to seek new challenges but slow down and reflect more between activities.

CASE STUDY ONE

Chief Executive Officer, Investment Consulting Firm, and Author

Peter Tanous is not your typical CEO and has the sense of humor to prove it. He likes to joke that "an economist is someone who didn't have the personality to become an accountant." He can say things like that because his books, *Investment Gurus* and *Wealth Equation*, have both been successful enough to be Money Book Club main selections and receive wide critical acclaim.

He started his business, Lynx Investment Advisory, LLC, a Washington, DC-based investment consulting firm, relatively late in life at age 54. The advantage was he brought wisdom, experience, and contacts to the table, making him able to cope with the old business school rule about starting a business: "Double the expense and halve the revenue of your plan and see if you still make it, because that's what's most likely to happen," he says. "As someone I know put it, I never met a business projection I didn't like. That's because they all look good!"

He set about drumming up business but found the conventional wisdom of making tons of business calls was not the most effective way. "I found you are better off concentrating on the ones where you have a high chance of success . . . that includes people you know or institutions to which you have privileged access," he says. "Anything else is an uphill battle." Red/Blue Extroverts are strong motivators of people, and this was critical to his success. Today, Peter's firm advises on over $1 billion of client assets.

"I understand markets," he says. "I am a very good salesperson and highly optimistic, which is essential." His Red side enjoys the changeable nature of the financial markets and the diverse needs of his clients, particularly his international ones. "I like dealing with their investment needs based on the political environment that they live and function in," he says.

His biggest energizer? "I enjoy making clients happy. I enjoy getting new clients by convincing them of the value of what we do for them." The duties he leaves to others include "most administrative, regulatory, and legal tasks. Pure research, as well."

Peter's top three strengths are typical of his Red/Blue Color. He lists them as enthusiasm, understanding what people really mean (as opposed to what they say), and being "not brilliant, but wise."

He serves on the investment committee of his alma mater, Georgetown University, and on the board of its University Library. He also serves as a trustee of Lebanese American University. Peter is on the corporate boards of General Employment Enterprises, Inc., and Worldcare, Ltd. "I very much enjoy serving in that capacity and helping management achieve the goals we set for them," he says.

You on the Job

AS A LEADER

"Straightforward, fair, and decisive" describes you. Collegial and persuasive, you back it up with a down-in-the-trenches management style. Breaking tension with humor keeps your staff productive.

You are realistic about problems and outcomes. To keep a negotiating process moving, you'll compromise. Projects move forward fast under your take-charge style, while you focus on bottom-line results.

AS A TEAM PLAYER

Having realistic expectations of people and challenges is how you operate. You make things happen and are skilled at persuading others to participate. While you appear fun loving, you are quietly adept at obtaining necessary resources to get things accomplished.

Look at figure 10–1 for a list of your natural work-related strengths.

FIGURE 10–1 *Natural Work-Related Strengths*

Approximately 80 percent of these attributes will apply to you. Check off those that do, and use them in your resume and interviews. This will set you apart from the canned responses of others. You:

- Bring energy and enthusiasm to projects
- Can work through a broad range of people
- Are easygoing and accepting
- Are self-reliant
- Are highly effective in negotiations and sales
- Observe and recall factual information
- Analyze situations quickly and find the most logical course of action
- React fast in crisis or under time pressure

CASE STUDY TWO

Career Coach/Entrepreneur

Reds are James Bond, risk-taking types, but they come in many forms. Laura Hill is not a spy, but there is plenty of risk taking, urgency, and crisis in her professional life. She is the principal of Careers in Motion LLC, a career coaching firm that helps people attain more rewarding careers through strategic career planning, more effective job searches, and building their personal brands.

Her Red primary enjoys the resume-writing process. "Resumes are very tangible; there is a finished product," she says. Reds often have trouble in mostly conceptual, service-oriented roles where finished, tangible products are rare, but Laura finds this serves her need.

Laura's Blue secondary personality provides strategic balance and an outlet for her analytical side. "I get clients to look at their longer-term career—not just their next job—and strategize how they can achieve their goals.

"One of the most engaging parts of my job is helping clients negotiate their job offers. This always involves a high sense of urgency; a crisis of sorts." Reds thrive on, and seek out, adrenaline rushes; Red/Blues particularly enjoy salary negotiations and can be fearless when discussing compensation.

Like most Reds, the (Gold's natural) ability to organize is anathema to Laura. "One of my least desirable tasks is cleaning up my desk and organizing my files!" she says. Although she lacks a Green's ability to read people well and deeply relate to their emotions, she enjoys interacting with a variety of people and the continual learning opportunities that provides.

Red collegiality counterbalances this. "I network well and can build rapport easily with my clients. I also inject practical common sense into their thought processes," she says. As an Extrovert, she has always gravitated to roles where people interaction is a key element of her day. Prior to establishing Careers in Motion, Laura moved through a few people-intensive careers of her own: sales, executive recruiter, bank operations/management, and outplacement consultant. "I think one of my most noteworthy career attributes as a Red is that about every seven years, I've made a major career shift," she says. "I can't imagine being in one job for a long time. I'm highly entrepreneurial, a risk taker." She recently became an angel investor in startup tech companies, a risky proposition that's not for everyone. "I enjoy analyzing the companies and supporting dynamic entrepreneurs while hoping that one of my investments will be a big winner."

But her chief Red/Blue Extrovert strengths really shine in her current role. "One of my best successes has been building a business and personal brand as a career coach," she says. "My reward is making a difference in the careers of my clients."

Ideal Work Environment

Freedom and fun define your ideal work space. Get as much of what follows in figure 10–2 as possible.

FIGURE 10–2 **The Ideal Red/Blue Extrovert Work Environment**

Compare your current work environment to the descriptions below. If these descriptions seem obvious, that confirms you've tested your individual color correctly. Other Colors, especially Golds, would find this environment uncomfortable and unproductive. The optimal Red/Blue Extrovert work environment:

○ Is relaxed, tolerant, and informal. You function best with a minimum of rules, paperwork, and supervision. You need freedom to move around.

○ Provides variety, excitement, and preferably a crisis or two. Repetitive, expectable work brings out the worst in you. You'll butt heads with bureaucracy.

○ Rewards entrepreneurial risk taking and a direct approach. You are valued for your ability to handle the unexpected. If you can work in multiple locations, you are happy and stimulated.

○ Focuses on short-term problems. You need results *now* to feel good about what you're doing; you dislike being forced to think or operate long term.

○ Permits working on tangible products with factual information. If you can't see it, touch it, taste it, hear it, smell it, or prove it, you are not interested. Brainstorming is frustrating, except for the camaraderie.

○ Has associates who are high energy and fun, and value practical experience. You are an enterprising individual who doesn't want to be held back.

○ Provides public recognition. Recognition fuels you to greater achievement.

A corporate culture integrating the above elements is fertile soil for your career advancement.

The worst type of work culture for a Red/Blue Extrovert is one that emphasizes long-term projects. The daily tone is overly serious; humor and play are frowned upon. You will find it nearly impossible to accomplish anything in hierarchical environments full of meetings and memos.

When Extroverted Red/Blues work in nonideal corporate cultures, productivity is stunted and career achievements become an uphill climb.

The Extroverted Red/Blue's Ideal Boss

Even a great job can be frustrating under the wrong boss; a mediocre job under a wonderful boss is pretty hard to leave. Red/Blues get along especially well with other Reds. But bosses of other Color types who possess the traits in figure 10–3 also can be good mentors.

FIGURE 10–3 *The Red/Blue Extrovert's Ideal Boss*

Check off if your boss:

○ Is action-oriented, outgoing, and focused on end results rather than schedules and timetables

○ Gives you the goal, and then leaves you alone

○ Creates rapport through a sense of humor

○ Encourages fun in the workplace and postwork activities

Careers That Attract Red/Blue Extroverts

Like Peter Tanous and Laura Hill, you are most attracted to careers that provide freedom, action, and the ability to be a troubleshooter.

Please note that not all the following careers will appeal to you, but recognize that each, in some way, draws on the strengths of your style and appeals to a significant number of your Color group. This is not a comprehensive list, but it will show underlying patterns of preference. If unlisted careers offer similar patterns, your chances of success increase. Text in parentheses at the end of each section highlights the Color style characteristics that create success in that broad area.

According to our research, jobs italicized in the lists below are predicted to benefit from an above-average growth rate over the next several years. This information is based on the continuously revised data provided by the U.S. Department of Labor and Bureau of Labor Statistics on their websites O*NET OnLine (www.onetonline.org) and http://www.bls.gov/CAREEROUTLOOK/. There you will find in-depth information about job requirements and salary ranges.

There are successful people of all Color styles in all occupations. In nonideal jobs, you can still shine by creating your own niche.

BUSINESS/FINANCE/MANAGEMENT/MANUFACTURING

advertising and promotion manager/sales agent ▶ *business/franchise owners of all types* ▶ career coach ▶ chief executive officer ▶ executive recruiter ▶ *financial advisor* ▶ financial securities trader (stocks, bonds, commodities, foreign currency options) ▶ industrial production manager ▶ insurance adjuster/broker/claim examiner/investigator ▶ *investment banker/consultant* ▶ *marketing manager* ▶ occupational health and safety specialist ▶ purchasing manager/agent ▶ risk management specialist ▶ *sales manager*/retail salesperson ▶ sales representative ▶ stockbroker ▶ *venture capitalist* ▶ wholesale and retail buyer (autonomy, making fast decisions, variety, and attractive money-making potential)

DIGITAL/HIGH TECH

audiovisual specialist ▶ *computer network support specialist* ▶ *computer systems analyst* ▶ *information security specialist* ▶ video game developer (applying technical expertise to immediate and practical problems)

ENTERTAINMENT/MEDIA

actor/dancer/comedian ▶ *agent/business manager of artists and performers* ▶ author ▶ director stage/motion picture/TV ▶ film/TV camera operator

▸ *film/TV producer* ▸ media specialist ▸ musician ▸ photographer ▸ special effects technician ▸ sportscaster ▸ talent director ▸ talk show host (using creative talents in team settings)

HEALTH SCIENCE

chiropractor ▸ *clinical laboratory technician* ▸ community outreach ▸ *emergency room physician* ▸ *paramedic* ▸ personal fitness trainer ▸ podiatrist ▸ *radiological technician* ▸ *respiratory therapist* ▸ *sports medicine specialist* (focus on observing concrete details of the body and practical methods for getting well)

HOSPITALITY/RECREATION

casino/club manager ▸ *chef*/food service manager ▸ cruise director ▸ food serving staff/bartender ▸ *hotel manager* ▸ tour agent (frequent small crises requiring pragmatic response, motivation of others, especially through humor)

INVESTIGATIVE WORK

detective/investigator ▸ insurance fraud investigator ▸ *intelligence analyst* (detailed visual memory, ability to size up problems)

LAW/POLITICS/GOVERNMENT

lawyer (especially criminal, election, entertainment, financial services, litigation, product liability, trial) ▸ lobbyist ▸ *mediator* ▸ negotiator ▸ politicians at all levels (flexibility, ability to persuade, adaptability to the needs of voters)

LAW ENFORCEMENT/GOVERNMENT

corrections officer ▸ criminologist and ballistic expert ▸ FBI agent ▸ firefighter ▸ *forensic science technician* ▸ military officer ▸ police officer ▸ tax examiner (acute visual memory, need for variety)

REAL ESTATE

building inspector ▸ land developer ▸ property manager ▸ real estate broker/agent (interaction with people in a fast-moving business)

SCIENTIFIC RESEARCH/ENGINEERING/LAND RELATED

civil/electronic/industrial/*petroleum engineer* ▸ conservation scientist and forester ▸ farmer and rancher ▸ industrial safety and health engineer ▸ landscape architect ▸ marine biologist ▸ mining engineer ▸ park naturalist/ranger ▸ product safety engineer ▸ technical trainer (for those with technical aptitudes, the opportunity to work close to nature or with other people in a generally collegial environment)

SPORTS RELATED

athletic coach ▶ professional athletes of all types ▶ sports news reporter ▶ sports promoter/agent (generally attracted to physical activity; Red/Blues with special athletic abilities are ideally suited to making this a profession)

TRANSPORTATION

air traffic controller ▶ aircraft mechanic ▶ commercial pilot/copilot/flight engineer ▶ flight instructor ▶ ship captain (appeals to your love of excitement, variety, and risk)

TRADES

carpenter ▶ craftsperson ▶ factory supervisor ▶ general contractor (variety, eye for detail, ability to coordinate resources)

CASE STUDY THREE

When a Career Isn't Working

Rick Jackson was the first child in his family to attend college. His family had high hopes that he would become a doctor, but the theoretical nature of his science classes simply didn't appeal to him. Nor did being stuck in a lab all day; Rick loved all sports and counted the minutes each day until he could get outside.

Rick compromised and became one of the first African Americans in biomedical engineering. He loved the concrete, practical nature of the field, working on real-world problems, often with immediate solutions. He still hated the theory part of his studies but graduated near the top of his class.

He was recruited in his senior year to a well-known, fast-growing firm in California. He relished the idea of adding several new sports to his repertoire.

In his first year, he found himself constantly fatigued. Long hours allowed for fewer sports to manage stress. He made his mark for handling crises well, but he had to do constant theoretical research and talk theory with other researchers. It drained him dry.

He was about to float a resume when a job opening for a biomedical community outreach person appeared on the cafeteria bulletin board. It featured lots of variety, outdoor events, people contact, and no research. Rick went straight to human resources and got the job. Today, Rick not only explains his company's products but brings back ideas he then designs for new ones as well. Some of these have become major profit centers for the firm.

Your Personality's Challenges

Red/Blue Extroverts have a unique set of potential work-related blind spots. We emphasize *potential* because no Red has all of them. Tone down a blind spot by deciding to see it, then choose more productive actions. (Suggestions for doing so are in parentheses below.) You:

- Tend to be casual about rules, procedures, and authority. (This is your number one career-derailing attribute. What makes your job easier may make someone else's much harder, and humor rarely solves that. Think about your salary-review time when tempted to skip a mundane procedure.)

- Sometimes do not follow through on commitments. (If a commitment bogs you down, you may skip it. In the professional world, however, instead of appearing focused on important things, you actually look like you don't have your act together at times. Write appointments down; review them each morning; call to cancel well ahead of time.)

- Hate having tight deadlines, repetitive work, and having to work alone. (Avoid or change jobs where these are the norm. This makes you pessimistic and joyless. If unavoidable, approach your tasks as if they were all ridiculous; this will lighten your mood. So will setting yourself up in a conference room near others.)

- Don't think much beyond today. (You are present centered; often an advantage, but sometimes not. Set long-term goals as a mental discipline.)

- Often do not prepare for a meeting or project. (The ability to wing it is vital in some circumstances. But being ill prepared for meetings and projects damages credibility. Schedule at least twenty minutes for prep beforehand.)

Your Job Search—the Good, the Bad, and the Ugly

You'd rather be out there taking action than reading this. But here are some quick, practical points to keep in mind.

Your natural strengths easily allow you to:

- Have an extensive network for job information and referrals and be adept at using it

- Get facts on different careers/companies

- Sell yourself well, impressing interviewers with energy and responsiveness

- Be specific and detailed about past work and achievements

- Respond to unforeseen opportunities without trepidation

- Logically weigh pros and cons of job offers

In order to tone down your blind spots, you need to:

- Force yourself to set long-term career objectives; enlist the help of friends or family, particularly Greens or Blues (to identify, read chapter 24, "Before I Do Something Stupid: Adjusting to Other Styles")

- Talk less, listen, and ask questions more

- Be patient with multiple interviews and slow decision making

- Follow through consistently with the details of a job search, such as phone calls, thank-you notes, company research; get a willing Gold to help you if possible

- Talk over and decide what's good for you and your family

The Red/Blue Extrovert's Interviewing Style

With an interviewer whose Color is close to your own, you will feel immediate rapport. However, if your interviewer seems to have a significantly different style, use the suggestions in parentheses. Mercilessly exploit your natural traits and you'll get more job offers.

In following your natural style:

- You speak with energy, excitement, charm, and humor. (You may be so energetic that you intimidate some interviewers. If yours seems to get defensive, sit back and answer the next few questions seriously to see if that puts him or her at ease.)

- You often give personal stories to make a point. (Watch to see if this is well received. If the interviewer gets antsy or breaks eye contact, cut it short.)

▸ You focus on the current situation and not on future or strategic issues. (Your ability to focus on the present is a valuable asset, but you may be too short when handling future-oriented questions. Answer slowly and thoughtfully. Then emphasize your talent for turning on a dime if things change.)

▸ You get to the point; you prefer to act rather than talk. (Ask for the job at the end of the interview, but don't rush things. Impatience will hurt you here. If your interviewer seems indecisive, take action. Offer to work a trial project or trial period.)

▸ You reply quickly and think on your feet. (Normally a plus, but some interviewers may want more thoughtful replies. Periodically sit back, look up at the ceiling, and pause a moment before speaking further.)

▸ You convince others with a sense of urgency and excitement. (Don't let your interviewer mistake your excited urgency for desperation. Try not to sit farther forward in your chair than the interviewer is sitting.)

▸ You make frequent jokes. (Gauge interviewer receptivity; stick with neutral subjects.)

Okay, go do something active and energizing. Later, check out chapter 14, "Blues Overall," if we've actually hooked you a little on this stuff. You can jot notes if you want to impress someone with your attention and interest in the Roadmap in chapter 27. The Roadmap is also a great tool to aid a job search.

CHAPTER 11

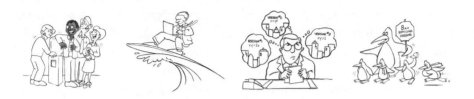

Red/Blue Introverts

YOU'RE NOT ONLY a Red, you also have strong secondary characteristics of the Blue personality. And you have tested as a Color Q Introvert, which means you recharge your batteries by being alone rather than being with others. It's likely you have little patience for this book and are just reading this to please someone. Unless we appeal to you logically and realistically, we know you'll dismiss all this material.

You Overall

Reflective, down to earth, and expedient, Red/Blue Introverts are convinced only by logical reasoning. Self-starting is as natural to you as breathing.

Sharing your thoughts only happens if someone asks. Often absorbed in your own world, you prefer working independently without interruption. Being part of a small, collegial team where hierarchy is secondary to getting the job done brings out your best.

You are unusually effective in times of crisis and change. Realistic and pragmatic, you trust only what you have personally observed. With your particularly acute visual memory, you excel at observing details. Oriented to the concrete, here-and-now world, you have no use for long-term projects or abstract visions.

Your communication style is succinct and informal. You may appear detached to others. Networking and socializing are low on your list of enjoyable activities. Others enjoy your deadpan humor but otherwise find you hard to read. Unorthodox approaches to problems intrigue you, which, coupled with the low visibility you prefer, may leave coworkers puzzled.

It's likely you couldn't care less; you view the process of getting involved with others as a waste of time (although this characteristic mellows somewhat in the second half of your life). Other Colors are intimidated by how quickly you lose interest and stop listening when topics don't appeal to you. You just want the facts and respond best to practical solutions.

Though very attentive in the moment, you have a short attention span. You resist making decisions under pressure. You quickly size up problems but like to keep all options open as long as possible, and this makes you a formidable negotiator. When ready, however, you decide with the speed of light.

You are most irritated by emotional and pompous people who moralize or get caught up in a single way of doing something. Living on the edge, seeking action and variety appeal to you.

In business, you tend to avoid opportunities leading to management positions in large organizations. You'll opt to sell or purchase a franchise while turning your attention to ever-new interests. For you, rising to a position of high responsibility is most likely under crisis conditions; here your flexibility and ability to see the core of a problem make you a most effective leader.

If we've been fairly accurate so far (and we should be since this system has been tested on millions of people worldwide for seven decades), give us a little more time. Read the rest of this chapter to see if it might change your life for the better.

CASE STUDY ONE

High-End Interior Designer

Bunny Williams's interior designs are in high demand by high-net-worth clients. "I do primarily residential work," she says. "My interior design style is quite varied, but it is really to create comfortable houses for people to live in."

Working out of her Upper East Side Manhattan offices, Bunny manages clients and her furniture-licensing business, Bunny Williams Home. Her designs are featured at Ballard's (tabletop and glassware), Dash & Albert (rugs), and Lee Josa (fabrics). She has published five books.[1] *An Affair with a House* reveals the aesthetics of her warm and tasteful style. Bunny's personality shines in this field, where a Red's appreciation of life's finer things supports success.

"I immediately knew this is the field I wanted to be in. I came to New York and got a job with a very prestigious antique firm, Stair and Company. Next I went to work for the one interior design firm that I most wanted to work for, Parish Hadley. I started out as Mr. Hadley's secretary and worked my way up to becoming a senior designer. After twenty years, I left and started my own design company, Bunny Williams, Inc."

Bunny's Blue secondary personality provides the analytical and strategic strengths necessary to her role as president of Bunny Williams, Inc. "I'm the senior designer," she says. "The most engaging part for me is the design element. I also manage the business. The business part interests me; every month I go through how we're doing financially, I'm very aware of it. But that isn't what I want to spend all my time doing. I have people in the accounting department who are better at accounting than I would be. I think any good leader figures out their own role."

Her Introvert side supports her work. "I sometimes just shut my office door, get off the computer and phone, and look at my books, new magazines, and catalogs. I get stimulated by new materials."

Although her career path has been strategically focused, Bunny dealt with the challenges of her early years in a Red's present-centered way. "You don't know what a career is at fifteen or eighteen. I pursued something I liked. Around thirty, I realized I was going to make a career out of it. You make a huge commitment to a career. I think a lot of people stay in a position early on because they need to pay the rent. They lose a lot of time trying to find their passion. The earlier you say to yourself, 'I don't want to do this,' the better it is to move on and try something else."

You on the Job

AS A LEADER

You lead your staff through action, by example. When assessing problems, you are logical and realistic about the easiest way to complete the task. Your communication style is precise, and you engage the skills of your staff efficiently.

When others need information, you are a factual warehouse. Those facts produce creative solutions and allow you to take well-calculated risks.

AS A TEAM PLAYER

You find working on a team draining and inefficient. Teammates get confused and threatened when you go off and return with your own solutions and ideas.

Your natural reserve is counterbalanced by your love of action. If your team is charged with handling a crisis, you may wind up being its leader, because moving others to action is a natural skill.

Brief meetings are the only ones you tolerate. You may irritate others by not completing tasks you have deemed low priority. They may mistake your detachment for disorganization.

Look at figure 11–1 for a list of your natural work-related strengths.

FIGURE 11–1 Natural Work-Related Strengths

Approximately 80 percent of these attributes will apply to you. Check off those that do, and use them in your resume and interviews. This will set you apart from the canned responses of others. You:

- ○ Bring people and tasks together in a way that inspires action

- ○ Are highly observant

- ○ Pay attention to factual information

- ○ Excel in assignments that are action oriented, practical, and nonrepetitious

- ○ Value and promote efficiency

- ○ Love to overcome obstacles using a logical approach

- ○ Combine a no-nonsense need for facts and figures with an openness to new strategies

- ○ Can be productive for hours when left on your own

Here are some Red/Blue Introverts in action in very different fields.

CASE STUDY TWO

Deputy Chief, Educational Support Team

Alex Lee is a Red with an eye for opportunity. But rather than purely seeking profit, Alex looks for ways to help higher education faculty teach more effectively.

Reds are the most playful of the personality types, always ready for sports and other games. The games Alex and his team of five program designers create support and improve the higher education process.

"We create scenarios and teach students and faculty to run real-world simulation games," says Alex. "We research existing games for potential use and sometimes create them to meet teachers' desires. I have coauthored two courses on teaching with games and coteach two other courses."

It's a great job for a Red, because it addresses hands-on needs that are constantly evolving. "The best part of my job," says Alex, "is that I get to do a variety of things I like to do: teach, provide tech support, design games. I get to go around and make people satisfied. It's a series of different challenges—never the same day in and day out."

Not all the games Alex works on are usable or accepted; this developmental part of his job involves some risk taking. But the Red/Blue's combination of risk taking and strategic thinking is ideally suited to tackling such demands.

"I make many major shifts in direction," says Alex. "I scan for opportunities, then try them to see whether they'll pan out. I tell myself I will never forgive myself if I don't try." Exploring uncharted territory invigorates Reds, while it can mentally exhaust other Colors (especially Golds).

Alex is more interested in being effective than always being right. "Our greatest success, surprisingly, is that not every teacher uses what we provide but that they know that we support them. They see we are not going to come into their classrooms and shove something down their throats. Forcing ourselves in would make us ineffective."

Red/Blues are particularly effective at circumventing rules and procedures they deem obstructive or unnecessary. Alex does so by assigning tasks to others who he feels do them better. "One of my team writes better official memos, and I have a team member who is better at day-to-day technical support," he says.

He has a uniquely Red way of dealing with tough clients. "One of the techniques I use is to officially agree with them and then say something they did not actually say. Then it sounds like their idea. If they contradict me, I can say, 'I am sorry—I misunderstood you.'"

But Alex has a strong work ethic. "I bring a questioning attitude to my own performance; I would not be effective if I thought I had all the answers."

Ideal Work Environment

Your ideal work environment offers routine crises and a private office to reflect in. Use all the leverage you can when a job offer is made to get as much of what follows in figure 11–2 as possible.

FIGURE 11–2 **The Ideal Red/Blue Introvert Work Environment**

Compare your current work environment to the descriptions below. If these descriptions seem obvious, that confirms you've tested your individual color correctly. Other Colors, especially Golds, would find this environment uncomfortable and unproductive. The optimal Red/Blue Introvert work environment:

○ Is easygoing. You function best with a minimum of rules, paperwork, and supervision.

○ Focuses on immediate results. You need results now to feel good about what you're doing.

○ Permits working on real things and tangible products. If you can't see it, touch it, taste it, hear it, or smell it, you are not interested. Brainstorming is a frustrating waste of time for you.

○ Encourages a blunt, direct approach. Small talk and beating around the bush make you impatient. Subtlety, nuance, and emotion are for other Colors, not you.

○ Offers opportunities to experiment.

○ Contains variety, excitement, and openness to high-stakes gambles. A crisis or two to share with action-oriented associates is your definition of a perfect day.

○ Allows for autonomy and private space. As an Introvert, your batteries get drained when dealing with others, even if your people skills are superb. If you have to share your work space, you will feel a lot more fatigue at the end of the day. You think and perform better in a private space; insist on one as a condition of employment if possible.

A corporate culture integrating the above elements is fertile soil for your career advancement.

The worst type of work culture for an Introverted Red/Blue is a strongly hierarchical one that runs on meetings and memos. It requires too much collaboration with others, especially if those others need constant reassurance.

When Introverted Red/Blues work in nonideal corporate cultures, productivity is stunted and career achievements become an uphill climb.

The Introverted Red/Blue's Ideal Boss

Even a great job can be frustrating under the wrong boss; a mediocre job under a great boss is pretty hard to leave. Red/Blues get along especially well with other Reds. But bosses of other Color types who possess the traits in figure 11–3 also can be good mentors.

FIGURE 11–3 **The Red/Blue Introvert's Ideal Boss**

Check off if your boss:

○ Points you in the right direction and then leaves you alone

○ Shares your sense of humor

○ Rewards logic and is not threatened by your independent ways

○ Is willing to take risks

Careers That Attract Red/Blue Introverts

Like Alex Lee, you are most attracted to careers that provide freedom, action, and variety. You'll often gravitate to positions where your negotiation skills are appreciated. Look for jobs that reward your key strengths: jumping in, acting immediately, and negotiating whatever it takes to get the job done.

Please note that not all the following careers will appeal to you, but recognize that each, in some way, draws on the strengths of your style and appeals to a significant number of your Color group. This is not a comprehensive list, but it will show underlying patterns of preference. If unlisted careers offer similar patterns, your chances of success increase. Text in parentheses at the end of each section highlights the Color style characteristics that create success in that broad area.

According to our research, jobs italicized in the lists below are predicted to benefit from an above-average growth rate over the next several years. This information is based on the continuously revised data provided by the U.S. Department of Labor and Bureau of Labor Statistics on their websites O*NET OnLine (www.onetonline.org) and http://www.bls.gov/CAREEROUTLOOK/. There you will find in-depth information about job requirements and salary ranges.

There are successful people of all Color styles in all occupations. In nonideal jobs, you can still shine by creating your own niche.

BUSINESS/FINANCE/MANUFACTURING/MANAGEMENT

budget analyst ▶ *entrepreneur/franchise owner* ▶ *financial advisor* ▶ financial securities trader (stocks, bonds, options, commodities, foreign currency, etc.) ▶ insurance adjuster/claim examiner ▶ *investment banker* ▶ *property manager* ▶ *purchasing agent* ▶ *retail buyer* ▶ risk management specialist ▶ *securities analyst* ▶ *stockbroker* (operate independently or with few people at a time, logical approaches and fast decision making rewarded, crises provide stimulation)

DIGITAL/HIGH TECH

computer systems analyst ▶ hardware engineer ▶ *educational computer simulations software engineer* ▶ *information security specialist* ▶ *Internet of Things solutions architect* ▶ *network systems administrator/analyst* ▶ *software designer/developer* ▶ *software engineer* ▶ *support specialist* ▶ *technical trainer* (for those with technical aptitudes, the opportunity to work with factual material coupled with spurts of action)

ENTERTAINMENT/MEDIA

agent/business manager of performers and special events ▶ *audio and video equipment technician* ▶ *audiovisual specialist* ▶ *film, video, and TV camera operator* ▶ photographer ▶ *sound engineering technician* ▶ special effects technician (appeals to your need for excitement, freedom, use of technical expertise, and unorthodox approaches)

HEALTH SCIENCE

anesthesiologist ▶ *cardiovascular technologist* ▶ *clinical laboratory technologist* ▶ *dentist/dental hygienist* ▶ *emergency room physician/technician* ▶ *exercise physiologist* ▶ *paramedic* ▶ *podiatrist* ▶ *radiologic technician* ▶ *sports medicine specialist* ▶ *surgical technologist* (hands-on activities with sensitive equipment, observing concrete details of the body, using technical expertise, quick-response situations)

HOSPITALITY/RECREATION

bar/club owner/manager ▶ chef ▶ restaurant owner/manager (frequent crises and pressure, need to jump in and act immediately)

INVESTIGATIVE WORK

detective/investigator ▶ forensic technician ▶ insurance fraud investigator/adjuster ▶ *intelligence agent/specialist* (allows independent operation, working alone for long periods)

LAW/LAW ENFORCEMENT/GOVERNMENT

ballistics expert ▸ corrections officer ▸ *criminal investigator* ▸ firefighter ▸ fire prevention specialist ▸ *lawyer* (especially in criminal, energy, litigation, real estate, transportation) ▸ mediator ▸ military officer/special forces ▸ police /correction officer (acute visual memory for details, logical approach to problems, action, and variety)

NATURE RELATED

agricultural inspector ▸ farmer/rancher ▸ forester ▸ landscape architect ▸ marine biologist ▸ park naturalist ▸ soil conservationist ▸ surveyor (love of the outdoors and physical activity, ability to work for long periods alone productively, dealing with problems flexibly and expediently)

SCIENTIFIC RESEARCH/ENGINEERING

engineer (civil, electrical, environmental, industrial, health and safety, alternative energy systems) ▸ occupational health and safety specialist (for those with technical aptitudes, the opportunity for hands-on applications)

SPORTS RELATED

athletes of all types ▸ *athletic coach* ▸ *business manager of athletes* (keen awareness of physical nuances, quick ability to respond and negotiate)

TRANSPORTATION

ambulance driver ▸ air traffic controller ▸ aircraft mechanic ▸ flight instructor ▸ pilot/flight engineer ▸ race car driver ▸ ship captain (appeals to your love of excitement and risk)

OTHER

automotive products retailer ▸ boat captain ▸ carpenter/cabinetmaker ▸ *electrician* ▸ general contractor ▸ interior designer (high end) ▸ *jeweler* ▸ plumber ▸ surveyor (need for flexibility, cool under crisis, getting things done expediently)

CASE STUDY THREE

When a Career Isn't Working

Hector Torres always knew he would one day manage his family's upscale Spanish restaurant. He really enjoyed working there as a teenager, sampling the fine foods on the menu. Reds appreciate good food and fine wine more than most other Colors. Hector enjoyed the pressure and crises, and his social life came to him—an excellent situation for an Introvert who is drained by parties. "Any job where I can move around as much as I do here—that's for me," he always said.

Hector attended the Culinary Institute of America after high school, paying particular attention to restaurant management. He was surprised to find some of it quite boring— inventory control and nightly account balancing in particular. But Hector's mind was set, and upon graduating, his parents retired and he took over the restaurant, eager to implement some new ideas.

He found he had less skill at dealing with employee schedules and temperaments than his parents, causing Hector constant irritation. Several long-time waiters quit, and the small crises Hector enjoyed became big ones he did not. Inventory and account balancing became daily realities. His relationship with his fiancée became strained when he asked to postpone the wedding until he got the restaurant under control.

It all came to a head the day the restaurant was robbed. The police came, but all they could determine was that it was an inside job. Impatient with their progress, Hector undertook his own internal investigation. Within forty-eight hours he'd identified the culprit and gotten a fair amount of money back. Hector hadn't been this energized since he took over the restaurant.

He went back to school and became a private detective. Today, he is married and has his own investigative agency, specializing in restaurant incidents. One of his siblings took over the restaurant, the old waiters returned, and it is thriving.

Your Personality's Challenges

Red/Blue Introverts have a unique set of potential work-related blind spots. We emphasize *potential* because no Red/Blue has them all. Tone down a blind spot by deciding to see it, then choose more productive actions. (Suggestions for doing so are in parentheses below.) You:

- Tend to be casual with rules and procedures valued by others, including meeting deadlines. (This is your number one career-derailing attribute. What makes your job easier may make someone else's much harder, and deadpan humor rarely solves that. Think about salary review time when tempted to push a deadline.)

- Sometimes step on the feelings of associates. (Getting involved with people is not a priority for you; being expedient is. Hurt feelings hinder results.)

▶ Hate not having control of your own schedule and being under tight deadlines. (This makes you cynical and frivolous. Give serious consideration to leaving any job in which these are a frequent occurrence.)

▶ May wing things that require preparation. (This undermines your credibility. People will dismiss your special qualities and contributions if they are inconvenienced by your loose approach to areas that are important to them.)

Your Job Search—the Good, the Bad, and the Ugly

You'd rather be out there hitting the pavement than reading this. But hang in there; you're almost done. You'll benefit from these concrete job-search tips:

Your natural strengths easily allow you to:

▶ Respond quickly and decisively to unforeseen opportunities

▶ Be specific and precise in your interview about past positions and achievements

▶ Make good career contacts through your love of adventurous hobbies

▶ Negotiate the terms of a new job well

In order to tone down your blind spots, you need to:

▶ Force yourself to set long-term goals; enlist the help of friends or family, particularly Golds or Blues (to identify, read chapter 24, "Before I Do Something Stupid: Adjusting to Other Styles")

▶ Prepare ahead for emotional, rapport-building questions; practice role playing with a Green

▶ Follow through on commitments, deadlines, and the nitty-gritty tasks of a job search such as keeping lists of contacts and sending thank-you notes; enlist the aid of a willing Gold to help

▶ Discipline yourself to think about how a job offer will affect you and your family in the future, not just this month or this year

▶ Be aggressive about soliciting referrals and leads from acquaintances and strangers, as your preferred circle of friends is small

The Red/Blue Introvert's Interviewing Style

With an interviewer whose Color is close to your own, you will feel immediate rapport. However, if your interviewer seems to have a significantly different style, use the suggestions in parentheses. Mercilessly exploit your natural traits and you'll get more job offers.

In following your natural style you:

▸ Are concrete and realistic about past responsibilities and accomplishments. (Some interviewers will dig for feelings: "Did you like your previous boss? How did you get along with your coworkers?" Ask a Green to help role play such questions ahead of time.)

▸ Avoid sharing personal information. (Keeping your distance will make you look as if you have something to hide. Take a moment if needed, then be honest.)

▸ Answer questions succinctly and informally. (Some interviewers look for more formal responses. If there's a pause and the interviewer seems to be waiting for something more, use your quick thinking to expand your answer with more facts.)

▸ Listen only when your interest is engaged. (Grit your teeth and listen to everything your interviewer says, no matter how irrelevant. Patience is a virtue in a job interview.)

▸ Use deadpan humor. (This works with people who know you well, but for those who don't know you, it can create social awkwardness. If a joke falls flat in an interview, quickly smile and say, "Just kidding.")

▸ Focus on the company's current situation and not on future or strategic issues. (Your ability to focus on the present is a valuable asset, but you may be too short when handling future-oriented questions. Answer slowly and thoughtfully. Then emphasize your talent for turning on a dime if things change.)

Congratulations for making it all the way through this chapter. Most Reds won't. Reward yourself by doing something active now. Later, check out chapter 14, "Blues Overall," if we've actually hooked you a little on this stuff. You can jot notes if you want to impress someone with your attention and interest in the Roadmap in chapter 27. This is also a good place to record the information you pick up when networking during a job search.

CHAPTER 12

Red/Green Extroverts

YOU'RE NOT ONLY a Red, you also have strong secondary characteristics of the Green personality. And you have tested as a Color Q Extrovert, which means you recharge your batteries by being with people rather than being alone. It's likely you have little patience for this book and are just reading this to please someone. So we'll make this realistic and fun, or we know you're out of here.

You Overall

Warm and energetic, Red/Green Extroverts have wide interests and many friends. You are active, sociable, and adaptable. In entrepreneurial startups or corporate crises, you shine.

Realistic and pragmatic, you trust only what you have personally observed. With a particularly acute visual memory, you excel at observing details. Yet you are easygoing and fun loving, and you enjoy the unexpected.

Of all the Colors, you are most in touch with the present moment. Because you are driven to achieve results *now*, you have low tolerance for procedure and routine. Bossy people who insist on having things done "the right way" annoy you mightily. Otherwise, you have an accepting, live-and-let-live attitude.

Others see you as exuberant, entertaining, and generous; they feel positive and enthused when you are around. Networking comes naturally to you.

Straightforward communication is your style. You want the facts but enjoy an anecdote or two (particularly a humorous one). Though very attentive in the moment, you have a short attention span. Making decisions under pressure is not for you; instead, you keep all options open as long as possible. When ready, however, you decide with the speed of light.

CASE STUDY ONE

Entrepreneur, Restaurant and Mail Order Businesses

Gregory B. Bidou didn't think racing motorcycles as a teenager would ever lead to a career. So he went to college and became an environmental engineer and industrial hygienist. But for thirty years this Red/Green Extrovert was dissatisfied because, "Even if I did my job perfectly—in terms of lives saved and illnesses prevented—it wouldn't be recognized statistically for decades."

So in his spare time, Greg sold parts for vintage British motorcycles. He enjoyed the immediate rewards of refurbishing rusty parts and diagnosing mechanical problems with customers.

Within two years, this side business outgrew his garage. Greg had to rent expensive warehouse space, some not secure from theft, for his rapidly growing inventory.

Greg enjoyed meeting these concrete challenges. One Sunday, deep in the countryside, he found a vacant, neglected coffee shop with an apartment above and two barns on the property. By Monday evening, he had purchased it, not even sure what he was going to do with the storefront but encouraged by the positive response of town hall authorities.

He sold his house for a good price, allowing him to pay cash for his new property and have funds left over to renovate. Members of his new community kept asking him, "Are you going to reopen the coffee shop?" Despite having no restaurant experience, he jumped in. It took a year for him to rebuild the little café essentially by himself.

His business plan became to sell motorcycle parts one-half of the week and operate a biker-friendly café the other half, both businesses helping to build each other.

His previous industrial hygiene career allowed him to deal with stimulating crisis situations. But, Greg says, "What drove me nuts was babysitting programs once I had implemented them." Red/Green Extroverts like startups but find ongoing administration repetitive and stifling.

Present-centered Red/Green Extroverts need immediate results. "In the café, I make a dish. Right away, customers can tell me if they like it." However, Greg does get frustrated by making the same dishes time and again.

The motorcycle-parts business offers constant change and challenge. "No two customers are alike, and no two bikes are alike," Greg says with satisfaction. "I really like diagnosing motorcycle problems over the phone and providing the parts to solve them."

He even likes coping with the heart-stopping cash flow problems new business owners can face. "I see it all as risk management. I've had to sacrifice compared to my old corporate income days, but so far no creditors have come knocking on my door."

Today, Greg's café has been very successful—enough for mention in the *New York Times* and *Men's Journal* magazine, and many glowing reviews, most notably by Jane Stern of *Roadfood* fame. His motorcycle-parts business picks up the slack in the winter when café traffic declines, and he lives a modest but much happier life.

You on the Job

AS A LEADER

Quick—that's you. You have a fast, down-in-the-trenches management style, breaking pressured moments with humor. You prefer collegiality over power plays.

Risk and change do not worry you, because you are realistic about problems and outcomes. Creative solutions that lack a track record intrigue, rather than frighten, you.

AS A TEAM PLAYER

Realistic and grounded, you make things happen—your enthusiasm inspires everyone to participate. Your image is fun loving, although you are adept at finding the necessary resources to get things accomplished.

You may irritate others by placing too much focus on fun or the adrenaline rush.

Look at figure 12–1 for a list of your natural work-related strengths.

FIGURE 12–1 **Natural Work-Related Strengths**

Approximately 80 percent of these attributes will apply to you. Check off those that do, and use them in your resume and interviews. This will set you apart from the canned responses of others. You:

○ Are realistic about what needs to be done

○ Notice and remember factual information

○ React quickly in crisis or under time pressure

○ Bring energy and optimism to projects

○ Enjoy collaborating with others

○ Are highly effective in negotiations and sales

Now see how two other Red/Green Extroverts use their strengths in very different fields.

CASE STUDY TWO

General Counsel and Chief Compliance Officer, Alternative Financial Investments

When things are new, trending, or in need of upgrading, Ria Davis, Esq., is the one to assign. These are the strengths she brought to her role as general counsel and chief compliance officer at Semper Capital Management, LP, a $1 billion New York City alternative investment firm for institutional and retail clients.

Normally, you don't find Reds like Ria doing detailed financial compliance work. "I'm a Red in a Gold job," she admits wryly. But how she got there was completely a Red story.

"Massive changes were happening in Semper's business in 2013," she says. "I spent eighteen months rebuilding an effective compliance program to reflect those changes, reconfiguring a lot of technology solutions. (I'm very intuitive about how things should work mechanically and technologically.) All the compliance manuals were rewritten, and we did an end-to-end audit of the compliance function."

But the Red personality's strengths lie in problem solving rather than maintaining a well-designed department. "My career choices have been all about the need for variety and change, to constantly be learning new things," she says. "I never had 'a plan' other than to avoid getting 'stuck' in a boring role." Reds prefer immediate challenges.

"I learned to speak Portuguese in a few weeks when my firm decided that Brazil was a 'hot market.' At my first client meeting, we discussed accounting matters. I had to figure out what a Japanese man was saying in heavily accented Brazilian Portuguese. Piece of cake!" she recalls. "My motto is: 'Been there, done that; what's next?' Once a challenge has been met, I am ready to move on to something else."

Reds are talented problem solvers who plunge in even when the odds are not good. They seem to make things happen with little effort that other Colors find require meticulous planning. She was an early adopter of digital tools. "I learned about the Internet and led a legal and technology team to build the first secure private bank client website at Citigroup in the late 1990s," she says. "None of the other lawyers wanted to do it."

Her career path has taken her from her start as an associate attorney at Houston law firm Baker and Botts to several firms in New York (Shearman & Sterling, Kaye Scholer, Brown & Wood [now Sidley-Austin], and Citigroup Private Bank) before joining Semper.

Ria speaks Spanish, French, and Portuguese; she would love to learn Japanese. When speaking English, she is direct and pulls no punches— typical of her Red personality type. "I'm a woman with a very direct, masculine communication style, which creates a lot of challenges for me in dealing with both men and women." Fortunately, her Red collegiality provides balance. Recently Ria changed careers. She is now the new Executive Director of the Financial Women's Association of NY.

CASE STUDY THREE

TV/Film Actor and Producer

Howard Platt's prolific show business career spans fifty years and has made him a recognizable face and voice in many American households. Howard is perhaps best known for his role as Hoppy the white cop on the classic sitcom *Sanford and Son*, but his work extends through radio, television, film, theater (acting and producing), and music. He has costarred with such well-known actors as Alan Alda, Gene Hackman, Hal Linden, Lee Marvin, Bob Newhart, Oliver Reed, Sissy Spacek, Connie Selleca, and John Travolta.

Howard currently stars in the long-running play *A Couple of Blaguards*, the story of *Angela's Ashes* author Frank McCourt and his brother Malachy. This often takes Howard on the road to destinations across America. Typical of adventurous and gregarious Reds, Howard enjoys the constantly new experiences and people he meets on road trips. His Red visual memory and observational skills serve him well when navigating unfamiliar back roads and big cities.

"I spend a lot of time in Chicago," he says. That's where he produced the theatrical hits *Pump Boys and Dinettes, Driving Miss Daisy, Shirley Valentine,* and *I'm Not Rappaport*. That's also where he worked with such luminaries as Shelly Berman, Ellen Burstyn, Garrett Morris, and Loretta Swit. "I have family I like to visit in Wisconsin and Dallas. I often go to New York and Los Angeles for auditions. But these days I live in Mexico."

Reds in general enjoy humor-filled conversations; Howard is an accomplished raconteur. His life stories are filled with celebrities and theatrical adventures. His Red crisis-management abilities always serve him well when he or a fellow actor forgets their lines; he can gauge and raise audience mood immediately using his Green secondary type's sensitivity to others. These traits together make him easily able to improvise onstage as the need arises.

His Green side has inspired him to create through multiple artistic outlets. He has composed ten songs; currently he is collaborating on (and will star in) a play about the famous Midwestern environmental activist known only as the Fox. Howard's original music will be included in the score.

Red/Greens thrive in flexible work environments. "I had the most fun working on *Flying High*," Howard recalled of his starring role in the 1978–79 television series. "The producers told the directors, 'Don't mess with Howard, let him do what he does.' So it was great! I had freedom to do what I wanted. I would put the other actors on notice: 'I'm going to do something, so just be ready for it.'"

Ideal Work Environment

Greg Bidou's motorcycle business and café both permit working on tangible products that focus on short-term problems—perfect for a Red/Green Extrovert. Red/Green Extroverts also like to operate by their own rules and need very flexible environments, like Howard Platt.

When a job offer is made, leverage as much as you can from the list in figure 12–2.

FIGURE 12–2 **The Ideal Red/Green Extrovert Work Environment**

Compare your current work environment to the descriptions below. If these seem obvious, that confirms you've tested your individual Color correctly. Other Colors, especially Golds, would find this environment uncomfortable and unproductive. The optimal Red/Green Extrovert work environment:

- ○ Is relaxed, tolerant, and informal. You function best with a minimum of rules, paperwork, and supervision.

- ○ Provides variety, excitement, and preferably a crisis or two. Repetitive, routine work brings out the worst in you.

- ○ Rewards those who move at a fast pace and solve problems. You enjoy the adrenaline rushes that drive other Colors crazy.

- ○ Gives opportunities to use troubleshooting skills. Your ability to work fast under pressure makes you the one for projects or departments in chaos.

- ○ Focuses on short-term problems. You need results *now* to feel good about what you're doing.

- ○ Permits working on real things and tangible products. If you can't see it, touch it, taste it, hear it, or smell it, you are not interested. A day of brainstorming feels like a waste to you, except for the camaraderie.

- ○ Is aesthetically appealing and colorful. More than for most Colors, unattractive surroundings will distract and irritate you, detracting from productivity. You appreciate the world's finer things, and they inspire you at work.

- ○ Has associates who are lively and action oriented. Energetic people stimulate your productivity.

- ○ Factors in needs of customers and staff. You'll burn out in workplaces that disregard human needs, squeezing every nickel out of each transaction and worker.

A corporate culture integrating the above elements is fertile soil for your career advancement.

The worst type of work culture for an Extroverted Red/Green is one that emphasizes long-term projects. Humor and play are frowned upon, and the daily tone is serious. You will find it near impossible to accomplish anything in environments that are hierarchical with many meetings and memos.

When Red/Green Extroverts work in nonideal corporate cultures, productivity is stunted and career achievements become an uphill climb.

The Extroverted Red/Green's Ideal Boss

Even a great job can be frustrating under the wrong boss; a mediocre job under a wonderful boss is pretty hard to leave. Red/Greens get along especially well with other Reds. But bosses of other Color types who possess the characteristics in figure 12–3 can also be good mentors.

FIGURE 12-3 **The Red/Green Extrovert's Ideal Boss**

Check off if your boss:

○ Is pragmatic

○ Points you in the right direction and then leaves you alone

○ Creates rapport through a sense of humor

○ Encourages fun in the workplace

Careers That Attract Red/Green Extroverts

Like the people in our case studies, you are most attracted to careers that provide freedom, action, and the ability to be a troubleshooter.

Please note that not all the following careers will appeal to you, but recognize that each, in some way, draws on the strengths of your style and appeals to a significant number of your Color group. This is not a comprehensive list, but it will show underlying patterns of preference. If unlisted careers offer similar patterns, your chances of success increase. Text in parentheses at the end of each section highlights the Color style characteristics that create success in that broad area.

According to our research, jobs italicized in the lists below are predicted to benefit from an above-average growth rate over the next several years. This information is based on the continuously revised data provided by the U.S. Department of Labor and Bureau of Labor Statistics on their websites O*NET OnLine (www.onetonline.org) and http://www.bls.gov/CAREEROUTLOOK/.

There you will find in-depth information about job requirements and salary ranges.

There are successful people of all Color styles in all occupations. In non-ideal jobs, you can still shine by creating your own niche.

ARTS/DESIGN/ENTERTAINMENT/MEDIA

actor/performer/comedian ▸ art director ▸ audiovisual/multimedia specialist ▸ *costume/wardrobe/set designer* ▸ craft and fine artist (painter, sculptor, illustrator) ▸ dancer ▸ entertainment agent (actor/performer) ▸ fashion/interior designer ▸ film/TV/stage producer and director ▸ landscape architect ▸ musician ▸ news anchor ▸ photographer ▸ radio and TV announcer/talk show host ▸ special effects technician ▸ stage manager ▸ tour guide/organizer ▸ TV/camera operator (use artistic talents to produce concrete and usable products)

ANIMAL CARE

animal breeder/groomer/trainer/service worker ▸ pet store owner ▸ *veterinarian* ▸ *veterinary technician* (tap into sensitivity to animals and their physical and emotional needs)

BUSINESS/FINANCE/LAW

buyer and purchasing agent ▸ corporate trainer ▸ *diversity manager* ▸ *entrepreneur* ▸ *financial advisor* ▸ *financial securities trader* (stocks, bonds, commodities) ▸ *insurance agent/broker*/claim investigator ▸ *labor relations mediator* ▸ *lawyer* (real estate, litigation, poverty) ▸ manufacturer sales representative ▸ *marketing specialist* ▸ *meeting and event planner* ▸ *public relations specialist* ▸ retail manager ▸ *sales manager* ▸ salesperson ▸ small business owner (draw on strong communications and selling skills)

DIGITAL/HIGH TECH

software engineer ▸ *support specialist* ▸ *video game designer* (ability to combine design and technical skills with other people in a generally collegial environment)

EDUCATION/HUMAN SERVICES

child care worker ▸ *child/family counselor* ▸ *community service manager* ▸ *fundraiser* ▸ *health educator and community health worker* ▸ *instructional coordinator* ▸ teacher (lower grades, special education, music, drama, and art) (enjoy counseling or teaching and have rapport-building skills)

EMERGENCY SERVICES
crisis center worker ▶ *emergency medical technician and paramedic* ▶ firefighter ▶ police officer (variety, change, and need for quick response in high-stress situations)

HEALTH SCIENCE
chiropractor ▶ *dental assistant/hygienist* ▶ *dentist* ▶ dietitian ▶ *emergency room physician* ▶ *gynecologist* ▶ hospice worker ▶ lab technician ▶ massage therapist ▶ *nurse* (especially emergency room) ▶ *nursing instructor* ▶ *obstetrician* ▶ *pediatrician* ▶ personal fitness trainer ▶ *physician assistant* ▶ *podiatrist* ▶ *primary care physician* ▶ *radiological technician* ▶ *respiratory therapist* ▶ *senior caregiver* ▶ *speech pathologist* ▶ *substance abuse counselor* ▶ *therapist (occupational, physical, recreational)* ▶ *veterinarian* ▶ *veterinarian technologist/technician* (observing concrete details of the body and practical methods for getting well; helping the sick deal with uncomfortable and frightening situations)

HOSPITALITY/RECREATION/HOTEL/SERVICE
casino manager ▶ *chef*/food service manager ▶ cruise director ▶ food server ▶ lodging owner/manager ▶ tour agent (frequent small crises requiring pragmatic response, motivation of others especially through humor)

ELECTED POLITICS
politicians at all levels (requires flexibility, ability to persuade, adaptability to the needs of voters)

REAL ESTATE
land developer ▶ property manager ▶ real estate agent and broker ▶ real estate lawyer (allows interaction with people in a fast-moving business)

SCIENCE
environmental scientist ▶ *geologist* ▶ industrial hygienist ▶ marine biologist ▶ zoologist (enjoy being outdoors, protecting animals and nature)

SPORTS RELATED
athletes of all types ▶ athletic coach (attracted to physical activity; those with special athletic abilities are ideally suited to making sports a profession)

TRANSPORTATION
air traffic controller ▶ flight attendant/instructor ▶ pilot/copilot (appeals to your love of excitement, movement, variety, and risk)

OTHER
cosmetologist ▶ farmer ▶ florist ▶ *hairdresser* ▶ mechanic ▶ rancher

CASE STUDY FOUR

When a Career Isn't Working

Bill Lloyd was a born salesman. In his freshman year at a university, he saw how much money college textbooks cost and was more excited by that than the engineering major his dad wanted him to pursue. Why go to college, Bill figured, when he could read all the texts and get paid for it? His parents disowned him when he quit to work at a major college textbook publisher.

Starting at the bottom selling the most esoteric titles, Bill quickly became a star salesman. Within three years he was the firm's number one sales producer. That's when the trouble began.

Bill was promoted to sales manager, overseeing twenty-five people selling nationwide. He had to read not just his titles but all of them, and he hated it. His shoot-from-the-hip style was no longer needed. Instead, he had to think strategically about what professors wanted, a task foreign to here-and-now Red/Green Extroverts. He had much less interaction with people, which made him restless. He started to daydream about the days when he was flying solo around the country, attending conventions and scoring huge sales coups.

At a meeting of top managers at the end of a stellar year, Bill's boss half-kiddingly bemoaned the lack of Porsche franchises in their area. The other managers laughed; Bill started thinking. He contacted Porsche and persuaded them to sell him an area franchise, citing his track record with the firm.

Today, Bill owns a Porsche franchise, belongs to the local country club, and has reconciled with his parents. His Red personality gets a kick every morning he walks into his upscale showroom. He oversees only two salespeople and handles a number of clients himself. He finds customers at the country club before they find him. He gets all the business he can handle with the line, "When you're ready for your Porsche, here's my card." He loves his work.

Your Personality's Challenges

Red/Green Extroverts have a unique set of potential work-related blind spots. Some you have, others you won't. Tone down a blind spot by focusing on it, then choose more productive actions and make them habits. (Suggestions for doing so are in parentheses below.) You:

▸ Tend to be casual about rules, procedures, and authority. (This is your number one career-derailing attribute. Your superiors may need rules and procedures to control their own job anxieties. Would that make you respond with more respect and compassion? Try it and see how your boss reacts.)

▸ Have difficulty planning ahead and sometimes do not follow through on commitments. (If a commitment bogs you down, you may skip it. You hate red tape, including making phone calls to cancel appointments. In the professional world, it can look like you don't have your act together at times. Write down commitments, call ahead of time to cancel.)

▸ Hate having tight deadlines, repetitive work, and working alone. (Reject or change jobs like this; they make you pessimistic and joyless. When deadlines or repetitive tasks cannot be avoided, pretend they are all ridiculous; this will lighten your mood. If possible, set yourself up in a conference room to be near others.)

▸ Get frustrated in overly serious environments where humor is not respected. (You withdraw and become moody. If exposed to such environments for too long and put under extreme stress, you may have violent, even abusive, outbursts.)

Your Job Search—the Good, the Bad, and the Ugly

You Red/Green Extroverts would rather be out there taking action than reading this. But hang in there; we're almost done. You'll benefit from these job-search tricks.

Your natural strengths easily allow you to:

▸ Have an extensive network for job information and referrals

▸ Establish a warm relationship with interviewers who allow it

▸ Sell yourself well

In order to tone down your blind spots, you need to:

▸ Force yourself to set long-term career objectives; enlist the help of friends or family, particularly Golds (to identify, see figure 19–1 in chapter 19, Golds Overall)

- Consider the long-term potential of a job, for you *and* your family, before accepting

- Take a hard look at the possible downside before jumping into a job

- Develop a thicker skin and don't take rejections personally

- Consistently follow through with details like phone calls, thank-you notes, company research; get a willing Gold to help if possible

The Red/Green Extrovert's Interviewing Style

With an interviewer whose Color is close to your own, you will feel immediate rapport. However, if your interviewer seems to have a significantly different style, use the suggestions in parentheses. Mercilessly exploit these natural abilities of yours and get more job offers.

In following your natural style, you:

- Speak with tact, excitement, charm, and humor. (Your immediate charm will intimidate some interviewers. If yours does not warm up, answer a few questions in a serious tone; see if that puts him or her more at ease.)

- Develop a rapport with people. (With an interviewer who seems distant, stick to the facts. Let him or her set the tone for any personal exchanges.)

- Are concrete and realistic about past responsibilities and accomplishments. (Some interviewers will dig for feelings: "Did you like your previous boss? How did you get along with your coworkers?" Ask a Green to help role play such questions ahead of time.)

- Focus on the current situation and not on future or strategic issues. (Your ability to focus on the present is a valuable asset, but your answer may be too short when handling future-oriented questions. Answer slowly and thoughtfully. Then emphasize your talent for turning on a dime if things change.)

- Get to the point; you prefer to act rather than talk. (Ask for the job at the end of the interview, but don't rush things. Impatience will hurt you here. If your interviewer seems indecisive, take action. Offer to work a trial project or period.)

▶ Reply quickly and think on your feet. (Normally a plus, but some interviewers may want more thoughtful replies. If so, sit back, look at the ceiling, and pause, even if you know what you want to say.)

Okay, go do something exciting now. Later, skim chapter 4, "Greens Overall," if we've actually gotten you a little hooked on this stuff. You can jot notes if you want to impress someone with your diligence in the Roadmap in chapter 27. The Roadmap is an excellent place to keep networking notes during a job search.

CHAPTER 13

Red/Green Introverts

YOU'RE NOT ONLY a Red, you also have strong secondary characteristics of the Green personality. And you have tested as a Color Q Introvert, which means you recharge your batteries by being alone rather than being with others. It's likely you have little patience for this book and are just reading this to please someone. So we'll keep it pragmatic.

You Overall

Warm and attentive, Red/Green Introverts have an unusual sensitivity to people and animals. A low need to lead or control, but a great desire to encourage others, is your style. Small collegial teams where hierarchy is secondary to getting the job done efficiently bring out the best in you. Where possible, you like to operate outside norms and rules followed by others.

Realistic and pragmatic, you trust only what you have personally observed. You have a particularly acute visual memory.

Your communication style is straightforward. You want the facts but enjoy an anecdote or two (particularly a humorous one). You are easygoing, fun loving, and enjoy the unexpected. Though very attentive in the moment, you have a short attention span.

You resist making decisions under pressure, keeping all options open as long as possible. When ready, however, you decide with the speed of light.

Others see you as speaking clearly without hidden agendas. They experience you as calm, modest, and cheerful. Although you are very tolerant of most folks, you get annoyed by bossy people who insist on having things done "the right way."

You on the Job

AS A LEADER

You lead your staff by example. Hierarchical power structures and ruling others with an iron fist are not your way.

Realistic about problems and outcomes, you prefer collegiality to conquest. Your first impulse is to break tension with humor. You'll find other Colors require more structure than you do.

AS A TEAM PLAYER

You have common sense and a knack for getting others to focus. They trust you—you really do want to accomplish the task at hand without playing political games. You provide a role model for your teammates.

All ideas floated by team members get a hearing before you begin drilling down to the final decision. You are most likely to irritate other teammates by being overly sensitive to people who disagree with you.

Look at figure 13–1 for a list of your natural work-related strengths.

FIGURE 13–1 *Natural Work-Related Strengths*

Approximately 80 percent of these attributes will apply to you. Check off those that do, and use them in your resume and interviews. This will set you apart from the canned responses of others. You:

- ○ Like to initiate and implement change

- ○ Bring people and tasks together in a cooperative style

- ○ Provide supportive feedback to others

- ○ Excel in assignments that are action oriented, practical, and nonrepetitious

- ○ Love to overcome obstacles using a tactical approach

- ○ Bring creativity and well-developed aesthetics to your work

- ○ Have a strong customer service attitude, no matter what level of job you have

- ○ Are most productive when left on your own

CASE STUDY ONE

Upper Management, Utility Field

Christopher L. Dutton has been president and CEO of Green Mountain Power Corporation in Colchester, Vermont, since 1997. Previously, he had been its general counsel, chief financial officer, treasurer, and vice president.

Chris started his career as a trial lawyer. He liked the work, he says, "because each case was different." Red/Green Introverts crave challenge and nonrepetitious work, especially if they can be involved on a personal level. Thus well suited to trial law, Chris spent the first decade of his career trying cases.

Today, he says, "I spend 45 percent of my time focusing on the policy issues that confront us because we are a regulated utility company. I have to be externally oriented; every decision we make affects the kind of power we buy or the generating facilities that we build."

He is constantly dealing with politics. Five months after taking the helm, a public service commission made a decision "that put us in extreme financial peril," Chris recounts. While Red/Green Introverts enjoy surprises and challenges, this stretched Chris to his professional limits. His solution? "We figured out how to convince the regulators to change their minds in a face-saving way without admitting they made a mistake." Red/Green Introverts are keen observers of human nature; this talent kept Chris's organization viable.

Chris spends an additional 40 percent of his time "on Board relations, as well as dealing with the financial community, investors, and ratings agencies." The Red/Green Introvert's tendency to listen to all sides before making a decision helps Chris here.

He offloads the detail work (an irritant to Red/Green Introverts) to his chief operating officer Mary Powell. "I recognize she has strengths I don't."

How does Chris create the egalitarian workplace he prefers? During the company's early crisis days, Chris led the decision to sell its lavish offices and move into its service center, where the line and bucket trucks were. "We wanted everybody on the same floor; we wanted no private offices, just low partitions where necessary. We wanted all employees to have the same amount of office space so there could be no hidden agendas."

Today, Chris and Mary are physically visible to 90 of their 195 employees. "If I get a call about a sensitive matter, I'll call back later," Chris says.

Answering to so many entities, Chris knows obstacles are a recurring part of the job. But these are stimulating rather than stifling to him. Red/Green Introverts are tactical, practical, and enjoy solving concrete problems.

They also value and welcome change, which gives Chris an edge in his role as CEO. So does his Red/Green flexibility and customer service orientation.

The open floor plan is ideal for helping Chris keep his finger on the pulse of his organization. Red/Green Introverts thrive when they can focus on the human side of things. As an Introvert, however, he expends extra energy coping with the resulting lack of privacy.

Chris's job makes ample use of his inborn Red/Green preferences. He doesn't have to try to be a success in this position; instead, his natural instincts provide the right response.

CASE STUDY TWO

Innkeeper

Bud owns a cozy, twenty-room inn in Maine. He is the kind of innkeeper who takes a personal interest in his guests and remembers them over the years. The rugged coast of Maine and the remoteness of the town appeal to Bud, his core of regulars, and celebrities alike. On any given night, artists may share a common wall with Supreme Court justices.

Bud has a quiet smile and is an intent listener. He loves running the inn, but it was never his life's ambition.

"I had no intention of buying an inn," Bud recalls. "After my divorce, I had lost both my job and my house. A guy called and offered it to me, knowing it was a way to be closer to my kids who live on an island nearby. So I looked at it, said, 'Whoa! This is a pretty good deal. It would give me a place to live, and it would give me a job.' I had enough money to buy the place mortgage free. So I did." Red/Greens respond well to unexpected opportunities.

True to his Color, Bud loves the flexibility of owning an inn. He enjoys the variety of people he meets. (As an Introvert, it gives him the advantage of having his social life come to him.) He posts no guest rules. "You don't make policy because one person does something upsetting," he says. Reds dislike policy in any case.

"The stressful part of running an inn is the things you have no control over, like electric power," Bud says. He is twenty miles from any major center of services; the town has an antiquated water system and no police department. But a true Red, Bud takes crises as they come. "I am the chairman of the water department here because I am the biggest user," he says.

Bud's top work-related strength is delegating, which he mainly exercises overseeing his housekeeping staff.

Most people find his life romantic. Bud is quick to dispel the myth in down-to-earth, practical Red fashion. "The main reason people fail as innkeepers is they are not realistic. They overromanticize it. There is nothing romantic about being an innkeeper. But I do like coastal life; I like looking at the ocean. It's a different scene every day."

Ideal Work Environment

Beautiful, private, and relaxed—who wouldn't want to work in a place like Bud's? Actually, some Colors are uncomfortable in relaxed, informal settings. Extroverts opt for bullpens or open cubicles. But for you, it's the most productive way to go.

Use all the leverage you can when a job offer is made to get as much from figure 13–2 as possible.

FIGURE 13-2 *The Ideal Red/Green Introvert Work Environment*

Compare your current work environment to the descriptions below. If these descriptions seem obvious, that confirms you've tested your individual Color correctly. Other Colors, especially Golds, would find this environment uncomfortable and unproductive. The optimal Red/Green Introvert work environment:

○ Is relaxed and informal. You function best with a minimum of rules, paperwork, and supervision.

○ Is supportive and harmonious. Backstabbing, confrontation, and malicious gossip really irritate and distract you from the task at hand.

○ Permits making an immediate contribution. You need real results with tangible products now and chafe doing grunt work in your early career years. Brainstorming feels like a waste of time to you.

○ Is aesthetically appealing. More than for most Colors, unattractive surroundings will distract and irritate you, detracting from productivity. While declining a job on the basis of ugly offices might sound frivolous, for you it is a genuine matter of mental health.

○ Allows for private space. As an Introvert, your batteries get drained when dealing with people, even if your people skills are superb. If you have to share your work space with others, you will feel a lot more fatigue at the end of the day. You think and perform better in a private space; insist on one as a condition of employment if possible.

A corporate culture integrating the above elements is fertile soil for your career advancement.

The worst type of work culture for a Red/Green Introvert is one where you are micromanaged on tight deadline projects that emphasize long-term strategic thinking. The daily tone is overly serious, and humor is frowned upon. You will find it draining to work in noisy environments that do not respect your real need for privacy.

When Red/Green Introverts work in nonideal corporate cultures, productivity is stunted and career achievements become an uphill climb.

The Introverted Red/Green's Ideal Boss

Even a great job can be frustrating under the wrong boss; a mediocre job under a wonderful boss is pretty hard to leave. Red/Greens get along especially well with other Reds. But bosses of other Color types who possess the characteristics in figure 13–3 also can be good mentors.

FIGURE 13–3 *The Red/Green Introvert's Ideal Boss*

Check off if your boss:

○ Points you in the right direction and then leaves you alone

○ Encourages rapport through a sense of humor

○ Rewards ingenuity and is not threatened by your free-wheeling ways

○ Offers a high degree of trust

○ Is appropriately interested in your personal life

Careers That Attract Red/Green Introverts

You are most attracted to careers that provide freedom, action, and the ability to be of service, like Chris Dutton.

Please note that not all the following careers will appeal to you, but recognize that each, in some way, draws on the strengths of your style and appeals to a significant number of your Color group. This is not a comprehensive list, but it will show underlying patterns of preference. If unlisted careers offer similar patterns, your chances of success increase. Text in parentheses at the end of each section highlights the Color style characteristics that create success in that broad area.

According to our research, jobs italicized in the lists below are predicted to benefit from an above-average growth rate over the next several years. This information is based on the continuously revised data provided by the U.S. Department of Labor and Bureau of Labor Statistics on their websites O*NET OnLine (www.onetonline.org) and http://www.bls.gov/CAREEROUTLOOK/. There you will find in-depth information about job requirements and salary ranges.

There are successful people of all Color styles in all occupations. In non-ideal jobs, you can still shine by creating your own niche.

ARTS/DESIGN/ENTERTAINMENT/MEDIA

actor/dancer/performer ▸ artist (painter, sculptor, illustrator, animator) ▸ *audio-visual specialist* ▸ costume/wardrobe/set designer ▸ craftsperson ▸ entertainment agent (actor/performer) ▸ interior decorator ▸ fashion designer ▸ *film/video editor* ▸ *graphic designer* ▸ jeweler ▸ photographer ▸ *producer and director* ▸ *web designer/art director* (use artistic talents to produce concrete and usable products)

ANIMAL CARE

animal breeder/groomer/trainer/service worker ▸ pet store owner ▸ *veterinarian* ▸ *veterinary technician* ▸ zoologist (draw on sensitivity to animals and their physical and emotional needs)

BUSINESS/FINANCE/LAW

bookkeeper ▸ *business coach/diversity manager* ▸ insurance appraiser/claim investigator ▸ *interpreter/translator* ▸ *lawyer* (not highly represented but found mostly in children, entertainment, real estate, poverty, and trial specialties) ▸ mediator ▸ museum curator ▸ paralegal ▸ product designer ▸ public relations specialist ▸ retail merchandise buyer ▸ retail/sports equipment salesperson ▸ small business owner ▸ upper management (draw on need to provide people with practical service and products)

DIGITAL/HIGH TECH/SCIENCE

computer game programmer ▸ multimedia artist and animator ▸ *software engineer* ▸ *support specialist* (combine design and technical skills)

EDUCATION/HUMAN SERVICES

child care worker ▸ *community service manager* ▸ counselor (*rehabilitation and substance abuse*) ▸ *health educator* ▸ religious leader ▸ *social worker* ▸ teacher (art, drama, lower grades, music, special education) (enjoy counseling or teaching and have rapport-building skills)

EMERGENCY SERVICES

crisis center worker/crisis hotline operator ▸ emergency medical technician and paramedic ▸ firefighter ▸ police officer (variety, change, and need for quick response in high-stress situations)

HEALTH SCIENCE

anesthesiologist ▸ *chiropractor* ▸ *dental assistant/hygienist* ▸ *diagnostic sonographer* ▸ *dietician/nutritionist* ▸ *emergency room physician* ▸ *gynecologist* ▸ *home health aide* ▸ hospice care worker ▸ lab technician ▸ massage therapist ▸ *nurse* (especially emergency room) ▸ *optometrist* ▸ *pediatrician* ▸ *personal fitness trainer* ▸ *pharmacist* ▸ *physician assistant* ▸ *primary care physician* ▸ *optician* ▸ *radiological technician* ▸ *senior caregiver* ▸ *speech pathologist* ▸ *surgical technologist* ▸ *therapist* (art, occupational, physical, recreational, respiratory, *substance abuse*) ▸ *veterinarian/veterinary assistant* (observing concrete details of the body and practical methods for getting well, helping the sick deal with uncomfortable and frightening situations)

HOSPITALITY/RECREATION/SPORTS

athletes of all types ▸ chef/food service manager ▸ innkeeper owner/manager ▸ restaurant host/hostess ▸ tour agent (provide variety and frequent small crises requiring pragmatic response)

SCIENCE

botanist ▸ *geologist* ▸ marine biologist ▸ soil conservationist ▸ zoologist (using practical skills and the ability to be outdoors to protect the environment)

REAL ESTATE

land developer ▸ property manager (fast-moving business)

OTHER

animal care ▸ antique dealer ▸ *cosmetologist* ▸ flight attendant ▸ florist ▸ gardener/landscape designer ▸ *hairdresser* ▸ jeweler ▸ tailor (focus on beauty, nature, and personal service)

CASE STUDY THREE

When a Career Isn't Working

Mallory, a Red/Green Introvert, was a real estate salesperson and a good one. She enjoyed the sales process and the people with whom she dealt. She even had that marvelous Red ability to enjoy a crisis every now and then.

But Mallory was feeling a seven-year itch. She was burning out on the unrelenting aggressiveness of making cold calls and drumming up business. She was a good negotiator, but pushing to close deals the way her boss taught her never felt natural. While she enjoyed people, her Introverted nature was feeling overwhelmed by sheer numbers, and the intrusions on her quiet time made her edgy.

One of the properties Mallory listed was a kennel with several beautiful surrounding acres. She found herself pointing out all its flaws to potential customers and steering them away. Finally, she realized she wanted to buy it herself.

Mallory pooled all her resources and purchased the property. She moved into its small caretaker's cottage and started a doggie day care sideline business. Red/Green Introverts adore animals and are very sensitive to their needs. Within the year, she had quit her real estate job to run her business full-time. Local celebrities loved her unique doggie pampering services; Mallory is now able to command top dollar and has a long waiting list.

Your Personality's Challenges

Red/Green Introverts have a unique set of potential work-related blind spots. We emphasize *potential* because you won't have all of them. Tone down a blind spot by deciding to see it, then choose more productive actions. (Suggestions for doing so are in parentheses below.) You:

- Tend to be casual with rules and procedures valued by others, including meeting deadlines. (This is your number one career-derailing attribute. Your superiors may need rules and procedures to control their own job anxieties. Would that make you respond with more respect and compassion? Try it and see how your boss reacts.)

- Either avoid conflict or become defensive when confronted. (You've got two great tools: humor and practicality. Get control over the tone of the interaction. Start with, or interject, humor. Then get practical about how to resolve the issue.)

▶ Hate not having control of your own schedule and having tight deadlines. (This makes you hyperactive, blunt, pessimistic, and joyless. For you, it is critical to avoid or change jobs where tight deadlines are the norm. When deadlines cannot be avoided, approach your tasks as if they were all ridiculous; this will lighten your mood.)

Your Job Search—the Good, the Bad, and the Ugly

You'd rather be out there hitting the pavement than reading this. But hang in there; you're almost done. You'll benefit from these concrete job-search tips:

Your natural strengths easily allow you to:

▶ Get the facts on careers and companies; you are particularly adept at Internet research

▶ Respond quickly and decisively to new opportunities

▶ Weigh whether a job meets your personal values

▶ Be detailed in your interview about past positions and achievements

▶ Appreciate and appropriately thank others for their help and introductions

▶ Assemble a small but loyal group of acquaintances who will provide referrals and leads

In order to tone down your blind spots, you need to:

▶ Force yourself to set long-term goals; enlist the help of friends or family, particularly Golds (to identify, read figure 19-1 in chapter 19, "Golds Overall")

▶ Prepare ahead for hypothetical questions; practice role playing rather than winging it

▶ Speak up in interviews, rather than just listening, to avoid appearing "too quiet"

▶ Sell, don't just state, your accomplishments; role play to reduce discomfort

▶ Follow through on commitments, deadlines, and the nitty-gritty tasks of a job search; enlist the aid of a willing Gold to help (to identify, read chapter 24, "Before I Do Something Stupid: Adjusting to Other Styles")

- Hang in there when the hiring process drags on through multiple interviews; avoid snap decisions to drop out of the race

- Be aggressive about soliciting referrals and leads from acquaintances and strangers as your preferred circle of friends is intimate but small

The Red/Green Introvert's Interviewing Style

With an interviewer whose Color is close to your own, you will feel immediate rapport. However, if your interviewer seems to have a significantly different style, use the suggestions in parentheses.

In following your natural style, you:

- Are a calm, quiet listener. (With an interviewer who asks short questions and expects long answers, take more of a lead. Practice selling your accomplishments. Rather than egotistical, you will appear self-confident.)

- Develop a rapport with people. (With an interviewer who seems distant, stick to the facts. Let him or her set the tone for any personal exchanges.)

- Are concrete and realistic about past responsibilities and accomplishments.

- Avoid sharing personal information until trust is established. (Keeping your distance or answering vaguely will make you look as if you have something to hide. Use humor to gain space, if needed, then be honest.)

- Focus on the current situation and not on future or strategic issues. (Your ability to focus on the present is a valuable asset, but you may be too brief when handling future-oriented questions. Answer slowly and thoughtfully. Then emphasize your talent for turning on a dime if things change.)

- Prefer to act rather than talk. (Ask for the job at the end of the interview, but don't rush things. Impatience will hurt you here. If your interviewer seems indecisive, take action. Offer to work a trial project or period.)

- Speak up when your values are threatened. (While this may lose you a job, never hide this valuable instinct of yours. You will save yourself wasted years working for firms you don't respect.)

Okay, go do something new now. Later, check out chapter 4, "Greens Overall," if we've actually hooked you a little on this stuff. You can jot notes if you want to impress someone with your diligence in the Roadmap in chapter 27. It's also a great place to keep notes during a job interview that will help with follow-through.

PART 4

BLUES

"Let's Change It"

Blues enjoy complex problems and work tirelessly to improve ideas and systems until they are just right.

CHAPTER 14

Blues Overall

BLUES REPRESENT 10 percent of the overall world population. If you are not a Blue but want to read about how to identify or improve communications with one, go to figure 14–1.

FIGURE 14–1 **How to Recognize a Blue**

- ○ Prefers talking about ideas or the future
- ○ Speaks in compound sentences
- ○ Uses precise vocabulary with lots of abstract words
- ○ Expresses clear and direct ideas
- ○ Reads voraciously
- ○ Is insatiably curious
- ○ Has jousting wit
- ○ Is competitive
- ○ Often has advanced degree(s)
- ○ Disregards opposition and what others think of him or her

How to Communicate with a Blue

○ Keep relationship professional, limit chitchat, be brief and concise

○ Acknowledge intellectual skills

○ Emphasize your own competence; use sophisticated vocabulary

○ Present the "big picture"

○ Outline the theoretical framework

○ Bring up comparative studies

○ Limit facts and details; reduce to essentials in executive summary

○ Show long-term potential of your new idea or solution

○ Use ingenuity and logic

○ Allow the Blue to challenge and question

○ Don't take critiques and challenges personally; these actually are signs of interest in the topic under discussion

○ Joust back with his or her jousting wit

○ Avoid emotional approach and words like *feel* or *believe*

○ Compose a strategy *with* the Blue, not *for* the Blue; use his or her input

Hillary Rodham Clinton—former First Lady of Arkansas, First Lady of the United States, U.S. senator from New York, and secretary of state, and the 2016 Democratic presidential nominee—is one of the most interesting women in the United States and one of the best-known Blues (who are the rarest of the four Color types).

Growing up in Park Ridge, Illinois, Hillary was seen even as a child to be assertive, purposeful, and determined, all in-born Blue characteristics. A tireless worker and consistent overachiever, she was a National Merit scholar in high school. Her teachers noted her exceptional ability to take in information, argue a point thoroughly, but change her mind when new input demanded it (core Blue abilities).

In her senior year, she was voted most likely to succeed. She went on to become a high achiever in both college (Wellesley student body president) and at Yale Law School.

Her Blue abilities served her well early in her career. Assigned as part of the impeachment inquiry staff investigating President Richard Nixon in

1974, she worked dawn to midnight seven days a week. Hillary is remembered as "determined and dutiful, grinding away in a mildewed office overlooking an alleyway."[1] This typifies the Blue ability to work relentlessly on a problem of interest, functioning without significant stress in solemn and tense environments.

That summer she worked on Bill Clinton's campaign for an Arkansas congressional seat, already emotionally involved with the young up-and-comer. Campaign manager Paul Fray struggled with the hard-nosed young woman over the strategies he deemed his turf, but later admitted, "She was an organizational genius."[2] During her time in the White House as First Lady, Hillary helped President Clinton draw and clarify battle lines. Her personal goals (healthcare reform, legal rights of children) were typical of a Blues: long term, strategic, and abstract. Hillary was and is not concerned about stepping on toes while pursuing the ability to set her own agenda.[3] When her two-decade marriage to Bill Clinton was tested in 1996 by the Monica Lewinsky scandal in the glare of international media, it endured, and many wondered why. Put in Color Q terms, the answer was simple. Hillary is a Blue/Gold; Bill is a Red/Green. (Note: Neither has reported taking the Myers-Briggs Type Indicator questionnaire or the derivative Color Q self assessment, but these personalities have been extrapolated by noted temperament specialists in the Myers-Briggs community[4] and author Shoya Zichy from a personal meeting with Hillary. These results are supported by extensive research, candid conversations with journalists, and Hillary's personal friends.) Bill Clinton loves politics; she prefers making policy. He is a quick study; she, like most Blues, has depth and focus. He looks for ways to compromise; she, in typical Blue fashion, weighs alternative strategies. He forgives and forgets; she remembers and keeps score. He dives into a crowd with the abandon of a Red/Green Extrovert; she reaches out but remains at the Blue/Gold's cool distance. He works from the gut; she is guided by logical analysis—again, another Blue tendency. He thrives on risk; Blue Hillary circles it cautiously.[5] It's a case of opposites attracting—and complementing each other in deeply important (and binding) ways for the challenges they have faced together. After her role as First Lady of the United States ended, Hillary did what comes naturally to all Blues: She took charge. She chose to run for a seat in the U. S. Senate and made it happen, tactically using her political contacts and name recognition. In 2006, when the first edition of *Career Match* was being written, we said, "As of this writing she continues to place herself strategically in the spotlight on carefully chosen issues, fueling the possibility that she herself eventually will run for President of the United States." We were right, solely based on an assessment of her personality type.

Other famous Blues in politics are Madeleine Albright, Catherine the Great, Dwight D. Eisenhower, Al Gore, Thomas Jefferson, Abraham Lincoln, Nancy Pelosi, Condoleezza Rice, and Lady Margaret Thatcher. Microsoft founder Bill Gates, IBM's Lou Gerstner, business magnate and inventor Elon Musk, and Facebook's Mark Zuckerberg represent Blues in the corporate world. George Carlin, Matt Damon, Celine Dion, Walt Disney, Mia Farrow, Tina Fey, Jodie Foster, Whoopi Goldberg, Valerie Harper, Tom Hanks, Katharine Hepburn, and Meryl Streep illustrate the Blue style in entertainment; former Citibank chairman John Reed, megainvestor George Soros, and Charles Schwab in finance; and Albert Einstein in academia.

One look at the innovative companies Elon Musk has cofounded and run prove this statement accurate: "His psyche is tied up in the idea of changing the world," says his brother. Elon was the founder of SpaceX, one of the first private companies in space travel and one with a $1.6 billion contract with NASA to send supplies into space and astronauts to the International Space Station[6]; Tesla Motors, one of the first private companies in the electric car industry; and a cofounder with Peter Thiel of PayPal, which has changed the way millions of people worldwide do commerce. Blues more than most Colors use money as a measure of self-worth; with a $12.4 billion net worth as of 2016,[7] Musk has little to worry about. Blues look farther out into the future and see more than any other Color type. "I started SpaceX because if we're not on a path of expanding to the stars, then what we're effectively saying is [that] we're going to consign ourselves to Earth until an extinction event wipes us out," Elon says. A Blue who grew rich on his talent for designing new systems is Charles R. "Chuck" Schwab, founder and chairman of Charles Schwab Corporation. The corporation is a leading provider of financial services, with more than 330 offices, 10.1 million client accounts, and $2.69 trillion in client assets.[8] When Schwab started his business in the 1970s, he was $100,000 in debt and going through a divorce. But he saw the baby-boomer demographics and their meaning: 28 percent of the U.S. population would be in the preretirement age range of 45 to 64 by the year 2010.[9] And he invested big in pre-Internet technology in the late 1970s, a bet-the-company decision which gave Schwab a crucial head start into Internet trading and investing. These two things together—demand and technology—grew into a trillion-dollar business and made Chuck Schwab a billionaire six times over.

Described by *Fortune Magazine* in 2005 as "private and aloof,"[10] Schwab has a demeanor that is typical of Blues who focus on systems and their improvement. After retiring, Schwab reclaimed the CEO position of his firm when his designated successor was deemed "not really inclined toward the visionary, blue-sky stuff,"[11] and the company floundered in the early 2000s. Blues are the visionaries of the world, just what the company needed at that time. He remained CEO until retiring again in 2008,[12] keeping the company focused on its strengths and improving internal processes so it "skates to where the puck is going to be,"[13] as he likes to say. As of this writing, he continues as chairman and the largest stockholder of the company he founded, funneling some of his personal wealth into the Charles and Helen Schwab Foundation he established a decade before retiring. Its $270 million in assets provided $13 million in grants to organizations that help young people reach their fullest potential and alleviate human suffering in his home state of California and elsewhere.[14]

You as a Blue will critique every point made in a book like this, preferring instead to deal with things more intellectual and less emotional. However, if you are interested in learning how to work more effectively and efficiently with other personality types, this book will be the key that unlocks those secrets. Color Q shows you how to handle even the most emotional and disorganized people in your life. It describes what to do when all your best efforts have failed. The most logical way to proceed with this book is to read about your own Color first, and then learn how you interact with others by reading their profiles as needed. You especially want to learn about Reds, with whom you are most likely to clash because they are relentlessly present-centered and view deadlines and commitments merely as loose guidelines in personal and professional life. Reds, however, will help you achieve more than you could on your own. Harness their strengths to handle crises in troubled teams, departments, or companies. Turn to their present-moment thinking when strategic, future-oriented logic breaks down.

You'll also get along better with Greens and Golds. They, too, have strengths with which you should become familiar. Successful Blue entrepreneurs and leaders know how to engage the strengths of each Color and hire accordingly.

Use this chapter to determine if you've tested your primary Color correctly. It also will help identify Blues among people you know, as will chapter 24, "Before I Do Something Stupid: Adjusting to Other Styles." We added figure 14–1 for other Colors to have a list of ways to identify and communicate with Blues.

As a Blue, you are the rarest of the four Colors. You are the most strategic of all personality types, thriving when grappling with complex theoretical challenges. Your talent for new system designs brings you recognition and appreciation.

CHAPTER 15

Blue/Gold Extroverts

YOU'RE NOT ONLY a Blue, you also have strong secondary characteristics of the Gold personality. And you have tested as a Color Q Extrovert, which means you recharge your batteries by being with people rather than being alone. Your Color group makes things happen in decisive and take-charge ways. A lifelong learner, you typically are quite well informed. It is likely you already are challenging and critiquing this profile, if you're at all interested in the material. Please note that the underlying components of this profile have been researched for nearly seven decades worldwide and verified across age, sex, ethnic, and socioeconomic boundaries.

You Overall

You are dynamic and capable, and your talents dominate at every step of a project, from creating the vision to making it happen. Along the way, your abilities to devise strategies, establish plans (and contingencies), and take charge are all quite strong. Blue/Gold Extroverts do well in a broader range of careers than other Colors, because of your love of lifelong learning, sharp logic, and executive abilities.

Two core strengths combine in you to create a fast rise to the top: a high need for control and strong leadership skills. Combined with your frank, direct, intuitive, and focused communication style, those qualities make you an executive dynamo but at times overly challenging and alienating to those around you. Most other Colors cannot keep up with your drive, which can make your entire staff uncomfortable and rebellious.

The world of theories, future possibilities, and bold new designs are your territory. Existing systems and assumptions are just jumping-off points. You create long-range plans that incorporate ideas others do not yet see. If such plans create complex problems to be solved, so much the better. Not only will you marshal all necessary resources, you will gleefully solve them all.

Your greatest challenge is managing and controlling how others respond to you. On the plus side, you often come across as articulate, vivid, and confident. You persuade others through clear logic and thoughtful debate. On the down side, you are impatient with people who focus on what you consider irrelevant, redundant, and obvious issues. Those who are intimidated by you instantly lose your respect; you can't imagine why anyone would personalize competition or debate.

To be an effective leader or team player, you will need to learn which other Colors do personalize such things and adopt alternate strategies for interacting with them. Such reactions are deep in their core, offer a different (and usable) strength than yours, and cannot be changed by choice or willpower.

CASE STUDY ONE

Executive Director, Youth INC

Rehana Farrell is the executive director of Youth INC, a venture philanthropy nonprofit that transforms the lives of New York City kids by empowering the grass-roots nonprofits that serve them in their communities.

Rehana is a builder. She likes to build new businesses, new functions, new teams. She intellectually owns every aspect of her work and considers how it can get better and better. The only thing she doesn't enjoy is standing still or maintaining the status quo.

As an executive director, or CEO, she loves the wide variety of issues on her very full plate. From the sales function of development to the relationship management function of a thirty-five-person board to the operational efficiencies that can be created internally or for her network of over sixty youth-serving nonprofits, it's all interesting to her, including particularly how things come together. This includes the team. She is an avid student of human behavior and actively seeks to optimize team performance through process and culture.

Like most Blue/Gold Extroverts, Rehana is most energized by system-level concepts and changes that have the broadest impact. She values innovation at all levels of the organization. In Blue fashion, Rehana enjoys focusing on the big picture, but as a backup Gold, she also appreciates that execution and process improvements really make a difference.

Rehana is a doer as well as a thinker. She considers herself a "servant leader" whose job is to advocate for the staff to help them all be successful. She values commitment to the organization, project, or goal, and is with you 110 percent if you demonstrate that. If you don't own the outcome, there are other jobs out there for you that would be a better fit.

You on the Job

AS A LEADER

"I don't take no for an answer" is a phrase that must first have been uttered by a Blue/Gold Extrovert. Once you create a vision, you spring into action, mobilizing the talents of others, eliminating confusion and inefficiencies, making the tough decisions. Understanding the inner workings of any organization is your special talent; you can manipulate most bureaucracies to achieve your ends.

You often are the first one who sees connections between unrelated facts and ideas, which gives you an edge at handling global issues. You recognize the potential of new ideas before others do, and your company profits accordingly.

AS A TEAM PLAYER

Your natural leadership comes to the fore even in teams. Your ability to see the big picture and energize the group to achieve shows itself, whether you are the team leader or not. Cutting to the core of issues saves your team time. In order to meet deadlines, you will encourage (and work to) high standards, avoid wasting resources, and even consider untried solutions rather than fail.

You can irritate your teammates by being overly controlling and at times pushing too hard to get the job done.

Look at figure 15–1 for a list of your natural work-related strengths.

FIGURE 15-1 *Natural Work-Related Strengths*

Approximately 80 percent of these attributes will apply to you. Check off those that do, and use them in your resume and interviews. This will set you apart from the canned responses of others. You:

○ Are outgoing and energetic

○ Can see the big picture, create compelling visions, and make it happen

○ Enjoy connecting unrelated variables when analyzing problems and developing new systems

○ Are willing, and eager, to take charge of challenging, complex problems

○ Are task oriented and organized

○ Constantly seek improvements

○ Make tough, logical decisions

○ See the long-term consequences of your decisions

○ Will push your team to achieve goals, whether you are the leader or not

Now see how some Blue/Gold Extroverts use these strengths in very different fields.

CASE STUDY TWO

Chief Executive Officer

Nobody is going to burst Michael Isaacs's balloon, at least not any time soon. He is the CEO of U.S. Balloon Company, the largest wholesale distributor of balloons and related accessories in the United States. The company, which Michael started with a $750 investment, now annually grosses $30 million. It has 100 employees and a catalog of products that is 592 pages long.

Michael sees his function as being answerable to all the company's constituencies: employees, suppliers, customers, and bankers. "I set the direction of the company," he says. "I determine the targeted market and profitability goals."

Although he views himself more as an entrepreneur than a manager, he works very hard at building his managerial skills. "Most of all," he says, "I try to get the job done by hiring the right team."

Originally a junior high science teacher, Michael had always run side businesses to augment his family's income. He started selling balloons in a shopping mall. The business got bigger, and he left to pursue it full-time. Michael attributes his success to his natural "persistence and persuasiveness; the ability to translate my vision into an action plan and be very serious about measuring results."

He is most energized when his team makes an outstanding effort. He prefers to deal with others in groups rather than individually, very typical of a Blue/Gold Extrovert. Also true to his Color, he likes finance and accounting and finds very few things boring about his business. "I try to improve every process, even if mundane," he says. "There is always a faster, cheaper, and better way of doing it."

Michael has achieved success by his own definition. "What I do must have economic benefit for my family, employees, and other stakeholders," he says. Beyond that, success to Michael is being recognized by industry peers and customers, as well as being viewed as a knowledge resource. U.S. Balloon Company became the largest distributor of foil balloons for the largest manufacturer. It also became the largest supplier to the largest party-store chain in the United States. It nurtured the party-store chain from a startup of two stores with no computer to now over 800 locations. "True to the law of unintended consequences," says Michael, "the big party chain purchased the big manufacturer of foil balloons. Then they purchased us to exclusively service their balloon distribution needs nationwide. At age 71 with a three-year agreement, not a bad way to ease into retirement . . . if I have to?"

Ideal Work Environment

If, like Rehana Farrell, you are surrounded at work by highly competent and independent people who meet their deadlines, you are in the right place. Your superiors must also be highly competent and professional and respect you enough to let you work autonomously.

When a job offer is made, leverage as much as you can from the list in figure 15–2.

FIGURE 15–2 *The Ideal Blue/Gold Extrovert Work Environment*

Compare your current work environment to the descriptions below. Check all that ring true for you. If these descriptions seem obvious, that confirms you've tested your individual Color correctly. Other Colors, especially Greens and Reds, would find this environment uncomfortable and unproductive. The optimal Blue/Gold Extrovert work environment:

○ Provides a demanding and competitive atmosphere

○ Has high standards

○ Has highly competent bosses and coworkers

○ Encourages creative approaches to long-range problems

○ Rewards innovation and drive rather than playing by the rules

○ Funnels you into a leadership role

○ Assists you in dealing with the emotional reactions of others

○ Is a well-respected institution in need of change

The worst type of work culture for a Blue/Gold Extrovert is overly bureaucratic and/or full of sensitive people who need exorbitant amounts of hand-holding. Too much emphasis is put on detail work, not enough on long-range thinking and strategizing.

When Blue/Gold Extroverts work in nonideal corporate cultures, productivity is stunted and career achievements become an uphill climb.

The Extroverted Blue/Gold's Ideal Boss

Even a great job can be frustrating under the wrong boss; a mediocre job under a wonderful boss is pretty hard to leave. Blue/Golds get along especially well with other Blues. But bosses of other Color types who possess the characteristics in figure 15–3 also can be good mentors.

FIGURE 15-3 *The Blue/Gold Extrovert's Ideal Boss*

Check off if your boss:

○ Is someone you respect

○ Enjoys a hearty exchange of views and does not react to debate as a personal challenge

○ Values your independence and energy

○ Grants you sufficient autonomy

○ Helps you deal with the emotional outbursts of others

○ Shelters you from bureaucracy and detail work as much as possible

Careers That Attract Blue/Gold Extroverts

Blue/Gold Extroverts cluster in fields that provide intellectual challenge, complex and theoretical problems, and mastering new technologies. Routine, repetitive tasks are minimized; risk taking and original projects predominate. Autonomy, competition, and people you respect characterize jobs that provide your highest degree of satisfaction.

Please note that not all the following careers will appeal to you, but recognize that each, in some way, draws on the strengths of your style and appeals to a significant number of your Color group. This is not a comprehensive list, but it will show underlying patterns of preference. If unlisted careers offer similar patterns, your chances of success increase. Text in parentheses at the end of each section highlights the Color style characteristics that create success in that broad area.

According to our research, jobs italicized in the lists below are predicted to benefit from an above-average growth rate over the next several years. This information is based on the continuously revised data provided by the U.S. Department of Labor and Bureau of Labor Statistics on their websites O*NET OnLine (www.onetonline.org) and http://www.bls.gov/CAREEROUTLOOK/. There you will find in-depth information about job requirements and salary ranges.

There are successful people of all Color styles in all occupations. In non-ideal jobs, you can still shine by creating your own niche.

ARCHITECTURE/LAW
architect ▸ *lawyer* (especially corporate, employment, entertainment, estate planning, intellectual property, mergers and acquisitions, product liability, project finance, securities, among others) (intellectual challenge, high need for control, complex problem solving, high standards)

BUSINESS/MANAGEMENT
chief executive officer ▸ *franchise/small business owner* ▸ insurance agent/examiner/underwriter ▸ *managers/executive directors of all types* (marketing, financial operations, human resources, sales, training and development) ▸ real estate manager ▸ upper management (private sector/government service/arts and entertainment) (decisive, focused, take charge, high standards, solving complex problems, long-range strategic thinking, natural leadership skills)

BUSINESS/FINANCE
accountant ▸ bankers of all types ▸ economist ▸ *financial planner* ▸ *investment banker* ▸ *investment/securities broker* ▸ loan officer ▸ venture capitalist (intellectual challenge, intuition, strategic thinking, complex problem solving, high

need for control, competition, insatiable curiosity, well-informed, logical thinking, make tough decisions)

COMPUTER/INFORMATION TECHNOLOGY

artificial intelligence design ▸ *chief technology officer* ▸ *computer firm executive* ▸ computer programmer ▸ *computer systems analyst* ▸ *database manager/administrator* ▸ *information research scientist* ▸ *information security specialist/manager* ▸ *information systems manager/administrator* ▸ *information technology project manager* ▸ *Internet of Things solutions architect* ▸ *mobile application developer* ▸ *network architect*/administrator ▸ *software developer* (mastering new technologies, solving complex and/or theoretical problems, autonomy, long-range planning, future possibilities, bold new designs, contingency planning, need for control)

CONSULTING

industrial psychologist/organizational development specialist ▸ *management consultant* (autonomy, solving complex problems, working with theories and future possibilities, long-range planning)

EDUCATION

educational administrator ▸ *higher education teacher/university professor* (especially law, political science, science, or social studies) ▸ university president (desire to deal with competent people, establish long-range visions, strategic planning, few routine tasks, autonomy, debate skills)

GOVERNMENT/PUBLIC ADMINISTRATION

community services manager ▸ emergency management director ▸ fire inspector ▸ government service executive ▸ judge ▸ urban and regional planner (ability to tackle complex issues, long-range planning, respect of community)

HEALTH SCIENCE/HUMAN SERVICES

anesthesiologist ▸ *dentist* ▸ *internist* ▸ *medical health services manager* ▸ *neurologist* ▸ *optometrist* ▸ philanthropic/*community service executive* ▸ *psychiatrist* ▸ *radiological technician* ▸ *surgeon* ▸ *veterinarian technician* (intellectual challenge, opportunity to lead, respect of community)

SCIENTIFIC RESEARCH/ENGINEERING/MATHEMATICS

engineer (aerospace, agricultural, biomedical, chemical, civil, *environmental,* geological, health and safety, industrial, mechanical, nanotechnology) ▸ engineering manager ▸ *geoscientist* ▸ microbiologist ▸ political scientist ▸ *statistician*

▶ *wind turbine architect* (insatiable curiosity, need for control, dealing with confusion and inefficiencies, tackling complex problems, interacting with people you respect)

CASE STUDY THREE

A Come-from-Behind Success: Associate, Vault 100 Law Firm

Kat Burke's is a story of success against significant odds. Although the Color Q system does not measure personal resilience (which Kat has in abundance), it does measure dynamism and leadership abilities. Kat used these, plus her innate Blue strategic and analytic abilities, to create a come-from-behind career path.

In order to escape a violent marriage, eighteen-year-old high school dropout Kat needed a job. But the only things on her resume were her stints in group homes, living on the streets, hitchhiking across the country, and waitressing. But Blues don't stay at the bottom long.

Waitressing left her vulnerable economically and to the threats of her violent husband. Logic dictated the option that would take her the furthest—both away from her past and toward her future. She enlisted in the U.S. Army, with the single focus of getting an education. (Blue/Golds, no matter where they start in life, have an insatiable desire for lifelong learning.) With rebuilt self-esteem, she set her sights on law school. Ultimately she was accepted into the University of Pennsylvania.

She leveraged a summer internship into a full-time position in structured finance. This evaporated during the 2008 financial crisis, but Kat rebounded. She secured a clerkship with a judge who had just been assigned to oversee the bankruptcy proceedings of Lehman Brothers. On her very first day, she was plunged into what was, at that time, the largest bankruptcy in history.

Despite this solid resume credit, restructuring positions proved elusive as the financial crisis took hold the next year. Kat's prior work with an Indian tribe casino paved her way to securing a rare open position with another tribe. Her Blue/Gold need for control over her life propelled her to identify opportunities where others could not.

Meantime, her partner was accepted into a postgraduate program in London. They lived apart for more than a year until Kat decided to explore opportunities there. Through a legal recruiter, Kat found a London position in restructuring with one of the highest-grossing law firms in the world.

Kat has a very Blue way of summing up the abilities that have enabled her to come as far as she has. "I can easily see the big picture, and the steps to get there," she says. "When confronted with a problem, I typically think of multiple solutions and often prefer to use creative, and sometimes untested, solutions." But she is also a secondary Gold. "Gaining employment in the restructuring community has been a pretty amazing feat," she acknowledges. "I couldn't have done it without my deep and caring social network and the support of family and friends."

Your Personality's Challenges

Blue/Gold Extroverts have a unique set of potential work-related blind spots. Some listed below you have, others you don't. No one has them all. Tone down a blind spot by focusing on it, then choose more productive actions and make them habits. (Suggestions for doing so are in parentheses below.) You:

- May decide too quickly and overlook practical considerations. (High intellectual capability is no substitute for street smarts. You are more than capable of determining practicalities if you decide to focus. Especially early in your career, doing things too fast may create inefficiencies.)

- May be too abrupt, harsh, or dogmatic. (Everyone needs allies at some point. Alienating others is a strategic error, even if they seem less competent or less intellectual. Patience is a [long-range] virtue.)

- May pay insufficient attention to human needs and concerns. (Learn the wisdom that lies in emotions. They underpin every successful product and team equally with all your best strategic thinking. Once a day, require yourself to have empathy for someone.)

- May manipulate others to achieve goals. (It is tempting, when navigating bureaucracy, to cut to the chase. But when those people realize you've manipulated them, there can be hell to pay, and no second chances.)

Your Job Search—the Good, the Bad, and the Ugly

Blue/Gold Extroverts create accurate and well-presented resumes that elicit positive responses. With some interviewers, particularly Blues and Golds, you will feel a comfortable rapport. But with those of other Colors, you need to prepare and rehearse responses outside your comfort zone. Many human resources people are Greens; make a study of how to communicate effectively with this Color group before your first interviews by reading chapter 4, "Greens Overall."

Your natural strengths easily allow you to:

▶ Have an unusually creative job-search plan that you implement in an orderly way

▶ Perform good research on prospective companies

▶ Have a wide network from which to draw job leads

▶ Impress new contacts with your energy, insight, and competence

▶ Predict future needs and trends, possibly creating new jobs for yourself

▶ Create time lines, daily status reports, and budgets to lessen stress on you and your family

▶ Handle obstacles with creativity and strategy

In order to tone down your blind spots, you need to:

▶ Think of what you can do in return for those who help you; your networking sometimes comes off as too self-serving

▶ Cushion your tendency to be abrupt by extending answers beyond a few words and listening longer

▶ Learn to control your tendency to come across as arrogant; role play with a willing Green

▶ Pay attention to the personal aspects of job hunting (i.e., creating rapport with the interviewer and sending thank-you notes)

▶ Get help with the nitty-gritty of the job search to temper your natural impatience with administrative tasks; ask a willing Gold for assistance

▶ Employ your creativity and strategic thinking to address unexpected delays and obstacles

▶ Postpone any job decision until effects on family and personal life are reviewed

The Blue/Gold Extrovert's Interviewing Style

With an interviewer whose Color is close to your own, you will feel immediate rapport. However, if your interviewer seems to have a significantly different style (and it's statistically likely that many will have a Green component), use the suggestions in parentheses. Exploit these natural abilities of yours and get more job offers.

In following your natural style, you:

- Focus on future strategies. (Be ready to handle more mundane questions with equal dynamism. Don't continually pull the conversation back to the future.)

- Will have multiple and well-defined long-term goals. (Also practice talking about how you plan to "hit the ground running.")

- Tend to talk too much and not ask enough questions about the job. (If it has been a while since the interviewer said anything, pause. Let him or her ask a few questions. Prepare a list of questions about the job ahead of time and refer to it.)

- May not pick up on critical dynamics of corporate culture that will impact you. Ignoring corporate culture can make a move disastrous. (Rehash interviews with willing Greens who will help you spot such intangibles.)

- Logically consider the pros and cons of a job opportunity. (Never accept a job offer on the spot. Go home and thoroughly consider how it will impact your family and personal life.)

Once you've critiqued this profile and decided we've gotten enough things right to make it worthwhile, read chapter 19, "Golds Overall." Then carefully read up on the Greens in chapter 4 to prepare for job interviews (a large number of human resources people are Greens). Also study the Reds in chapter 9 if you have to interact with any at work or at home.

If you are actively engaging in a job search, keep notes in the Roadmap in chapter 27. Recording your strengths and strategies is a concrete and results-oriented way to navigate the minefields of a job search and promote creative thinking.

CHAPTER 16

Blue/Gold Introverts

YOU'RE NOT ONLY a Blue, you also have strong secondary characteristics of the Gold personality. And you have tested as a Color Q Introvert, which means you recharge your batteries by being alone rather than being with people. People in your Color group rise to the top of any profession that requires strategic thinking because you work tirelessly to very high standards. You excel at creating new systems and ideas.

You already have begun challenging and critiquing the last few claims, especially if you have any interest in this material. Please note that the underlying components of the following profile have been researched for nearly seven decades worldwide and verified across age, sex, ethnic, and socioeconomic boundaries.

You Overall

Creative, focused, and quite independent, you are superior at establishing links between seemingly unrelated ideas and facts. From such mental intricacies you construct models of anything from the cities of tomorrow to the conspiracy theories of yesterday.

Like your cousins the Blue/Gold Extroverts, you, too, have strengths to apply at all phases of a project. You can create the vision, devise the strategy, establish plans and contingencies, and make it all happen.

Unlike them, you come across as more calm, self-reliant, and enigmatic. Your deep powers of concentration make it seem as if you are in another world at times, but that's just you working with tireless focus on your latest project. Opposition does not intimidate you or shake your utter faith in your own insights. Your impressive scope of knowledge usually overcomes any challenges.

The world of theories, future possibilities, and bold new designs is your territory. Existing systems and assumptions to you are just jumping-off points. Departments or companies that need new direction will flourish using your long-range plans that incorporate ideas others do not yet see. If such plans create complex problems to be solved, so much the better. Not only will you marshal all the necessary resources, you will gleefully solve all the problems.

Your greatest challenge is managing and controlling how others see and respond to you. On the plus side, you come across as clear thinking, thoughtful, and insatiably curious. You persuade others through clear logic and convincing debate. On the down side, you are impatient with people who focus on what you consider irrelevant, redundant, and obvious issues. To avoid these irritants, you prefer written communications over face-to-face ones.

To be an effective leader or team player, however, you will need to adopt alternate strategies for working with Colors who do personalize things. Such reactions are deep in their core, offer a different (and usable) strength than yours, and cannot be changed by choice or willpower.

CASE STUDY ONE

Coach for Small and Medium-Size Businesses

Jeannette Hobson's high-powered New York career has made her a visible force in the small- and medium-size business communities. It all started with a young woman who lacked courage. "I considered a career in international business," says Jeannette. "But I didn't have the courage actually to go alone, find a job, and live on my own in a different land."

Instead, she found a training program for female college graduates at AT&T, moving eventually into a twenty-year career as a vice president of investment management at the Bank of New York. There, Jeannette sold economic- and investment-strategy services to corporations, a natural fit for a Blue. "I enjoy blue-sky thinking," she says. She progressed to managing investment portfolios for high-net-worth individuals and small pension funds, ultimately managing a team of eight.

But Jeannette envisioned a broader future. Today, she runs CEO peer advisory groups for Vistage International, the world's largest CEO membership organization. She also coaches, on a monthly basis, fifty CEOs of small-to-medium-size companies. "Coaching and facilitating meetings draws on my natural strengths," says Jeannette. "I just ask probing questions."

At one of her sessions, for example, those probing questions helped a leading provider of commercial coin-operated laundry equipment realize that technology would be the company's single greatest competitive advantage. Strategizing around this theme doubled the company's growth rate and resulted in a very lucrative acquisition.

As an Introvert, Jeannette finds it stressful to network in groups of complete strangers and to make cold prospecting calls to form new CEO groups. She admits to overpreparing for presentations: "Impromptu is very stressful for me." Her top three strengths, typical for her Color group, are thinking/analyzing, listening, and planning future strategies.

Today, if given the opportunity, she would live and work in a foreign land. But her family and the job of her passion keep her in New York. Instead she travels for fun.

You on the Job

AS A LEADER

"I don't take no for an answer" is a phrase that must first have been uttered by a Blue/Gold. Once you create a vision you spring into action, mobilizing the talents of others, addressing confusion and inefficiencies, making the tough decisions. Understanding the inner workings of any organization is one of your unique talents, and you can manipulate most bureaucracies to achieve your ends.

You often are the first one who sees connections between unrelated facts and ideas, which gives you an edge at handling global issues. You recognize the potential of new ideas before others do, and your company profits accordingly.

AS A TEAM PLAYER

While not keen on the rapport-building aspects of working on a team, your contributions nevertheless are substantial. You bypass small talk, going straight to the big picture. After a few precise and penetrating questions, you've cut to the core of even the most complex problems and begun synthesizing a strategy. Often you leave your teammates in the dust. If they have to ask what you consider to be obvious or incompetent questions, your impatience flares. Often you tap your foot waiting for others to catch up and see what's been obvious to you from the start.

To amuse yourself, you formulate unusual insights and run through untried and unique solutions. When your teammates finally understand the problem, you're there, ready with (one or more) solutions. You make fast decisions once you have reviewed all known data.

This may make team members feel rushed or pressured; it also can excite and galvanize them to action. Often you find yourself in the role of catalyst, moving the group to timely completion of deadlines using minimal time and resources yet working to highest standards.

Look at figure 16–1 for a list of your natural work-related strengths.

FIGURE 16–1 *Natural Work-Related Strengths*

Approximately 80 percent of these attributes will apply to you. Check off those that do, and use them in your resume and interviews. This will set you apart from the canned responses of others. You:

- ○ Are often the first to see the big picture

- ○ Are highly focused and goal oriented

- ○ Deal well with complex problems

- ○ Develop sophisticated new systems using the latest technology

- ○ Strategize final outcomes accurately

- ○ Work well with other competent people

Now see how some Blue/Gold Introverts use these strengths in very different fields.

CASE STUDY TWO

Vice President, Applications Development

If the technological singularity (in which superintelligent computers evolve beyond human control and intelligence capabilities) ever happens, Larry Spencer might be one of its survivors. He has been a programmer of business software for most of his life, making significant contributions, especially during the digital industry's early years.

"In the late 1980s," he says, "I wrote insurance quotation software that was bought and used by large insurance companies."

Larry worked for a large insurance company, performed his own contract programming, and ran his own company for three years. Like most Blue/Golds, he focuses intently on his selected tasks, with an eye toward making a significant impact on the world. Programming has held his fascination for close to four decades. "One unfulfilled goal I have is to get involved in artificial intelligence work," he says. Ultimately, he would like to be considered a famous software programmer.

Today, Larry has set his sights on one of those distant horizons that Blues perceive better than other personality types. "I would like to stay healthy enough to benefit from new technology that will enable me to go to age 200," he says.

When he's not planning this (long) future, Larry is a programmer, team leader, and mentor at ScerIS in Sudbury, Massachusetts. The software his company creates enables organizations to quickly develop, deploy, modify, and manage business practices critical to the needs of internal and external corporate clients.

Larry leads an international team of software developers, but this Introvert admits the mostly solitary activity of programming is his first love. "The design and programming of software is the most absorbing to me," he says, "because it is aesthetically satisfying."

What does someone fascinated by technological singularity and artificial intelligence do in his spare time? Besides going to the gym and hiking (which support the health he is planning to extend technologically), Larry says, "I read and go to meet-up groups on philosophy."

Being able to inject the deepest and best of human thought into the digital world while operating at optimal strength in a mostly bionic body could be why he may just survive—or even exploit—the singularity.

CASE STUDY THREE

Music Composer, Television and Motion Pictures

Joshua Stone can take still pictures and make a piano describe what's in them. He can sit at a keyboard, ask you to name an emotion, and create it through his fingertips. He can play the same fifteen-second music bridge over and over for seven days, improving it with each pass, and never get bored. And yet this Emmy Award winner describes his achievements writing music for movies and television with great modesty: "As a child, I didn't think, 'I am going to grow up and write music that nobody notices.' That is essentially what I do."

Music is a very direct conduit to Joshua's emotions. He is highly disciplined about codifying those emotions to enhance movies and TV programs. He has written for CBS News, A&E Network, the Smithsonian Institute, and Nickelodeon, and scored films about fine artists, among other projects.

"I have to understand the period of the time these people lived in to adequately compose music about them," Joshua says. Like most Blues, he enjoys the research phase of his work. He has composed in many musical styles, from 1930s swing music to various African styles. "I now actually feel there's no style I couldn't compose in," he says. "I found that if I subjugated my personality in service of the project at hand, it broadened the boundaries of what I had previously thought was possible."

Joshua is the founder of Song Book World (SBW), which creates cross-cultural collaborations with Africa, New Zealand, and his New England home area, the Berkshires. The organization is dedicated to the notion that songs connect everyone to everyone else. SBW (songbookworld.org) continuously invites community organizations, teachers, and students to play together for concert events and in-school programs.

Joshua can talk about music endlessly, attributing his continuing fascination to his curiosity and insatiable desire to keep learning, both typical Blue qualities. "There's no amount that's too much to learn to be good at what I do. Generally speaking, I'm not good at marketing, but people can see my curiosity and the passion I have," he says.

Like most Blues, Joshua is very into using technology in his work. "There are production techniques enabled by widespread Internet access now that provide many more ways to collaborate with partners around the world," he says. "Also within my own software programs are many things I didn't know could be done. When I discover them, I can't wait to tweak the results in my studio and share it with others around the globe."

Fortunately for Joshua, the business and bookkeeping side that Blues hate is minimal for him. "It's not too much fun," he says, "but with the advent of computers, the billing isn't bad."

He works alone for hours and often works for clients he's never met. That suits his Introverted side just fine. "When clients have musical knowledge, it can be even worse than when they don't," he says.

Joshua's top three strengths would sound surprising to anyone but another Blue. "I can take criticism," he says. "My biggest strength is my curiosity. And I always had great self-discipline."

Ideal Work Environment

Key to your job satisfaction are four conditions: smart, competent, competitive, and independent coworkers, like Larry Spencer has; control over your own projects, like Joshua Stone has; intellectual stimulation from complex problems and continuous learning, like Jeanette Hobson has; and privacy to think things through in great depth. If all these conditions are present within your workplace as they are at Jeannette Hobson's, your success (barring politics) is inevitable.

When a job offer is made, leverage as much as you can from the list in figure 16–2.

FIGURE 16–2 *The Ideal Blue/Gold Introvert Work Environment*

Compare your current work environment to the descriptions below. Check all that ring true for you. Don't be deceived if these descriptions seem obvious. It confirms you've tested your individual color correctly. Other Colors, especially Greens and Reds, would find this environment uncomfortable and unproductive. The optimal Blue/Gold Introvert work environment:

- ○ Must provide privacy for uninterrupted thought
- ○ Affords ability to work independently
- ○ Permits control of your own projects
- ○ Must be intellectually challenging with high standards
- ○ Values creativity
- ○ Rewards your strategic skills
- ○ Contains competent and competitive people
- ○ Compensates you for meeting your goals

The worst type of work culture for a Blue/Gold Introvert is overly bureaucratic. It is full of sensitive people who need exorbitant amounts of handholding. Too much emphasis is put on detail work, not enough on long-range thinking and strategizing. You need private space with unbridled creativity and competition in order to feel comfortable at work.

When Blue/Gold Introverts work in nonideal corporate cultures, productivity is stunted and career achievements become an uphill climb.

The Introverted Blue/Gold's Ideal Boss

Even a great job can be frustrating under the wrong boss; a mediocre job under a wonderful boss is pretty hard to leave. Blue/Golds get along especially well with other Blues. But bosses of other Color types who possess the characteristics in figure 16–3 also can be good mentors.

FIGURE 16–3 *The Blue/Gold Introvert's Ideal Boss*

Check off if your boss:

- ○ Is a well-respected expert in the field
- ○ Can make the tough decisions
- ○ Sets high standards for you and him- or herself
- ○ Encourages creative problem solving
- ○ Gives you a high degree of autonomy
- ○ Trusts and respects your competence

Careers That Attract Blue/Gold Introverts

Autonomy is critical to you. Environments that reward original thinking, solving complex problems, and mastering new technology provide fertile soil for a stellar career like Joshua Stone's.

Please note that not all the following careers will appeal to you, but recognize that each, in some way, draws on the strengths of your style and appeals to a significant number of your Color group. This is not a comprehensive list, but it will show underlying patterns of preference. If unlisted careers offer similar patterns, your chances of success increase. Text in parentheses at the end of each section highlights the Color style characteristics that create success in that broad area.

According to our research, jobs italicized in the lists below are predicted to benefit from an above-average growth rate over the next several years. This information is based on the continuously revised data provided by the U.S. Department of Labor and Bureau of Labor Statistics on their websites O*NET OnLine (www.onetonline.org) and http://www.bls.gov/CAREEROUTLOOK/. There you will find in-depth information about job requirements and salary ranges.

There are successful people of all Color styles in all occupations. In non-ideal jobs, you can still shine by creating your own niche.

ARTS/ARCHITECTURE/COMMUNICATION/MEDIA

architect ▶ composer ▶ art/movie/theater critic ▶ editor/literary agent ▶ film producer/director ▶ *multimedia specialist* ▶ music composer ▶ news analyst/reporter ▶ *web designer* (see complex interconnections, insatiably curious, have many facts at your fingertips, gifted strategic thinker, autonomy, deep concentration powers, faith in own insights, high standards)

BUSINESS/MANAGEMENT/FINANCE

accountant and auditor ▶ *actuary* ▶ bankers of all types ▶ budget analyst ▶ chief financial officer/controller ▶ coach (business/executive) ▶ compensation and benefits manager ▶ credit analyst ▶ economist ▶ executive (private sector, government) ▶ *financial analyst* ▶ *franchise/small business owner* ▶ *investment analyst* ▶ *investment banker* ▶ *investment/securities broker* ▶ insurance underwriter ▶ financial branch or department manager ▶ *marketing manager* ▶ *market research analyst* ▶ *operation research analyst* ▶ *personal financial advisor* ▶ strategic planning ▶ venture capitalist (decisive, focused, take charge, high standards, need for control, solving complex problems, long-range strategic thinking, natural leadership skills)

COMPUTER/INFORMATION TECHNOLOGY

applications developer ▶ artificial intelligence designer ▶ *data scientist* ▶ *database administrator* ▶ *hardware/software engineer* ▶ *information research scientist* ▶ *information systems manager* ▶ *Internet of Things insights strategist* ▶ network and computer systems administrator ▶ *network systems and data communication analyst* ▶ programmer ▶ security specialist ▶ software quality assurance engineer and tester ▶ *support specialist* ▶ *systems analyst* ▶ *web developer* (mastering new technologies, solving complex and/or theoretical problems, autonomy, clear and direct communications, long-range planning, future possibilities, bold new designs, contingency planning, high need for control)

CONSULTING

management consultant ▶ political consultant ▶ *telecommunications security consultant* ▶ training and development specialist (see the big picture in unrelated facts and concepts, solve complex problems, at ease with theories and future possibilities, long-range planning, contingency planning)

EDUCATION

higher education teacher/university professor (especially economics, science, or social studies) ▶ university president (need to deal with competent people, establish long-range visions, strategic planning, few routine tasks, autonomy, debate skills)

GOVERNMENT/PUBLIC ADMINISTRATION

government service executive ▶ intelligence analyst ▶ judge ▶ tax examiner ▶ urban or regional planner (ability to tackle complex issues, long-range planning, respect of community)

HEALTH SCIENCE

anesthesiologist ▶ *biomedical researcher/engineer* ▶ *cardiologist* ▶ *geneticist* ▶ *internist* ▶ *neurologist* ▶ nuclear medicine technologist ▶ *pathologist* ▶ pharmacologist ▶ *psychiatrist* ▶ *surgeon* (intellectual challenge, need for control, ability to tackle complex problems)

LAW

lawyer (corporate, estate planning, employment, entertainment, intellectual property, product liability, project finance, among others) ▶ *paralegal* (solving complex problems, intellectual stimulation, high compensation)

SCIENTIFIC RESEARCH/ENGINEERING/MATHEMATICS

aerospace engineer ▶ agricultural engineer ▶ astronomer ▶ biochemist ▶ biophysicist ▶ economist ▶ engineer (*biomedical*, chemical, civil, electrical, *environmental*, health and safety, industrial, mechanical, nanotechnology) ▶ *environmental scientist* ▶ *industrial psychologist* ▶ inventor ▶ *mathematician* ▶ medical scientist ▶ microbiologist ▶ *operation research analyst* ▶ political scientist ▶ *robotic and manufacturing engineer* ▶ space scientist ▶ *statistician* (strategic thinking, long-range planning, intellectual challenges, little routine or repetitive work, insatiable curiosity, need for control, ability to tackle complex problems, opportunity to interact with people you respect)

CASE STUDY FOUR

When a Career Isn't Working

Web designer Rory MacAfee was having a bad day. The design he knew from research and testing would work best for his firm's biggest client had just been shot down. Even Rory's boss was shocked. Rory knew there would be some long hours and difficult challenges ahead.

The client had insisted on "something more artistic and less logical-sounding; something more today and less futuristic." All the appreciation Rory had been anticipating for his long hours and deep strategic thought had evaporated. In its place came a nightmare of requests he had no clue how to fulfill. He wished he owned the brilliant design and its vast potential. But all his work was copyrighted by his employer. Rory had no alternative but to struggle with the client's requests.

After college, he had been so enthused about web design. He saw it as a way to spend the day doing what he loved: programming and being around other techies. This had happened, but Rory never anticipated the amount of artistic demands he had to handle, for which he frankly had little aptitude. Today's dressing down was the worst yet; he could feel his temples start to throb with yet another of the excruciating tension headaches he'd started having since he took this job.

Rory knew that day he had to make a change. He started talking to Tetiran, his cubicle neighbor, about the idea of starting a firm of their own. Tetiran was enthusiastic. So were Tetiran's rich relatives, who bankrolled the two young programmers to start their own company designing security software for financial corporations.

Rory's role in the new firm was strategic planning and implementation. He took to it like a fish to water. Today he loves his job and deals with matters of future rather than artistic direction. He and Tetiran own all the programs they've created and are well on their way to making their first million.

Your Personality's Challenges

Blue/Gold Introverts have a unique set of potential work-related blind spots. Some listed below you have, others you don't. No one has them all. Tone down a blind spot by focusing on it, then choose more productive actions and make them habits. (Suggestions for doing so are in parentheses below.) You:

▶ May be too abrupt, harsh, or dogmatic. (Everyone needs allies at some point. Alienating others is a strategic error, even if they seem less competent or less intellectual. Patience is a [long-range] virtue. Emotions underpin every successful product and team equally with all your best strategic thinking. Once daily, require yourself to show empathy to someone and note the results.)

▶ Can be unwilling to open your complex thought processes to review or challenge. (You may find it difficult even to get people to understand your deep and brilliant insights, much less agree with or sign off on them. But refusing to discuss them until the end of a project, then being unwilling to change them at that point, is a bad strategy. Break your plan down into steps, and then share it from the beginning to prevent opposition.)

▶ Believe you must do things yourself because no one else is capable. (This comes off as arrogance, which coworkers and bosses resent. They may not do things your way, but each Color brings strengths to the table that you may or may not recognize. There are many paths to the same destination, some even better than yours. Don't you at least want to know what they are?)

▶ May irritate others by being overly skeptical when information is presented. (Many Colors take this as a personal challenge, thinking you don't trust or respect their work. Ask all the questions you want, but soften them with the lead-in phrase, "This seems like good work that you've spent considerable time on. I have some questions, if you don't mind.")

Your Job Search—the Good, the Bad, and the Ugly

Blue/Gold Introverts are direct and to the point, creating resumes that follow a systematic process of presenting career achievements. With some interviewers, particularly Blues and Golds, you will feel a comfortable rapport. But with those of other Colors, you need to prepare and rehearse responses outside your comfort zone. Many human resources people are Greens; make a study of how to communicate effectively with this Color group before your first interviews.

Your natural strengths easily allow you to:

▶ Create measurable and long-term goals for your career

- Research and integrate new trends into your job-search plan

- Get jobs created for you by presenting enough innovative ideas

- Follow through on leads

- Create time lines, daily status reports, and realistic budgets for your job search that reduce stress on you and your family

In order to tone down your blind spots, you need to:

- Think outside your select but limited network of associates; overcome your reluctance to ask for job leads from those you don't know

- Pay attention to the personal aspects of job hunting (i.e., establishing rapport with the interviewer, sending thank-you notes, overtly appreciating the efforts of secretaries and support staff you encounter)

- Cushion your tendency to be abrupt by extending answers and listening without interrupting

- Realize when you're sounding arrogant so you can control it at will; role play with a willing Green

- Request support from friends and family to stay on track when setbacks and obstacles upset you

The Blue/Gold Introvert's Interviewing Style

With an interviewer whose Color is close to your own, you will feel immediate rapport. However, if your interviewer seems to have a significantly different style (and it's statistically likely that many will have a Green component), use the suggestions in parentheses.

In following your natural style, you:

- Will impress interviewers as competent and insightful. (A Green interviewer will ask emotion-based questions like, "Did you enjoy those duties?" Be prepared with answers more extended than "Yes." A Red interviewer also will want to establish some kind of rapport.)

- May come across as arrogant or too abstract. (It is not necessary to humble yourself, but don't attempt to build up your accomplishments at anyone's expense. Show respect for previous colleagues so future ones know they can expect it too. You'll gain no points by overwhelming your interviewer with highly technical jargon. Keep in it plain English; let your resume communicate your abilities.)

▶ Might not convey enough enthusiasm during the interview. (You are passionate about ideas, but don't express it freely. Role play sharing just a little of that passion; ask a willing Green or Red. You'll come across as really wanting the job. This also will overcome your tendency to appear enigmatic.)

▶ May need to be more flexible when considering a job offer. ("My way or the highway" is not a good strategy for negotiating duties and compensation. Listen, counteroffer, take a day to think through what's right for you and your family, and counteroffer again. Establish in advance realistic boundaries for what is acceptable; don't make it a competitive fight to the death.)

Once you've critiqued this profile and decided we've gotten enough things right to make it worthwhile, read chapter 19, "Golds Overall," then carefully read chapter 24, "Before I Do Something Stupid: Adjusting to Other Styles," to learn about the strengths of other Colors. Read up on the Greens to prepare for job interviews (a large number of human resources people are Greens) and the Reds if you have to interact with any at work or at home.

If you are actively engaging in a job search, keep notes in the Roadmap in chapter 27. Recording your strengths and strategies is a logical and results-oriented way to navigate the minefields of a job search. You also can keep track of contacts for follow-up.

CHAPTER 17

Blue/Red Extroverts

YOU'RE NOT ONLY a Blue, you also have strong secondary characteristics of the adventurous Red personality. And you have tested as a Color Q Extrovert, which means you recharge your batteries by being with people rather than being alone. Your Color group prides itself on finding innovative ways to do things. You take initiative and surmount all limitations with a can-do attitude. Please note that the underlying components of the following profile have been researched for nearly seven decades worldwide and verified across age, sex, ethnic, and socioeconomic boundaries. So if we don't get you right, nobody will.

You Overall

Blue/Red Extroverts radiate a contagious enthusiasm for anything that captures their interest. You constantly scan the universe for those new and unusual ideas that fire your vivid imagination. Creative and insightful, you love the challenge and excitement of pursuing your latest goal—until it ceases to interest you. But until then, you are tireless, energizing others as you charge ahead.

Whether you've got advanced degrees or not, you are blessed with high intellectual energy, constantly on the alert for the latest and greatest opportunities. When you see them, you pounce. Inquisitive and clever, you need a great deal of freedom to use your many talents. A flexible environment is key. Unconventional approaches are fun for you, and you will bend or break rules as needed to make things happen. Following through to the bitter end once the project has been launched, however, is of little interest.

You are used to people disagreeing with your perceptions. Whether others agree with you is not important. Since childhood you've enjoyed an inborn ability to debate from either side of an issue, confounding opponents at times by jumping back and forth. You are naturally quick on your feet. Ultimately, your enthusiasm and the compelling power of your ideas persuade all.

You are unique among the Colors for your ability to be both serious and humorous, speaking with passion and wit. However, you prefer logic to emotion and are irritated by others who require too much hand-holding. People who refuse to consider new ways of doing things really annoy you.

CASE STUDY ONE

Vice President, Human Resources/Social Services

There are few jobs as challenging as meeting the special needs of troubled youths and their families. The can-do attitude Blue/Red Extroverts like Deborah Finley-Troup possess has helped hundreds of New York City families find their way to become educationally proficient, economically productive, and socially responsible community members.

A thirty-year veteran of nonprofit human resources and training, Deborah today handles human resources for the Children's Village in New York City. She began her career there as a direct care worker at their school for troubled children. Her Blue/Red Extrovert's unique blend of seriousness and humor engaged and managed her young clients very effectively. But Blues never linger at the junior level. Deborah quickly advanced to manager, then director of training and development.

One of her greatest successes came during her time at the New York Foundling Hospital. There, her Blue strategic gifts met their perfect challenge. "I led a strategic planning process which resulted in large organizational change," she says. "One large organization was split into three more effective and mission-targeted organizations." For a Blue personality, making a positive impact on the world is a primary goal and a source of deep fulfillment.

Today, Deborah is responsible for all the diverse human resources aspects of the Children's Village and CV Management Services. This includes managing the human resources and learning and development departments administering for four not-for-profit organizations—everything from attracting, hiring, and training 1,500 employees serving thousands of children and families annually to running a day care program for employees. "I am good at designing new strategies for recruitment, retention, and development of staff and managers," says Deborah.

Being a red secondary type enables Deborah to identify problems and support employees who are difficult or challenging. When unconventional approaches are called for, this personality type jumps right into the thick of things, quickly able to identify opportunities and solutions.

State and federal audits fall under her purview—a task better left to detail-oriented Golds. Such focus on detail work stifles a Blue/Red's intellectual energy. "I don't like to do them," Deborah says simply.

What Deborah does enjoy currently is an initiative for undoing institutional racism. "I find that challenging and exciting," she says. "I do leadership training and development, and create succession planning programs. I like to develop new programs," she says. This is not unusual for Blues, who can visualize a broader horizon than the other Color types.

But it is her Red secondary personality that leads the way when it is time to kick back, relax, and recharge. Reds are the most physically oriented; for Deborah, relaxing does not mean staying still. "I walk, I bike, I kayak, and I canoe," she says.

Through working with others, Deborah is able to support the Children's Village and four other not-for-profit organizations to offer a continuum of services that serve diverse populations of children and families. Programs address a variety of issues such as behavioral problems, mental illness, homelessness, education, domestic abuse, substance abuse, life skills, housing, and employment. Deborah says, "We work within systems of immigration, juvenile justice, and child welfare with the primary goal of keeping children and families together."

You on the Job

AS A LEADER

"Let's exceed goals!" would be the theme of any pep talk given by a Blue/Red Extrovert. You lead and motivate with energy, taking initiative, making the tough decisions, being comfortable with risk. Your well-developed problem-solving skills and tendency to challenge conventional wisdom move everyone forward.

You set the bar high for your people, and you don't hire the marginally competent. Your people exceed limitations and quickly adapt to changing conditions because you respect their independence. This is especially critical since you often gravitate to global issues.

AS A TEAM PLAYER

A can-do approach is how you begin each project. You are apt to suggest high standards and encourage everyone to go the extra mile. Contributing best at the first half of a project, you ask imaginative questions and provide clear analysis. Your ability to think strategically long term always helps set team direction. When coping with fatigue and tension, humor is your tool of choice.

Finding unique ways of solving problems is another strength, and you will generate many options for consideration. While it is unusual for team-mates to dislike you, you occasionally may irritate them by proposing too many possibilities.

Look at figure 17–1 for a list of your natural work-related strengths.

FIGURE 17-1 *Natural Work-Related Strengths*

Approximately 80 percent of these attributes will apply to you. Check off those that do, and use them in your resume and interviews. This will set you apart from the canned responses of others. You:

- ○ Are particularly good at startups or the initial stage of a project
- ○ See the big picture
- ○ Inspire others through energy, enthusiasm, and colorful communication
- ○ Take an interest in complex problems
- ○ Are energized when seeking new and more creative solutions
- ○ Enjoy brainstorming and are one of the most effective Colors at it
- ○ Can work with a broad range of people
- ○ Analyze situations objectively
- ○ Reduce tension with humor
- ○ Are willing to take risks

Now see how some Blue/Red Extroverts use these strengths in very different fields.

CASE STUDY TWO

Surgeon

Charles "Chuck" Sheaff is a classic Blue/Red Extrovert. He got his undergraduate degree in engineering and intended to become a biomedical engineer. "In medical school, I got sidetracked," he says. "I ended up getting a Ph.D. in biochemistry instead. Then I became more interested in surgery, because there's a lot of immediate gratification in it. At the end of an operation, the problem is fixed and the person usually gets well and goes home."

With his Red backup, Chuck was drawn to emergency surgery, which he taught for two years. "When I am faced with a patient who is bleeding to death and a lot of things have to be done in a short period of time, that tends to make me more focused and organized," he says. "I tend to be almost easier to get along with then than I am in some other situations."

One thing Chuck's Red side enjoys is flying. "I like instrument flying," he says, "and solving the navigational problems." This is an excellent combination of his Blue and Red characteristics.

Chuck served in leadership positions at his hospital for ten years. "I like politics," he says. "It's rewarding to solve problems in a political arena." Blue/Red Extroverts make excellent politicians and are drawn to the politics of any field in which they work.

In classic Blue/Red Extrovert fashion, Chuck uses his engineering skills to create innovative solutions wherever he is. "I saw a Christmas tree hanging upside down in a shop, and it made more sense that the ornaments could hang so they were easily seen," he recalls. "I devised a way to keep the tree better watered upside down, and the project worked out well. The tree stayed alive until Easter." A true Blue innovator, Chuck fantasizes about establishing a small think tank organization. "It would be fun," he says, "to have some people working for me to solve problems, invent new things, and take them to market."

CASE STUDY THREE

Chair/CEO, Executive Recruiting

Some people's resumes are too big for ordinary jobs, and such is the case with Charles W. B. Wardell III. If you don't know his name, you are not high enough up in the corporate food chain. Chuck is chair and CEO of the top ten executive search firm Witt/Kieffer. He is also former global chairman for the Association of Executive Search Consultants and former managing director for the Northeast Region of Korn/Ferry International, the world's largest recruiting firm. He reached the top of the ladder in his field because his own background brought him into contact with many high-level people and he fostered these relationships. Today he knows who to call for almost any executive placement or leadership need.

After a distinguished career in the military and graduation from Harvard University, Chuck worked for Henry Kissinger as deputy assistant secretary of state. He served in the White House under two presidents. He was the chief operating officer of American Express's private bank and ran its Middle East credit card division. He also managed the Business Diversification Group, a large division of Travelers Insurance. "Executive search requires years of assessing and leading people," he says, "dealing with their successes and failures, formulating the building blocks of what they need to get ahead in their careers."

Chuck likes meeting the demands of today's changing workforce, dealing with baby boomers, whose experience now suddenly is back in vogue—or with millennials, who embrace innovation. "Firms are beginning to realize they have to invest [in] and keep good people," he notes. "Companies are demanding experience and performance over academic credentials."

Chuck most enjoys the variety his work affords him, something important to his Color style. He especially likes working with those at senior levels on important issues, where the people he manages and advises have real-world impact. "What I do helps to influence how the capitalist system works," he says. But Chuck has three priorities for himself—maintaining his health, keeping his independence, and enjoying his work—all hallmarks of his Color style.

Blues enjoy complex challenges more than many Colors, and that's a good thing because Witt/Kieffer operates in sectors like healthcare and education that are undergoing major overhauls. "Healthcare is changing from an industry that used to do almost all of its business in hospitals to one that operates in specialized centers and clinics and even Walgreens or CVS. How do you help clients find executives to run organizations that look nothing like they did in the past?"

Ideal Work Environment

The opportunity to meet stimulating, powerful, and influential people often is the key that gets you to accept a job. Working on cutting-edge ideas is right where you want to be.

When a job offer is made, leverage as much as you can from the list in figure 17–2.

FIGURE 17–2 **The Ideal Blue/Red Extrovert Work Environment**

Compare your current work environment to the descriptions below. If these descriptions seem obvious, that confirms you've tested your individual Color correctly. Other Colors, especially Golds, would find this environment uncomfortable and unproductive. The optimal Blue/Red Extrovert work environment:

○ Provides a variety of tasks and projects

○ Is creative, entrepreneurial, and nonstructured

○ Rewards expertise and quick thinking

○ Creates new products and solutions

○ Is a continuous opportunity for new learning

○ Lets you assemble a competent staff of people who do not need to be micromanaged

○ Offers the opportunity to interact with powerful or influential people

---

The worst type of work culture for a Blue/Red Extrovert is one in which you are micromanaged and surrounded by coworkers who lack initiative. It emphasizes detailed work with predictable results.

When Blue/Red Extroverts work in nonideal corporate cultures, productivity is stunted and career achievements become an uphill climb.

The Extroverted Blue/Red's Ideal Boss

Even a great job can be frustrating under the wrong boss; a mediocre job under a wonderful boss is pretty hard to leave. Blue/Reds get along especially well with other Blues. But bosses of other Color types who possess the characteristics in figure 17–3 also can be good mentors.

FIGURE 17–3 **The Blue/Red Extrovert's Ideal Boss**

Check off if your boss:

○ Can make tough decisions

○ Is competent and respected

○ Keeps bureaucracy at bay

○ Has a sense of humor

○ Does not micromanage you

○ Sets high standards

○ Values and rewards innovation

○ Provides all necessary resources to ensure tasks are accomplished

Careers That Attract Blue/Red Extroverts

Blue/Red Extroverts are most productive in environments that reward their intellectual energy, original ideas, and risk taking. You especially enjoy original projects dealing with global issues.

Please note that not all the following careers will appeal to you, but recognize that each, in some way, draws on the strengths of your style and appeals to a significant number of your Color group. This is not a comprehensive list, but it will show underlying patterns of preference. If unlisted careers offer similar patterns, your chances of success increase. Text in parentheses at the end of each section highlights the Color style characteristics that create success in that broad area.

According to our research, jobs italicized in the lists below are predicted to benefit from an above-average growth rate over the next several years. This information is based on the continuously revised data provided by the U.S. Department of Labor and Bureau of Labor Statistics on their websites O*NET OnLine (www.onetonline.org) and http://www.bls.gov/CAREEROUTLOOK/. There you will find in-depth information about job requirements and salary ranges.

There are successful people of all Color styles in all occupations. In non-ideal jobs, you can still shine by creating your own niche.

BUSINESS/FINANCE/ADMINISTRATION

executive (business, entertainment, financial services, healthcare) ▸ *financial analyst* ▸ *financial planner* ▸ *executive/human resources recruiter* ▸ *insurance sales agent* ▸ *investment banker* ▸ *management consultant* ▸ *new business development specialist* ▸ real estate, property, and community association manager ▸ *sales manager* ▸ *securities, commodities, and financial services sales agent* ▸ training and development specialist ▸ venture capitalist (inquisitive, take initiative, compelling interest in everything around you, insightful, open to new and unusual opportunities, quick on your feet)

COMMUNICATIONS/CREATIVE/MARKETING

actor ▸ *advertising, promotion, and marketing manager* ▸ art director ▸ *business manager* (artists, entertainers, athletes) ▸ editor ▸ industrial designer ▸ journalist ▸ literary agent ▸ photographer ▸ *public relations director* ▸ *stage/film producer* ▸ *talk show host* ▸ writer (high intellectual energy, love of excitement and challenge, responsive to new opportunities, clever, enjoy company of influential people)

COMPUTER/INFORMATION TECHNOLOGY

computer analyst/engineer/programmer ▸ *computer security specialist* ▸ *information and systems manager* ▸ *Internet of Things solutions architect* ▸ robotics designer/engineer ▸ *support specialist* ▸ *systems analyst* ▸ *web developer* (variety of projects, creation of new products and solutions, autonomy, opportunity to brainstorm, problem solving, flexible environment, need for unconventional methods)

EDUCATION

athletic coach ▸ lecturer ▸ *professor/teacher* (upper levels) ▸ school psychologist (high intellectual energy, flexible environments, see both sides of issues, quick on your feet, prefer logic)

ENTREPRENEURSHIP/HOSPITALITY

hotel/lodging manager ▸ inventor ▸ restaurant/bar owner ▸ *small business/franchise owner* (make tough decisions, flexible entrepreneurial atmosphere, turn innovative ideas into reality, responsive to new opportunities and unusual ideas, contagious enthusiasm, freedom, quick on your feet)

HEALTH SCIENCE/PSYCHOLOGY

chiropractor ▸ *emergency room doctor/surgeon* ▸ *family practitioner* ▸ *health services manager* ▸ *industrial psychologist* ▸ *internist* ▸ *psychiatrist* ▸ *radiological technologist* (variety, autonomy, flexible environment, quick on your feet, high intellectual energy, problem solving)

POLITICS/GOVERNMENT

political analyst ▸ politician/political manager ▸ regional and urban planner (quickly see possibilities of new situations, provide clear analysis to issues, generate many options, strategic and long-range thinking, enjoy company of powerful and influential people)

LAW

lawyer (especially bankruptcy, immigration, intellectual property, litigation, mergers and acquisitions, among others) (analytical ability, insightful, see both sides of issues, quick on your feet, enjoy company of influential people)

PROFESSIONS

architect ▸ detective ▸ environmental scientist ▸ industrial/aerospace engineer (high standards, clear analytical ability, love excitement and challenge, insightful, always looking to increase competence, ability to debate from both sides of an issue, autonomy, responsibility for own projects, quick on your feet)

CASE STUDY FOUR

When a Career Isn't Working

Brad Kittering's great-grandfather had founded the First National Bank in the town where he grew up, and Brad determined to go into banking to follow family tradition.

From the day Brad started at First National as a bank teller, it looked to the world like another young Kittering was on his way up the ladder to the bank president's office. Brad was great with the customers and rapidly developed a loyal group of depositors who never complained if he made a mistake. Behind the scenes, he was a disaster. Try as he might, Brad miscounted money, was terrible at following the bank's many arcane rules, and was bored out of his skull dealing with the details of his drawer. He was warned several times to shape up and would have been fired but for his last name.

Brad was intrigued by the internal bank newsletter and on a whim contributed an article on how to deal with difficult customers. It was very well received, and a highly regarded banking trade journal asked to run it nationwide. Blue/Red Extroverts make excellent journalists because they are interested in people to the point of nosiness and often are good writers.

Brad continued submitting articles and was asked to be a regular columnist to the trade journal. Today he writes and lectures on banking customer service through his own consulting company.

Your Personality's Challenges

Blue/Red Extroverts have a unique set of potential work-related blind spots. Some listed below you have, others you don't. No one has them all. Tone down a blind spot by focusing on it, then choose more productive actions and make them habits. (Suggestions for doing so are in parentheses below.) You:

- Initiate too many projects, some of which don't get completed. (You can get swept away by your own enthusiasm. A good rule for you: Don't start something until you've finished the last project.)

- Can be too casual about deadlines and commitments. (Work is fun, but it's still work. If you're getting paid to meet deadlines, then meet them. Your work ethic will incorporate this value more as you mature and get yelled at by your bosses.)

- Intimidate those less quick witted. (You have little use for those less competent than yourself. Particularly when you're young, it's a sport to run them around verbally. But one of them could end up as your boss.)

- Sometimes change plans and strategies too frequently. (If you're working on your own, you will lose focus; within a company, you will upset all those whose talents you need to make things happen. Lost focus often equals lost money.)

- Want too much of the limelight. (Put yourself out to be noticed when someone else deserves the attention and you create bad blood. Be sure to share the limelight once you have it with those who deserve applause—or else watch your back.)

Your Job Search—the Good, the Bad, and the Ugly

Blue/Red Extroverts create succinct, objective resumes but prefer talking in person. With some interviewers, particularly Blues and Reds, you will feel a comfortable rapport. But with those of other Colors, you need to prepare and rehearse responses outside your comfort zone. Many human resources people are Greens; make a study of how to communicate effectively with this Color group before your first interviews.

Your natural strengths easily allow you to:

- Find multiple paths to explore during job searches

- Have an extensive network to tap for referrals and job leads

▶ Rebound quickly from obstacles and rejections

In order to tone down your blind spots, you need to:

▶ Write down long-term goals and your plans for getting there; include priorities and checkpoints

▶ Limit your time off to play during the job search

▶ Remember your goals while networking and don't get lost in the fun of it

▶ Make a budget for your job search based on a realistic timeframe

▶ Follow through on all administrative details of the job search; ask assistance from a willing Gold

▶ Temper initial excitement about a prospective job; review impact on your family and personal life before accepting

The Blue/Red Extrovert's Interviewing Style

With an interviewer whose Color is close to your own, you will feel immediate rapport. However, if your interviewer seems to have a significantly different style, use the suggestions in parentheses.

In following your natural style, you:

▶ Come across as energetic, flexible, adaptable, and creative. (You establish rapport with interviewers easily. With cooler ones, address them by their last names until invited to use first names, then let them set the tone.)

▶ Might talk too much and not ask enough pertinent questions. (Write critical questions down on a list and refer to them. Slip them in between the fun parts of the conversation.)

▶ May overwhelm more concrete types with possibilities and theory. (If your interviewer seems to glaze over when you go into theoretical areas, back away. Let the person lead the conversation until you can assess his or her areas of interest.)

If you're having fun with this material, read chapter 9, "Reds Overall," to understand your backup. Then carefully read chapter 24, "Before I Do Something Stupid: Adjusting to Other Styles," to learn about the strengths of other Colors. Read up on the Greens to prepare for job interviews (a large number of human resources people are Greens) and the Golds if you have to interact with any at work or at home.

If you are actively engaging in a job search, keep notes in the Roadmap in chapter 27. Recording your strengths and strategies is a logical and results-oriented way to navigate the minefields of a job search and brain-storm some unconventional approaches. It also will help keep your net-working activities focused.

CHAPTER 18

Blue/Red Introverts

YOU'RE NOT ONLY a Blue, you also have strong secondary characteristics of the Red personality. And you have tested as a Color Q Introvert, which means you recharge your batteries by being alone rather than being with others. Much, but not all, of this material will focus on human and emotional subjects, which your Color finds irritating. You will be more open to this if you are in the second half of your life but will need it more if you are younger. But since you respond to new ideas, the aim will be to surprise you with our accuracy.

You Overall

Did the previous paragraph surprise you? Okay, let's see what else we can say to rock your highly logical world. After all, you are open minded. Mental stimulation is as necessary to you as breathing. Color Q is a new derivative of a decades-old, tried-and-true system of personality profiling. It goes back to concepts proposed by Carl Jung. There are a lot of perspectives in here for you to debate, so get a friend to read this chapter with you and go at it from all angles. You're good at that.

Your group of friends is small but intimate. Few see your real feelings. Emotional stuff is usually last on your list, but many of your friendships are formed over shared projects. Privacy is important, though, because when concentrating on something, you find interruptions irritating. So just view reading this as a new project on which you've decided to risk twenty minutes (or fewer; it's likely you skim or read fast).

New projects draw you like a magnet, often propelling you to the cutting edge of your field. Independent, resourceful, and a skeptic at heart, you are unafraid to take controversial positions.

It's necessary for you to have flexibility to critique, redesign, and improve; whether others understand or agree with your changes is irrelevant. You are confident of your ability to improvise your way through difficult problems that you doubt others even understand. Project follow-through, however, is of low interest.

Your unusual insights make you, at times, almost psychic about future trends, so people count on you for the most innovative systems and solutions. In your interest areas, you communicate with speed and enthusiasm; otherwise, you may not communicate at all.

People see you as clever, critical, challenging, and sometimes disorganized. You are most irritated by people who refuse to consider new ideas, who are overly emotional, or who apply faulty logic.

CASE STUDY ONE

Entrepreneur, Small Business Expert

Jack Rubinstein "views the world at 50,000 feet" and aspires to view it at 60,000. He is chairman of the board of credit card processing company Pipeline Data and general partner of DICA Partners, an investment hedge fund. For fifteen years, he has been an advisor to small public entities through his company Capital Market Advisory Network. He employs his ability to see three years out to mold small firms into multibillion-dollar entities.

"My function," says Jack, "is to create alternate solutions for people who are too involved in the day-to-day nitty-gritty."

Jack's father owned a small business, and Jack remembers discussing the day's problems with him at the dinner table when he was eight years old. When Jack began his career, he trained as a research analyst. "It's a curiosity, analyzing businesses of all sorts," Jack says.

Jack helps business owners navigate the capital markets and finds innovative ways to help them expand. "I was an advisor to a $20 million company, showing them how to 'creep the market' making thirty-seven different acquisitions over a twenty-four-month period," Jack recalls. "Then they were sold to GE Capital for over $1 billion.

"I was also an original backer of Sirius Satellite Radio when they had three employees, a driven entrepreneur, and virtually no money. I saw a combination of possibilities that allowed me to get the vision, whereas very few other people could. Now their market capitalization is $10 billion."

Jack has the Blue/Red Introvert's vision for small companies that can become large. He delegates all his detail work and record keeping to a Gold family member.

You on the Job

AS A LEADER

High quality is the cornerstone of your leadership. Whether it applies to the new ideas you propose, the people you hire to implement them, or the work standards you set, high quality is always the theme. To meet standards, you'll even challenge conventional wisdom or push your people to develop themselves intellectually.

Flexible and quick to adapt to change, you will be the first to see and solve problems. Understanding global issues is your real talent.

AS A TEAM PLAYER

Asking imaginative questions, generating many unique solutions, and accepting the good contributions of others are characteristics for which you are valued.

You may not be valued for pointing out every flaw or inconsistency or for indulging in overly intellectual or complicated descriptions.

Look at figure 18–1 for a list of your natural work-related strengths.

FIGURE 18–1 *Natural Work-Related Strengths*

Approximately 80 percent of these attributes will apply to you. Check off those that do, and use them in your resume and interviews. This will set you apart from the canned responses of others. You:

○ Keep creating and improving ideas

○ Evaluate situations logically and analytically

○ Provide calm amid emotional storms

○ Solve complex problems creatively

○ Are open to new information and will change decisions if necessary

○ Demand high-quality and rigorous intellectual application

○ Rarely get sidetracked into chitchat

○ Focus intensely for long periods

Here are some Blue/Red Introverts in action in very different fields.

CASE STUDY TWO

Medical Research Scientist and University Professor

The resume of Bruce I. Terman, Ph.D., is replete with long lists of medical research experience, grants awarded, and papers published. Behind the credentials is actually a likable guy (not unusual for those with a Red backup) who cares about doing the right thing.

Between the classes he teaches as associate professor of the medicine/cardiology division and associate professor of pathology at the Albert Einstein College of Medicine in the Bronx, New York, Bruce strives to be a good citizen at his university. Along with his main work in research, "I try to serve on administrative committees and participate in teaching and research seminars," he says.

As an Introvert, he especially enjoys the activities he performs on his own. Of his three top natural strengths, he does two of them alone. "I'm best at performing experiments and planning the scientific direction of the laboratory," he says. His third strength is teaching. He is energized by successfully obtaining grants, getting his papers published, and having his laboratory experiments produce expected or interesting results.

Another aspect of his job that well suits his Introvert side is obtaining funding to support his research. He applies for numerous grants. He also must keep abreast of his field by constantly reading scientific literature and attending national meetings of his peers (the latter he says is one of his least interesting duties). In the laboratory, he supervises the research activities of five individuals (a task that includes training of students and mentoring of other scientists). Typical of a Blue who chooses a scientific career, he is persistent about achieving his goals.

Bruce's three biggest stressors are "supervising or interacting with noncooperative, nonproductive, or obnoxious individuals; waiting to hear about or having grants and manuscripts rejected; and getting poor experimental results."

That doesn't happen often. In 1994, he was named the winner of the American Cyanamid Scientific Achievement Award. Bruce is straightforward about his successes. "I am smart and honest," he says, a very typical Blue/Red combination. Then it's back into the lab to continue his life's work.

CASE STUDY THREE

Hedge Fund Manager, Investment Industry

Ari Levy is well on his way to recognizing and developing his unique Blue/Red Introvert strengths. He is the founder, president, and chief investment officer of Chicago-based Lakeview Investment Group. Additionally, he functions as portfolio manager of the firm's limited partnership, Lakeview Fund, a long-short equity product focused on long-term investments in small- and micro-cap-value securities.

True to his Blue/Red nature, he prefers the portfolio management and research functions over marketing and governmental compliance demands. "There is nothing more satisfying than doing thorough research on a stock and finding some inefficiency that makes it undervalued before Wall Street discovers it," Ari says.

Ari finds marketing less interesting, especially when "I don't find the person that I'm marketing to particularly interesting, or he or she doesn't understand what we do," he admits. This is typical of Blue/Red Introverts.

He prides himself on his understanding of financial risk and reward and his management skills. Blue/Red Introverts are deeply disciplined in their areas of interest. Ari is very disciplined in the portfolio-management process, "although I am not as organized in certain areas of my personal life!"

Ari is a typical Blue/Red Introvert in other ways. He enjoys probability-based activities like gambling, investments, and card playing. His enjoyment of cutting-edge activities is indulged every day at his hedge fund, forever trying to perfect investment models. Even at leisure, his interest lies in sports statistics.

Ideal Work Environment

Jack Rubinstein's ability is to think innovatively about business is supported by a flexible environment. He also has the administrative support he needs to stay focused on what he does best. Ari Levy, too, has created his own firm and sets his own agenda.

When a job offer is made, leverage as much as you can from the list in figure 18–2.

FIGURE 18-2 *The Ideal Blue/Red Introvert Work Environment*

Compare your current work environment to the descriptions below. If these descriptions seem obvious, that confirms you've tested your individual Color correctly. Other Colors, especially Golds, would find this environment uncomfortable and unproductive. The optimal Blue/Red Introvert work environment:

○ Is flexible with a minimum of rules, procedures, and meetings. Nothing should impede the intellectual process.

○ Values independent and creative thinking. You look at a problem as if it were a Rubik's cube—from all sides. Then you rearrange it until a solution becomes evident.

○ Focuses on startup phase of projects. Implementation and administration are left to the support staff in place for that purpose.

○ Allows privacy and ability to work alone without too much time pressure. You really hate interruptions and people breathing down your neck. You're much more productive without them.

○ Is a nonemotional, logical culture that rewards competence and risk taking. Emotions take time and energy. You'd rather put those resources into the risk taking and analysis.

○ Contains an informal network of scholarly, independent, and motivated associates. You need to verbalize all sides of a problem and debate solutions. That's hard to do by yourself, or with less-competent coworkers.

The worst type of work culture for a Blue/Red Introvert is overly bureaucratic and controlled. Strict time management and required work-area tidiness drive you to distraction. When coworkers are emotionally sensitive, or less competent than you, it stresses you to the limits of your patience.

When Blue/Red Introverts work in nonideal corporate cultures, productivity is stunted and career achievements become an uphill climb.

The Introverted Blue/Red's Ideal Boss

Even a great job can be frustrating under the wrong boss; a mediocre job under a wonderful boss is pretty hard to leave. Blue/Reds get along especially well with other Blues. But bosses of other Color types who possess the characteristics in figure 18–3 also can be good mentors.

FIGURE 18–3 *The Blue/Red Introvert's Ideal Boss*

Check off if your boss:

○ Permits complete autonomy

○ Treats employees as equals

○ Is smart, quick witted, and stimulating

○ Shields you from the organization's bureaucracy

○ Does not saddle you with administrative work

○ Is open to improving existing systems and procedures

○ Asks you to come up with ideas, then has others implement them

○ Recognizes and respects your expertise

○ Lets you have a say in how you are evaluated and compensated

---

Careers That Attract Blue/Red Introverts

You, like Bruce Terman, are most attracted to careers that require intellectual energy, original ideas, and achievement. You prefer involvement with theoretical problems and new technologies. Original projects are a must; routine and repeated tasks are sorely taxing.

Please note that not all the following careers will appeal to you, but recognize that each, in some way, draws on the strengths of your style and appeals to a significant number of your Color group. This is not a comprehensive list, but it will show underlying patterns of preference. If unlisted careers offer similar patterns, your chances of success increase. Text in parentheses at the end of each section highlights the Color style characteristics that create success in that broad area.

According to our research, jobs italicized in the lists below are predicted to benefit from an above-average growth rate over the next several years. This information is based on the continuously revised data provided by the U.S. Department of Labor and Bureau of Labor Statistics on their websites O*NET OnLine (www.onetonline.org) and http://www.bls.gov/CAREEROUTLOOK/. There you will find in-depth information about job requirements and salary ranges.

There are successful people of all Color styles in all occupations. In non-ideal jobs, you can still shine by creating your own niche.

ARCHITECTURE/CREATIVE/MEDIA
architect ▶ art director ▶ artist ▶ broadcast news analyst ▶ columnist ▶ creative writer ▶ critic ▶ dancer ▶ editor ▶ entertainment agent ▶ *film/stage/motion picture producer and director* ▶ graphic designer ▶ industrial designer ▶ journalist ▶ multimedia artist or animator ▶ musician ▶ photographer ▶ writer and author (enjoy play and surprises, intense focus on everything around you)

BUSINESS/FINANCE
accountant ▶ auditor ▶ *budget analyst* ▶ *business analyst* ▶ business coach ▶ chief financial officer/controller ▶ credit analyst ▶ economist ▶ entrepreneur ▶ *financial analyst* ▶ franchise/small business owner ▶ hedge fund manager ▶ insurance underwriter ▶ *interpreter/translator* ▶ *investment banker* ▶ *investment/securities broker* ▶ *management consultant* ▶ *market research analyst* ▶ *new market/product designer* ▶ *personal financial advisor* ▶ *security analyst* ▶ *statistician* ▶ strategic planner ▶ think tank member ▶ training and development consultant ▶ venture capitalist (intellectual and insightful about future trends)

COMPUTER/INFORMATION TECHNOLOGY
computer programmer/researcher ▶ *cybersecurity specialist* ▶ *data scientist* ▶ *database administrator* ▶ hardware/software engineer ▶ *information research scientist* ▶ *Internet of Things insight strategist* ▶ *mobile application developer* ▶ *network and computer systems administrator* ▶ *network integration specialist* ▶ *network systems and data communication analyst* ▶ new product conceptualizer ▶ software quality assurance engineer and tester ▶ *systems analyst* ▶ *web developer* (flexible environments where you can create, critique, redesign, and improve)

EDUCATION
higher education teacher/university professor ▶ *online educator* ▶ *researcher* (intellectual stimulation, colleagues who enjoy debate)

HEALTH SCIENCE/PSYCHOLOGY

anesthesiologist ▸ *biomedical researcher* ▸ *cardiologist* ▸ *health specialist/teacher* ▸ *medical scientist/researcher* ▸ *neurologist* ▸ pharmaceutical researcher ▸ pharmacist ▸ *physician* ▸ *psychologist/psychiatrist* ▸ *surgeon* ▸ *veterinarian* (independence and intellectual stimulation, plus need for your ability to concentrate for long periods of time)

LAW

lawyer (especially banking, corporate finance, energy, estate planning, intellectual property, product liability, among others) ▸ *legal mediator* (enjoy difficult problems, intellectual stimulation, love of debate)

SCIENTIFIC RESEARCH/ENGINEERING/MATHEMATICS

archaeologist ▸ astronomer ▸ biologist ▸ biophysicist ▸ chemist ▸ economist ▸ engineer (aerospace, biomechanical, *biomedical*, chemical, civil, electrical, geological, health and safety, industrial, mechanical, nanotechnology) ▸ *environmental scientist* ▸ *geneticist* ▸ *geoscientist* ▸ inventor ▸ *mathematician* ▸ medical research scientist ▸ microbiologist ▸ physicist ▸ *robotic and manufacturing engineer* ▸ space/rocket scientist (opportunities to apply your love of solving difficult problems, be on cutting edge)

CASE STUDY FOUR

When a Career Isn't Working

Gretchen Kinderhook's father was a property manager for a large Midwestern office building. As a teenager, Gretchen used to join her dad after school to help out. She became fascinated anticipating the problems of the tenants and being ready to solve them as they arose. She also enjoyed the charged atmosphere when a tenant crisis arose. She thought her dad had the best job in the world.

When Gretchen was in her junior year at college studying business, her father died unexpectedly. With little life insurance in place, the family's security was threatened. Using all her secondary Red crisis-management skills, Gretchen dropped out and took over his job.

It was just as she had remembered it, and most of the tenants knew her by her first name. What Gretchen had not anticipated were the tasks her father had performed: They were so structured and stifling. Her Blue/Red Introvert's ability to see far into the future and strategize got little use as she dealt with getting the trash out, the leases renewed, the vendors contracted, the security staff hired, and the cleaning crew to show up.

Gretchen felt trapped by her obligation to help support her family. Dutifully, she went around to the tenants to renew leases. On the eighteenth floor was a small think tank with fifteen employees whose job was to predict market trends for their blue-chip clients. Gretchen lingered here, throwing out so many free ideas that the company president joked he would start paying her as well as the rent. Gretchen's heart leapt at the idea, surprising her. But she didn't think he was serious and did not feel she could let her family down.

Two years of valuable free ideas later, Gretchen actually accepted a genuine job offer from the think tank. The salary was substantially higher than what she made managing the property and would allow her to help her family even more. The choice was a no-brainer, and today the new property manager frequently comes up to the eighteenth floor to take Gretchen to lunch when he has a problem. Her job at the think tank puts her right in her strategic-thinking element, and she has completed her degree online.

Your Personality's Challenges

Blue/Red Introverts have a unique set of potential work-related blind spots. Some listed below you have, others you don't. No one has them all. Tone down a blind spot by focusing on it, then choose more productive actions and make them habits. (Suggestions for doing so are in parentheses below.) You:

- Can be too casual about deadlines and/or commitments when lost in intellectual projects. (Set aside time in the morning when you focus on such things; then you can concentrate on more important things.)

- May initiate too many projects that cannot be completed. (So much interest, so little time. Give yourself permission to work on more than two major projects only if you have adequate staff on projects three and up, and your role is to oversee.)

- Intimidate those less quick witted. (Admit it, you like the power your braininess gives you over your less-blessed colleagues. Just don't make a habit of humiliating them—one of them could eventually become your boss.)

- Can be overly critical, complex, and competitive. (The competitive drive is necessary in your preferred fields, but know where to draw the line. Same goes for critical and opinionated behavior. Pick your battles.)

- Change plans and strategies too frequently. (Changing course with each new fact can be overwhelming for other Colors and subordinates. Admit that you're not an expert implementer. Show respect for and cooperate with those who are.)

- When fatigued, you become bitingly sarcastic and have uncontrolled emotional outbursts. (Apologize and say, "I think it's time for a break." Don't talk to anyone until you're in a better frame of mind; you'll save allies this way.)

Your Job Search—the Good, the Bad, and the Ugly

Abundant creative ideas for pursuing your job search come easily to you. You think it unlikely we'll have anything new or useful in such a generalized book. But aren't job searches about improvising your way through a series of difficult problems? To improvise, you need background material and strategy. Thus, your natural strengths easily allow you to:

- See future trends and incorporate them into a career plan

- Find unusual ways of getting interviews

- Impress interviewers with your insights and competence

- Logically evaluate the future of different job opportunities

In order to tone down your blind spots, you need to:

- Pay attention to details

- Express more enthusiasm during interviews instead of just trying to wow the interview intellectually (which may backfire)

- Create a job-search plan and stay with it as much as possible

- Reign in your tendency to act smug with an interviewer you judge less intellectually competent than you

- Express appreciation to those who have helped you through thank-you notes, follow-up calls

The Blue/Red Introvert's Interviewing Style

With an interviewer whose Color is close to your own, you will feel immediate rapport. However, if your interviewer seems to have a significantly different style, use the suggestions in parentheses.

In following your natural style you:

▸ Summarize and identify root causes. (A job interview may be too early for critiquing how an organization works. Preface such remarks with the phrase, "As an outsider looking in . . ." That way, you are excused from knowing the political implications of your opinions.)

▸ Avoid personal chitchat. (While you downplay its importance, chitchat is meaningful to other Colors looking to see if you are compatible within the corporate culture. Practice beforehand with a willing Green; to identify, read chapter 4, "Greens Overall").

▸ Talk about insights and unusual approaches. (Your ideas flow like water. But beware the competitor who has "recruited" you out of the blue. He or she may only want to know what you know, and there's no job to be had at the end of it. Your ideas often are worth thousands of dollars; allude to them, but get a real paycheck before sharing details.)

▸ Frequently debate the pros and cons of various options. (A job offer is on the table. Now's the time to know the difference between debate and negotiation. Role play negotiation techniques with a willing Red— to identify, read chapter 9, "Reds Overall," which will also outline more of your own secondary strengths. You'll see the difference and understand debating is impolitic.)

Use this book to learn how to leverage your own strengths with those of other Colors. Select a few colleagues whose skills you'd like to make better use of. Read chapter 24, "Before I Do Something Stupid: Adjusting to Other Styles," to recognize their Colors, or ask them to take the self assessment. Study figure 1 in each "Overall" Color chapter, and experiment with a few new approaches. Do it scientifically; see if they work.

If you are actively job hunting, keep notes in the Roadmap in chapter 27. It will keep your strengths in front of you for encouragement and help you cultivate that elusive rapport-building function.

PART 5

GOLDS

"Let's Do It Right"

Golds are precise and organized and admire all those qualities in others.

CHAPTER 19

Golds Overall

GOLDS REPRESENT 46 percent of the overall world population. If you are not a Gold but want to learn how to identify or improve communications with one, go to figure 19–1.

This chapter will help you determine if you've tested your primary or backup personality Color correctly. It also will help you identify other Golds among people you know, as will chapter 24, "Before I Do Something Stupid: Adjusting to Other Styles."

FIGURE 19–1 How to Recognize a Gold

- ○ Always on time
- ○ Solid-seeming personality
- ○ Dresses conservatively with quality clothing
- ○ Clean desk, maybe one family picture
- ○ Thinks and speaks in linear fashion
- ○ Likes to devise and follow rules and procedures
- ○ Frequently found in administrative and managerial roles

○ Detail-oriented

○ Logistically skilled

○ Accountable

○ No-frills type

○ Well-organized files

○ Skeptical and cautious

○ Thrives on recognition and appreciation

How to Communicate with a Gold

○ Acknowledge his or her power, position, and achievements

○ Make your points sequentially or chronologically

○ Be factual and accurate

○ Be precise and down to earth

○ Avoid vague information and abstract theories

○ Be reliable; show up on time and do what you commit to

○ Have your own act together and presentations running smoothly

○ Follow procedures; respect the hierarchy

○ Be socially and materially responsible; do not waste resources

A Successful Gold: Joan Shapiro Green

Focus and organization were never issues for Joan Shapiro Green. For ten years, she was president and CEO of BT Brokerage, a subsidiary of Bankers Trust, trading stocks and bonds for institutional clients. During that decade, revenues increased sevenfold. Apart from leading the staff to achieve the company's objectives, what Joan enjoyed most was acquiring new clients and meeting with them to solve their problems.

Today she uses her well-developed Gold managerial abilities to support the Central Park Group registered hedge funds, the Financial Women's Association, and the American Red Cross in Greater New York. While colleagues frequently poke fun at her calendar—a sweep of multicolored sticky notes that regulate a complicated life—none dispute her passion or the Gold drive to consistently deliver superior performance. Joan describes her top strength as motivating and inspiring teams to accomplish their goals. Serving on boards enables her to apply her energy and enthusiasm for important and valuable organizations.

Joan is able to identify key issues and bring others on board to solve them. These are all hallmarks of the Gold personality. Golds pay attention to details and hold themselves accountable for results. You are the most solid of all personality types, thriving on having many responsibilities for which you are recognized and appreciated. You typically are no-frills types who are loyal and procedurally oriented. While demanding top productivity from others, you expect no less from yourself.

Golds make up 46 percent of the world's population, are the largest of the four Color groups, and are the most grounded. You are the backbones of corporate and public institutions. Society's administrators, you are naturally talented at protecting others and directing the logistics of people, goods, schedules, and services. You value detail and procedures, are known for your follow-through ability, and can mobilize others to achieve well-defined goals. Golds shine when establishing policy and aim for status, respect, and power. "Let's do it right" is typical of the Gold mentality.

Beauty Queen, Business Owner, and Philanthropist

From an early age, Monica Lakhmana had something extra going for her, and it wasn't just her exceptional looks. She had a drive to make the world around her a better, and more beautiful, place.

"I became Miss India when I was twenty years old and went on to represent my country at the Miss Asia Pacific Pageant in the Philippines," she says. "It was a wonderful experience to be an ambassador of your country, attend charity functions, and visit different cities. To this day, I am still friends with some of the contestants."

The beauty of her jasmine-scented childhood home in Jamshedpur inspired an interest in design and fashion. After earning an honors degree in English literature from Stella Maris College, Madras University, India, she began working as a magazine journalist. In 1991, she was selected as a Rotary scholar for an exchange program that brought her to the United States for a year. Upon her return, she joined the Indian Hotels Company Ltd. (Taj Group of Hotels). "At age 34, I received a National Award for Hotel Operations," she says. "I have impacted over seventy-five hotels through my operational expertise." Monica was director of operations at the Taj Group for twenty-three years.

She has attended management programs at the Indian Institute of Management in Bangalore, the University of Michigan, and Cornell University, to name a few. "I have always valued education and knowledge," she says. "For me, learning never ends; the more you interact with a diverse lot of people, the more you learn."

In 2013, she decided to put her personal values into action. "I started the not-for-profit Monica Lakhmana Foundation for empowering rural Indian women through economic opportunity," she says.

Monica left the Taj Group in 2016 to form her own eponymous design company based in Mumbai, India, specializing in fashion and interior design. Her fashion company creates ready-to-wear couture, shoes, handbags, and accessories under the brand promise Carry Elegance. This creates work opportunities for the women served by her foundation. "I am inspired by the colors, fabrics, embroidery that create beautiful accessories for women. My handbags are colorful and quirky, and through them I hope to tell a story about India and the women who create them." Her interior design division concentrates on hotel interiors, restaurants, and residence designs.

"Networking and meeting interesting people are most engaging," Extrovert Monica says. "I attend several women-related conferences and workshops. I am invited as speaker and panelist at diversity events, forums, and investment events, and I have launched my own forum, Women's Leadership Network World."

Monica has been profiled by leading publications in India. She sits on several boards, including the Indian Crafts Village Trust and the advisory board of the Academy of Art University in San Francisco.

A typical Gold, she identifies some of her strengths as "professionalism, commitment, dependability, accountability, holding on to friends forever, and a principled approach to life and honesty." Golds are often self-described perfectionists; Monica is no exception. "Going into too many details at times slows me down," she says.

Her Blue side wants to sit in the Indian Parliament one day and speak at the United Nations on gender-equality issues. "I hope to leave a legacy behind of good work," she says.

Author and Playwright Betsy Howie

Plays and novels flow out of Betsy Howie; in true Gold fashion, she keeps them all well organized. "I have seventeen binders of unpublished and unproduced work," she says. "I have another shelf for the things that have gotten out there successfully."

But her Gold do-it-right nature holds her to high standards. "It takes focus, energy, and determination to complete a project," she says. "I hate seeing it on my to-do list. But I do love the rush of completion."

Betsy's involvement with the arts began as a child; she had two years of acting in summer stock before she graduated from high school. After graduating from college in three years, her goal was to be an actress. She did many commercials for companies like American Express, Clorox, Microsoft, Monster.com, and Wendy's.

Her involvement with theater expanded into writing. Her best-known production, the musical *Cowgirls*, spent only three years working its way up through regional theaters to become an off-Broadway hit in 1996. "Most musicals spend ten years before they make it to New York," Betsy explains. "But we fast tracked it."

During *Cowgirls*, Betsy met the publisher of Harcourt Brace & Company. This gave her the entrée she needed to publish her first novel, *Snow*, in 1998, inspired by Betsy's successful fight against a cancer diagnosis in her younger years.

To even out cash flow, Betsy went to work for Scholastic Reading Club in 1996. She has spent the last twenty years contributing blog posts, writing children's books (under a pseudonym), and running contests for Scholastic's book club division, where her Gold administrative talents get a regular workout.

Betsy's daughter, Calpurnia ("Callie"), was born in 2001, bringing fresh artistic inspiration for her Gold mother. "I wrote *Callie's Tally*, tracking how much my daughter cost me in the first year of her life," says Betsy. Picked up by Penguin/Putnam in 2002, its subtitle, *An Accounting of Baby's First Year (or: What My Daughter Owes Me)*, boosted sales and even brought her to the attention of the producers of *The Oprah Winfrey Show*. "I never expected the controversy it generated," Betsy says.

For the next decade, with the daily help of her mother, she raised her daughter in a small Connecticut town. The death of Betsy's mother in 2011 brought profound changes to her life, including far less time and emotional space to write.

"But now I'm turning the page," she says. "Callie is a young, talented tap dancer, and we're moving back to New York City to give her the greatest possible opportunities."

This move may do the same thing for Betsy. "I feel like all my dreams are still unfulfilled," she says, not realizing how much she has truly accomplished.

Sometimes Golds' very high standards make them forget past laurels as they pursue even greater ones.

Golds will be skeptical reading a book like this, preferring instead to deal with things more concrete and less abstract. However, if you are interested in learning how to work more effectively and efficiently with other personality types, this book will be a key that unlocks the secret to motivating even the most unfocused and disorganized people in your life. It will show you what to do when all your best efforts have failed.

The best way to proceed with this book is to read about your own primary and secondary Colors first, then learn how you interact with others by reading their profiles as needed.

Famous Golds in politics are President George H. W. Bush and his wife, Barbara; President Harry Truman; President George Washington; and Britain's Queen Victoria and Queen Elizabeth. Former chairman of IBM Thomas Watson Jr., Sam Walton, and J. C. Penney represent Golds in the corporate world. Kareem Abdul-Jabbar illustrates the Gold style in sports; Colin Powell in the military; Warren Buffett in finance; Natalie Portman, Jimmy Stewart, Martha Stewart, and Taylor Swift in entertainment; Sandra Day O'Connor and Sonia Sotomayor in law; and Barbara Walters in journalism. Kate Middleton, the commoner who has seldom made a misstep in her advancement into the circles of British royalty, is also a Gold.

This chapter should help you determine if you've tested your primary and backup personality Colors correctly. You now have tools for identifying Golds among the people you know. Chapter 24, "Before I Do Something Stupid: Adjusting to Other Styles," gives additional tips for Color coding others, as do the other "Overall" Color chapters.

CHAPTER 20

Gold/Blue Extroverts

YOU'RE NOT ONLY a Gold, you also have strong secondary characteristics of the Blue personality. And you have tested as a Color Q Extrovert, which means you recharge your batteries by being with people rather than being alone. Your Color group values efficiency, tradition, accuracy, predictability, and structure. Achieving goals on time and under budget is a strong inner drive in you.

You Overall

In your community, you are a pillar: indispensable, well respected, and firmly represented in important volunteer positions. You are realistic, grounded, and responsible, getting things done no matter how difficult. This does not make you stodgy, though; the hallmarks of your Color are boldness and drive.

Reinventing the wheel is not your style. Working on real as opposed to intangible things and going with your own experience instead of new theories are your usual choices. You value "the system" and prefer to organize life around procedures and contract agreements.

Your inner need for control makes it virtually inevitable that you will hold responsible positions during your career; administrative skills are second nature to you. Creating security and stability for family and coworkers is a priority.

Once in charge, you relish mapping out what needs to be done. Task assignments make best use of each staff member's strengths. Woe to those who fall short of your expectations: You show little sympathy for the ineffective and inefficient.

With a direct and clear communication style, you are gifted at implementing policies and ensuring things remain orderly and on track. Planning ahead, setting goals, and controlling schedules are activities that come naturally. Highly observant of details, you let little fall between the cracks.

You are not shy about criticizing those who break rules, dress flamboyantly, or behave in unusual ways. What you see as appropriate, right, or wrong comes from a place of deep moral certitude. Traditional and conservative ways keep the universe organized and orderly, and you cannot understand why anyone would ever want to disturb that. People who are disloyal, unreliable, or disorganized, or who miss deadlines irritate you.

You don't just celebrate but honor rituals, traditions, holidays, birthdays, and religious or cultural events. To you, these are symbols of continuity to be passed on to the next generation, and they require appropriate fanfare. Family is your central focus.

CASE STUDY ONE

Senior Executive, Investment Management Firm

Without a doubt, forty-seven-year-old Mellody Hobson is a "golden girl." President of the $10 billion Chicago-based investment firm Ariel Investments, she is also a regular financial contributor for CBS News. *Vanity Fair* and *Time* magazine have both written features on her.[1] In 2015, Mellody was named to *Time's* annual list of the 100 most influential people in the world. Mellody is chairman of the board for DreamWorks Animation SKG, Inc., as well as a director of Estée Lauder Companies, Inc., and Starbucks Corporation. She also is charismatic, personable, and an admitted "fashionista."

Gold/Blue Extroverts are driven to succeed from an early age. Mellody was no exception. At age five, she set herself the goal of attending an Ivy League university. By fifth grade she was staying up into the early morning hours doing homework. "Slow and steady wins the race" became her mantra, and at Ariel Investments she frequently wears a whimsical little turtle symbol incorporated into her otherwise classic dress style. The firm shares this theme for its highly recognized branding. "Slow and steady" also was how she rose to become president of Ariel Investments fourteen years after she started there as a college intern.

In typical Gold/Blue Extrovert fashion, Mellody lists her top three strengths as communication, organization, and energy. "I'm very decisive. Waffling and indifference drive me crazy."

Mellody's family background was not privileged. She grew up with five siblings and was the first to graduate from college. She does not know how she came by the drive to achieve all that she has. But Gold/Blue Extroverts have an innate need for control, which impels them to acquire responsible positions. They also value security and stability, things Mellody did not have as a child. "I hated not having money," she says of her formative years. "I hated the insecurity of being evicted. The great thing about money is freedom; you have choice. That's all I ever cared about. . . . I'm going to work until I die."

Mellody also says, "You really have to stay diligent about your values and beliefs and not compromise." Some of her deepest values are reflected in her work to educate young black children and their families about the investing process. To this end, her firm created and funded Ariel Community Academy in Chicago. Here, the first-grade class is given $20,000 to invest; by eighth grade the kids control the whole amount. Upon graduation, they return their initial $20,000 to the incoming first-graders and distribute their profits to charities and academic scholarships. Mellody's stated goal is to make investing into dinner table conversation among black families. A top priority of Golds is to render community service.

In December 2004, Senator Bill Bradley told *Time* magazine, "Mellody has a deep set of values about what's right and what's wrong."[2] She definitely puts this into practice on a daily basis. This is a core Gold/Blue characteristic.

You on the Job

AS A LEADER

Getting the right things to the right people, in the right amounts, to the right place at the right time—that is the crux of your talent. Outstanding logistical skills are the hallmark of Gold/Blue Extroverts in leadership roles. With a clearly defined chain of command and well-defined expectations and duties for the staff, you can achieve anything. Those who play by the rules and perform up to your exacting standards are rewarded in fair measure.

Like Mellody Hobson, you are decisive, providing for your organization's practical needs in a reliable and consistent manner. Getting to the core of a situation quickly, managing fairly, providing consistent feedback, and crafting clear and measurable goals are your tools for getting things done.

AS A TEAM PLAYER

Your positive attributes as a team member are many: defining problems quickly; clarifying issues, obstacles, and goals; bringing logic to the table; preventing important details from falling through the cracks; ensuring needed resources are available; acting as a reality check about feasibility and costs. No team functions at its peak without a Gold/Blue Extrovert.

You are able to make the tough decisions when needed. However, you may irritate team members by taking charge without being asked or being too blunt.

Look at figure 20–1 for a list of your natural work-related strengths.

FIGURE 20–1 *Natural Work-Related Strengths*

Approximately 80 percent of these attributes will apply to you. Check off those that do, and use them in your resume and interviews. This will set you apart from the canned responses of others. You:

- ○ Are predictable and stable

- ○ Are decisive

- ○ Expect and have high work standards

- ○ Use resources efficiently

- ○ Respect rules and established procedures

- ○ Get results through good time and task management

- ○ Imbue confidence in your people or coworkers

- ○ Finish projects on time and on budget

Now see how other Gold/Blue Extroverts use these strengths in very different fields.

CASE STUDY TWO
Fitness Business Owner and Novelist

Max Calder has spent almost thirty years improving life for hundreds of others. But before he did, he had to learn how to improve his own. His Gold strengths of passion, enthusiasm, competence, confidence, and knowledge have made him a successful owner of a growing Pennsylvania business.

Some of his best successes came early. "Athletic achievements," he says. "I was a competitive triathlete." Then several sports injuries benched him. "I shattered my right ankle," he says. "They told me I would never run again. I also endured a fully torn tendon in my shoulder."

He followed his doctors' orders exactly but found himself becoming less and less active. This did not sit well with him, and his Blue secondary personality started strategizing. "Doctors are very good at what they do, but they only prescribe certain things," Max says. "I decided to see what more I could do for myself." He started stretching to maximize his remaining flexibility, then added a strengthening regimen to restore his muscles gradually. When he began to see results from both, he worked on creating a balance between the two.

"It took a lot of rehab," Max says, "but not only did I run again, I've now run in over 100 races and countless track events. And although surgery was suggested for my shoulder, I rehabbed it back to 90 percent mobility with just stretching and strengthening."

His fellow athletes took notice, and he started showing them how to be safely active even with pain or injury. Eventually this led to formal training in fitness science and nutrition, and a career as a personal fitness trainer. Today, Max is the owner and manager of one of Anytime Fitness's 3,200 locations worldwide. He is planning to add two more centers shortly to his current location in Villanova, Pennsylvania.

Golds are the world's top administrators; half of Max's time is devoted to bringing in new business, sustaining current projects, designing and implementing fitness programs, and, most recently, learning how to delegate effectively. "I need help with the computer skills needed to conduct gym business," he says. In typical Gold fashion, he adds, "I experience impatience and lack of tolerance for people who are not fulfilling their responsibilities."

To recharge, Max enjoys the artistic pursuit of writing. He has written a coming-of-age novel, *Brotherly Love*, under the name Peter Maxwell Calder, which he self-published through XLibris in 2005. "I love to write fiction, and wish I had more time to do so," he says. But being a disciplined Gold, most of his time still goes to developing new revenue streams, improving his leadership skills, and mentoring other trainers.

CASE STUDY THREE

Literary Agent

New York City–based literary agent Linda Konner is a woman who knows what she wants and gets it. "For me, it means not having a boss, not working in an office/corporate environment, and choosing the people with whom I wish to work," she says.

Linda defines her principal functions as finding suitable publishers for her clients' books (mainly adult practical nonfiction), negotiating their contracts, editing clients' book proposals and sample chapters, troubleshooting with and providing information to clients and publishers, helping clients find cowriters and publicists if needed, and brainstorming ideas for future books. These draw on her true-to-form Gold/Blue Extrovert strengths of editing, creating ideas, negotiating, problem solving, and networking.

She has always gravitated to what most recognize as glamorous careers. Previously, Linda was a successful author of eight books, including *Just the Weigh You Are: How to Be Fit and Healthy Whatever Your Size* (Houghton Mifflin), *The Last Ten Pounds* (Barnes & Noble), and *Your Perfect Weight* (Rodale). She also served as editor in chief of *Weight Watchers Magazine* and features editor at *Redbook, Seventeen Magazine*, and *Woman's World*.

Her columns have appeared in *Glamour* and *Fitness* magazines and her articles in the *New York Times, Woman's Day*, the *Boston Globe*, the *Christian Science Monitor*, and *Playboy*, among others. She has been in the publishing field for over thirty years.

A natural editor, Linda is precise in her words. When asked for her top three strengths, her Gold desire to answer precisely shows: "Do you mean things like intelligence, creativity, sense of humor? Or writing, editing, and problem solving? Take your pick! They all apply." The most energizing for Linda are brainstorming ideas, editing, and negotiating, true to her Gold/Blue core.

Her Extroverted and Blue sides enjoyed the success and media attention she received as an author. Her Gold side comes into play in editorial positions. "I love editing, and I'm good at it," she says simply.

She is a precise, thorough, and assertive negotiator, bringing all aspects of her personality Color to the table in her current job. She recently celebrated her twentieth anniversary as a literary agent, no mean feat in an industry that inspires more burnout than longevity. Linda Konner illustrates how working through, instead of against, your Color optimizes career success.

Ideal Work Environment

A stable and well-respected institution with a predictable future is where Gold/Blue Extroverts like Mellody Hobson feel most at home.

When a job offer is made, leverage as much as you can from the list in figure 20–2.

FIGURE 20–2 **The Ideal Gold/Blue Extrovert Work Environment**

Compare your current work environment to the descriptions below. Don't be deceived if these descriptions seem obvious. It confirms you've tested your individual color correctly. Other Colors, especially Greens and Reds, would find this environment uncomfortable and unproductive. The optimal Gold/Blue Extrovert work environment:

○ Is a stable and well-respected institution with a predictable future. You work hard and want to be rewarded with money and respect. Small, growing companies or distressed companies can't offer this. You are the quintessential corporate worker.

○ Provides job security. Life change is a slow process for you; having it forced upon you is harder on you than other Colors.

○ Involves concrete and practical projects and products. Intangible services are tough for you to quantify and measure. Stick with the things you can touch and see.

○ Has clear rules and expectations. Valuable time is wasted making up rules as you go along. You don't want to be bothered by this.

○ Is organized and efficient. You cannot respect or work effectively within a company that isn't.

○ Includes hardworking coworkers who pride themselves on doing things right. You see crises and emotionalism as unnecessary weakness, even slacking, on the part of others.

○ Allows you to work within a group or team. You need people to organize.

○ Rewards those who are steady, accountable, and focused on results. Others may have time for drama and politics; you're the one who gets things done.

○ Offers progressively higher levels of responsibility. A clear career path gives you focus and helps you concentrate on the tasks at hand.

A corporate culture integrating the above elements is fertile soil for your career advancement.

The worst type of work culture for a Gold/Blue Extrovert is loose and disorganized. It does not allow you access to reliable and critical information. Constant change and ambiguity diminish your great administrative and organizational strengths. You need facts, bottom-line costs, and rules in order to feel comfortable at work.

When Gold/Blue Extroverts work in less-ideal corporate cultures, productivity is stunted and career achievements become an uphill climb.

The Extroverted Gold/Blue's Ideal Boss

Even a great job can be frustrating under the wrong boss; a mediocre job under a wonderful boss is pretty hard to leave. Gold/Blues get along especially well with other Golds. But bosses of other Color types who possess the characteristics in figure 20–3 also can be good mentors.

FIGURE 20-3 **The Gold/Blue Extrovert's Ideal Boss**

Check off if your boss:

○ Always knows and clearly states what needs to be done

○ Reliably provides needed resources

○ Has clout with superiors

○ Will confront workers who don't deliver on commitments

○ Gives more responsibility and perks when you've earned them

Careers That Attract Gold/Blue Extroverts

Gold/Blue Extroverts like Linda Konner cluster in fields that provide professional respect, require high levels of competence, and contribute in a meaningful way to society. You need the ability to create predictability and stability to be at your best.

Please note that not all the following careers will appeal to you, but recognize that each, in some way, draws on the strengths of your style and appeals to a significant number of your Color group. This is not a comprehensive list, but it will show underlying patterns of preference. If unlisted careers offer similar patterns, your chances of success increase. Text in parentheses at the end of each section highlights the Color style characteristics that create success in that broad area.

According to our research, jobs italicized in the lists below are predicted to benefit from an above-average growth rate over the next several years. This information is based on the continuously revised data provided by the U.S. Department of Labor and Bureau of Labor Statistics on their websites O*NET OnLine (www.onetonline.org) and http://www.bls.gov/CAREEROUTLOOK/. There you will find in-depth information about job requirements and salary ranges.

There are successful people of all Color styles in all occupations. In non-ideal jobs, you can still shine by creating your own niche.

ARTS
Literary agent ▶ writer (involvement with people, opportunity for fame and respect, keen observer, good memory for details, organization, business acumen, negotiating skills)

BUSINESS/FINANCE
accountant ▶ bank officer (all types) ▶ corporate finance lawyer ▶ *financial analyst* ▶ *financial advisor* ▶ *financial examiner* ▶ *investment banker* ▶ president/CEO ▶ *stockbroker*/securities/commodities sales agent ▶ venture capitalist (efficiency, observant of details, moral certitude and appropriateness, low tolerance for unconventionality)

BUSINESS/MANAGEMENT/MANUFACTURING
actuary ▶ *administrative services manager* ▶ *auditor* ▶ *business owner* ▶ chief financial officer/treasurer ▶ *chief information officer* ▶ compensation and benefits manager ▶ *human resources manager* ▶ *insurance claim examiner/underwriter* ▶ *insurance sales agent/broker* ▶ *management consultant* ▶ *managers of all types* (construction, database, factory, financial institution, hospital, office, industrial, production) ▶ project manager ▶ purchasing manager/agent ▶ real estate sales agent and appraiser ▶ *sales manager* (tangible products) ▶ top executive (accurate memory for details, bottom-line and cost oriented, well-developed administrative skills, need for order, give clear directions)

DIGITAL/HIGH TECH

computer network architect ❯ *computer systems analyst/security specialist* ❯ *information system manager* ❯ *network and computer systems administrator* ❯ *software quality assurance engineer* (good memory for details, efficient, solid administrative skills, keep things orderly and on track)

EDUCATION

athletic coach/trainer ❯ *business professor* ❯ *school principal/administrator* ❯ university president ❯ vocational teacher (administrative skills, respect for "the system," common sense, thoughtfulness, practical experience)

HEALTH SCIENCE

dentist ❯ *diagnostic medical sonographer* ❯ *gynecologist* ❯ *health services administrator* ❯ *medical and health services manager* ❯ *medical laboratory technician* ❯ nursing director ❯ *optometrist* ❯ *pharmacist* ❯ *primary care physician* ❯ *surgeon* (accuracy, keen observation of details, practical and measurable work, organizational skills)

LAW/LAW ENFORCEMENT/GOVERNMENT

compliance officer/*regulatory affairs specialist* ❯ division manager ❯ firefighter ❯ government employee ❯ *investigator* ❯ IRS agent ❯ judge ❯ *lawyer* (particularly administrative, criminal, corporate, employment, energy, product liability, real estate, securities, transportation) ❯ military officer ❯ *police/correctional* officer ❯ security consultant/guard (respect for rules and procedures, good administrative skills, observant of details, fact oriented, boldness)

SCIENCE RESEARCH/ENGINEERING/MATHEMATICS

civil/industrial/mechanical *engineer* ❯ electrical engineer ❯ flight engineer ❯ food scientist/technician ❯ geologist (respect for clear procedures and rules, high standards, respect for contracts, sense of appropriateness, drive, ability to make tough decisions)

OTHER

building inspector ❯ carpenter ❯ cost estimator ❯ electronic repair ❯ funeral director ❯ general contractor ❯ *hotel manager* ❯ mechanic ❯ pilot ❯ plumber ❯ *restaurant owner/manager* ❯ ship captain ❯ surveyor

CASE STUDY FOUR

When a Career Isn't Working

Three of eight students were crying—loudly—and a fourth was starting. Early childhood development teacher Jeanine Beckwith could see no earthly reason for the outburst—but started to feel like joining in. She had hoped her second year would be easier than her first, but it all seemed to be going downhill.

All Jeanine's female relatives had been teachers, and she was proud when they applauded her on graduation day. Her celebration afterward had made her feel so important, so much a part of a long family tradition. Now she was on her own in a sea of slobbering three-year-olds, trying to maintain order.

What she didn't want to admit was that kids drove her nuts. From the time she started babysitting at age 12, she always felt awkward trying to follow their nonlinear thinking, being sensitive to their changing needs. As a teacher, there was no way to maintain order, everyone's learning happened at different levels, and nothing about her day was ever predictable. Jeanine was at wit's end; such an environment will drive any Gold/Blue Extrovert crazy.

Confiding in her aunt, Jeanine explored how to use her education degree to find a job more organized and predictable. Her aunt suggested that Jeanine apply for an assistant principal position in a nearby town. Jeanine was ecstatic when she got the job. Being in charge, in control, and with the ability to manage and organize was very satisfying to her Gold/Blue Extroverted nature. She is in line for the principal's job in a few years and well respected by her peers. Life is under control again.

Your Personality's Challenges

Gold/Blue Extroverts have a unique set of potential work-related blind spots. Some listed below you have, others you don't. No one has them all. Tone down a blind spot by focusing on it, then choose more productive actions and make them habits. (Suggestions for doing so are in parentheses below.) You:

> • May prematurely dismiss new ideas. (Dismiss nothing until you investigate the who, what, where, when, why, and cost of a new idea. Profitable ventures start with untested ideas; learn how to allow others to brainstorm and present their conclusions to you.)

▸ May focus on the flaws in the efforts of others and not give credit where credit is due. (Make a point of affirming the efforts of deserving colleagues after listing flaws.)

▸ Are fixed in supporting established ways of doing things. (The tried-and-true contribute to efficiency, but they may not keep your company alive when the market is moving or changing. When faced with change, focus on details and costs—your areas of strength.)

▸ Push through your own ideas by being verbally aggressive. (Getting things done well requires buy-in, not submission. Study the art of persuasion, since you already have a natural talent for the art of ruling. Read about how to persuade other Colors in figure 1 of each Color's "Overall" chapter.)

Your Job Search—the Good, the Bad, and the Ugly

Gold/Blue Extroverts create accurate and well-presented resumes that elicit positive responses. With some interviewers, particularly Golds and Blues, you will feel a comfortable rapport. But with those of other Colors, you need to prepare and rehearse responses outside your comfort zone. Many human resources people are Greens; make a study of how to communicate effectively with this Color group before your first interviews.

Your natural strengths easily allow you to:

▸ Have a wide network of friends for job leads

▸ Set measurable, realistic, and well-defined goals

▸ Create time lines, daily status reports, and budgets that reduce job-search stress on you and your family

▸ Adequately research prospective employers

▸ Be well prepared for interviews

▸ Come across as hardworking and bottom-line oriented in an interview

▸ Logically consider pros and cons of job offers

In order to tone down your blind spots, you need to:

▸ Balance networking with research

- Do something in return for those who help you; your networking sometimes comes off as too self-serving

- Cushion your tendency to be abrupt; rehearse some areas of small talk

- Prepare to talk about yourself on a personal level (ask a willing Green to role play with you)

- Think about a prospective company's future direction (ask a willing Blue to help)

- Be willing to consider career opportunities in other industries

- Don't allow unexpected delays and obstacles to frustrate you

- Plan a "think-through day" when tempted to jump on a job offer

The Gold/Blue Extrovert's Interviewing Style

With an interviewer whose Color is close to your own, you will feel immediate rapport. However, if your interviewer seems to have a significantly different style (and it's statistically likely that many will have a Green component), use the suggestions in parentheses. Mercilessly exploit these natural abilities of yours and get more job offers.

In following your natural style, you:

- Describe past accomplishments in appropriate detail. (A Green interviewer may draw you out with questions like, "Did you enjoy those duties?" Be prepared with answers more thorough than "Yes.")

- Tend to talk too much and not ask enough questions about the job. (If it has been a while since the interviewer said anything, pause. Let him or her lead. Prepare a list of job questions ahead of time and refer to it.)

- Focus on the present. (Especially if interviewing for a senior-level position, you will need to prepare for questions on future planning. Take a Blue colleague to lunch and run a few ideas by him or her before an interview. At least read public statements about company direction prior to an interview.)

- May not think outside the box. (Your orderly mind knows what your next career step should be but tends to close off other possibilities. New fields, or even established ones you haven't considered, may allow you to ascend higher and faster than your planned career path.)

Take a break now to do something administratively important. Later, check out chapter 14, "Blues Overall." Then carefully read chapter 24, "Before I Do Something Stupid: Adjusting to Other Styles," to learn about the strengths of other Colors.

Like all Colors, you need the strengths of others, and you can put them to work for you if you know where to look and how to ask. If you invest time learning how to recognize the Colors who can best assist you (visit figure 1 in each of the "Overall" Color chapters), it will make everyone more effective and productive.

If you are actively engaging in a job search, jot notes in the Roadmap in chapter 27. Recording your strengths and strategies is a concrete and results-oriented way to navigate the minefields of a job search.

CHAPTER 21

Gold/Blue Introverts

YOU'RE NOT ONLY a Gold, you also have strong secondary characteristics of the Blue personality. And you have tested as a Color Q Introvert, which means you recharge your batteries by being alone rather than being with people. You are most happy when things are orderly, efficient, and predictable. Because of your innate talent at it, you have a strong drive toward managing.

You Overall

A pillar of whatever organization or community you join, you are thorough, responsible, and hardworking. Your unusually accurate memory records what others say and do with astonishing precision. While thoughtful, you can overlook such formal niceties as thank-you notes or praise for jobs well done by others.

Realistic and practical, you take your commitments seriously. You value "the system" of whatever organization you are in, trust contracts, and organize your life and work around procedures. Your children and coworkers all feel secure and stable under your watch—that is, if they measure up to your high standards. You can be the classic Type A personality, demanding much of others at home and work. But those demands are never made capriciously; you think things through and always are cautious about changes.

With your highly developed administrative skills, duty-bound work ethic, and great ability to concentrate, you float to top-level positions wherever you invest your efforts. Fierce loyalty to your company cements your status.

When undertaking a task, you bring to it logic, impersonal analysis, common sense, and practical experience. You gravitate to situations where you have to plan ahead, set goals, and control the schedule. You are gifted at implementing well-defined policies and ensuring that things remain orderly and on track. Because doing a good job is your primary focus, you expect to be judged and compensated on your own merits. You are fair and consistent when dealing with others.

Family is your central focus. You honor traditions and rituals, observing holidays, birthdays, and religious and cultural events with appropriate fanfare. For you, these times are important symbols of continuity to be passed on to the next generation. Gold/Blue Introverts often trace their roots and record the family heritage for their progeny.

Appropriateness is your watchword. Your strong morals lead you to judge others and speak up if they seem to blur right and wrong. You simply want the world to stay organized, free from the chaos that follows when rules are broken. Even flamboyant dress and unconventional behavior try your tolerance.

CASE STUDY ONE
University President

Dr. Kathleen Waldron is president of William Paterson University in Wayne, New Jersey. The public university serves over 11,000 students and is a residential suburban campus. Kathleen moves effortlessly between her many constituencies: students, faculty, staff, alumni, donors, and public officials. She is a natural and graceful leader with superior management skills.

A Fulbright scholar who received her doctorate in Latin American history in 1977, she had a thirteen-year career at Citibank, capped by her turn as president of Citibank International in Miami from 1991–1996. She then spent six years as dean of the School of Business at Long Island University and five years as president of Baruch College before joining William Paterson University in 2010.

She has achieved success by leveraging, rather than working against, her Introverted nature. For instance, others describe her as a great listener. "I am a fairly private person who can read three books a week. Now that is very hard to do with all the evening entertainment and events that take away my private time," she reflects. "But I knew that going in." While quite reserved in her early years, today her people skills are superior. "It's been a long process," she says, "to develop a comfort level for public speaking, of going forward to people with my hand outstretched, taking the initiative to do that. That was hard."

Fund-raising is a substantial part of her job, one where her banking background and Gold/Blue strengths are useful. When she sits down to solicit corporate leaders, "they know I am a business person who sets goals, measures accomplishments, and is a serious manager. They feel more comfortable that their donations are going to be properly utilized." Kathleen stresses to them and her staff the importance of "accountability, stewardship, and reporting back to people." She is known for expressing her opinions with tact. All these are prime Gold/Blue values.

She is also very involved with instituting proper instruments for educational evaluation. This typical Gold/Blue interest in results and accountability helps her nearly 1,000 faculty members institute assessment models that work within their particular disciplines. "Getting a job is such a narrow definition of a successful education," says Kathleen. "I changed the dialogue to broaden those evaluation measures to instill in students analytical capabilities, communications skills, and a broader sense of life including art and music."

She also has a typical Gold/Blue approach to organizing her work. "I have all my systems in place; I am very structured in getting to my goals. I keep very careful agendas, crosschecked to be certain things are on schedule. I know exactly where I'm going to be a year from now."

Early in her career, Kathleen was a natural analytical problem solver. Now, her feeling/intuitive side is coming into play. "I believe that leadership is people developing people. What gets me excited is to watch people do better than they have." Kathleen exhibits most of the key characteristics of her Color style, especially in her aptitude for taking the helm and running a smooth ship.

You on the Job

AS A LEADER

Getting the right things to the right people, in the right amounts, to the right place at the right time—that is the crux of your talent. Outstanding logistical skills are the hallmark of Gold/Blue Introverts in leadership roles. With a clear chain of command and well-defined expectations and duties for the staff, you can achieve anything. Those who play by the rules and live up to your exacting standards are rewarded in fair measure.

You see your role as reliably providing for your organization's practical needs. You are accurate, decisive, and know how to get things done.

Your decision-making style is to absorb and assess as many facts as possible. Then you measure the cost of each possible solution before choosing the optimal one.

AS A TEAM PLAYER

Your positive contributions are many. Getting to the core of problems quickly; clarifying issues, obstacles, and goals; bringing logic to the table; preventing important details from falling through the cracks; ensuring needed resources are available; acting as a reality check about costs—no team functions optimally without a Gold/Blue Introvert as one of its members.

You feel responsible and loyal to your teammates. You know how important your contributions are, and you work hard not to let others down. However, you may irritate team members by not sharing information until too late in the process and/or being rigid about how things should be done.

Look at figure 21–1 for a list of your natural work-related strengths.

FIGURE 21-1 *Natural Work-Related Strengths*

Approximately 80 percent of these attributes will apply to you. Check off those that do, and use them in your resume and interviews. This will set you apart from the canned responses of others. You:

○ Adapt naturally to the role assigned to you, be it leader or follower

○ Are accurate about all parts of a task

○ Create and enforce policies, procedures, and schedules that keep everyone effective and on track

○ Are fair with others and earn their respect

○ Are decisive, organized, and get things done

○ Have deep powers of concentration and can work alone for long periods of time

Now see how some Gold/Blue Introverts use these strengths in very different fields.

CASE STUDY TWO

Investment and Real Estate Advisor

Sergio I. de Araujo has the classic Gold/Blue Introvert resume, with clear corporate loyalty and few career changes. This satisfies a Gold's need for continuity, tradition, and stability. Prior to his retirement, he had been with U.S. Trust Company for twenty years. His final position there was managing director and senior investment officer for the Southeast region until he retired in 2008.

But later in life, one's primary personality traits soften; there is exploration of other Colors' neighborhoods. Sergio's resume since retirement looks like that of an active twenty-year-old. He dabbled briefly with his son, Andrew, in running a long-only fund investing in Brazil. "I have subsequently established a relationship with Evercore Wealth Management, a part of Evercore Partners in New York," he says. "A year ago, I obtained a Florida real estate license and associated myself with K-2 Realty, a successful, relatively young firm with a strong presence in north Palm Beach County and Palm Beach Island."

In his work with Evercore, Sergio's sales and relationship skills are put to use introducing prospects to the organization and may have a continuing support role in advising and maintaining the relationship. Golds follow established policies to the letter, an important characteristic in financial services.

Client relationship initiatives such as wealth advice, planning, and relationship reviews are some of Sergio's strengths, drawing on his attention to detail and organizational skills. He put these to good use when he helped found Citigroup's international private banking division in 1971; he spent the first half of his career there before aligning with U.S. Trust. Early on, Sergio realized how to make himself indispensable in an industry where there were always younger, brighter, better-educated, and less highly paid managers waiting to step into one's shoes. "I enjoy working with clients," he says, "and soon realized they are the anchor of one's career." Where others might compete in the ability to provide strong investment performance, keep up with technological and professional advances, or implement compliance initiatives, Sergio found there was no substitute for superior client service.

Sergio brings the same client relations capabilities to his new endeavors at Evercore and K-2 Realty. "These two activities are proving to be most enjoyable and also keep me engaged," he says. Perhaps this Gold is now beginning another twenty years in a third, long-term, stable career.

CASE STUDY THREE

Chemical Engineer, Manufacturing Company Owner

In Germany, all little Martin Deeg wanted to do was play in the dirt. His family had different ideas. "I grew up with parents who were both technically trained," says Martin. "It was an environment that discouraged anything other than being a scientist; an engineer was marginal, but nevertheless acceptable." His family moved to the United States in the 1960s when his father took a job as director of materials research at American Optical Corporation in Southbridge, Massachusetts.

Martin's adolescent rebellion led to a college major in archeology. "I would have loved to have been an archeologist. I like digging in the dirt." But parental expectations prevailed. After studying chemical engineering in college, Martin worked in product development for Celanese Corporation. He began as a process development engineer and ultimately attained the position of staff scientist. He holds more than ten patents in the fields of high-performance composite materials and PET/PBT melt spinning.

Martin branched out when he joined Scott Paper Company. Starting there as technology manager, Martin eventually expanded into director of business development–worldwide and concentrated on the marketing side. Following Scott Paper's merger with Kimberly Clark, he was given the title senior research fellow.

In 1999, he established and became president of Icarus West, Inc., a niche business manufacturer handling supplies for the polysilicon industry. "We make very clean, very pure, very expensive, extremely specialized polyethylene gloves," he says. Martin is involved in all parts of the business, handling all customer contact. "We have no competition," he says. Other companies "have not been able to meet the same kind of quality standards." No doubt his Gold/Blue process skills keep those standards high.

Being company president has its down side, however. "Bookkeeping, dealing with suppliers . . . taxes are downright stressful!" he says. "But probably the most stressful thing is dealing with ongoing requests to decrease price. I hate negotiating—I like things black and white, nice and straightforward."

Martin doesn't define what he's doing now as success. "I'll have success once I retire. The definition of success for me is being able to wake up in the morning and feel good about whatever it is I'm going to do for the day." To accomplish this, Martin plans to go back to his roots. "Doing relatively basic clearing, constructing, excavating . . . something outside, pushing dirt around, seems to be potentially a fun thing to do . . . it justifies buying big mechanical toys."

Ideal Work Environment

For both Kathleen Waldron and Sergio de Araujo, a stable and well-respected institution with a predictable future is their chosen environment; Martin Deeg owns his own business and frequently works at home.

When a job offer is made, leverage as much as you can from the list in figure 21–2.

FIGURE 21–2 **The Ideal Gold/Blue Introvert Work Environment**

Compare your current work environment to the descriptions below. If these descriptions seem obvious, that confirms you've tested your individual color correctly. Other Colors, especially Greens and Reds, would find this environment uncomfortable and unproductive. The optimal Gold/Blue Introvert work environment:

○ Has clear rules and expectations. It wastes valuable time trying to make up rules as you go along. You don't want to be bothered by this.

○ Includes hardworking coworkers who pride themselves on doing things right. It's much easier when everyone is on the same page about how to get things done. You see crises and emotionalism as unnecessary weakness, even slacking, on the part of others.

○ Is a stable and well-respected institution with a predictable future. You work hard and want to be rewarded with money and respect. Small, growing companies or distressed companies can't offer this. You are a quintessential corporate worker.

○ Rewards dependability and precision. You're on time, have a well-planned schedule, and do your job with consistency. No company runs well for long without a Gold/Blue Introvert on staff. You deserve recognition.

○ Involves concrete and practical projects and products. Intangible services are tough for you to quantify and measure. Stick with the things you can touch and see.

○ Is results oriented. You are frankly a bit skeptical of any work that can't be evaluated with a spreadsheet.

○ Has a clear hierarchy. Structure gives you comfort and frees you to concentrate on the task at hand.

○ Values loyalty and commitment. These are a deep and natural part of the core of who you are. In today's workplace, they are less valued. Now you are better off choosing to place your loyalty with a mentor rather than a company.

○ Allows for private space. As an Introvert, your batteries get drained when dealing with people, even if your people skills are superb. If you have to share your work space with others, you will feel a lot more fatigue at the end of the day. You think and perform better in a private space where you can reflect in-depth on projects; insist on one as a condition of employment if possible.

A corporate culture integrating the above elements is fertile soil for your career advancement.

The worst type of work culture for a Gold/Blue Introvert is loose and open ended with regard to goals and measures of success. "You're only as good as your last (fill in the blank)" describes a work environment that would make you tear out your hair.

You also hate working with people who take things too personally. You want to stay focused on the task; emotional situations are cloudy and distracting. Never work for a company that values intuition over hard data. You need facts, bottom-line costs, and rules in order to feel comfortable at work.

When Gold/Blue Introverts work in nonideal corporate cultures, productivity is stunted and career achievements become an uphill climb.

The Introverted Gold/Blue's Ideal Boss

Even a great job can be frustrating under the wrong boss; a mediocre job under a wonderful boss is pretty hard to leave. Gold/Blues get along especially well with other Golds. But bosses of other Color types who possess the characteristics in figure 21–3 also can be good mentors.

FIGURE 21-3 **The Gold/Blue Introvert's Ideal Boss**

Check off if your boss:

 ○ Is highly respected personally and professionally

 ○ Values your experience, thoroughness, and hard work

 ○ Gives you clear overall directions

 ○ Does not micromanage

Careers That Attract Gold/Blue Introverts

Like Sergio de Araujo, you want to find a place to call home, where you can work comfortably for many years under the guidance of clear rules, procedures, and expectations. You require predictability and stability to be at your best. You are happiest upon reaching a high level of responsibility, like Kathleen Waldron, in a culture where there's a clear chain of command. Like Martin Deeg, you particularly need to be rewarded for your abilities to be accurate and get things done.

Please note that not all the following careers will appeal to you, but recognize that each, in some way, draws on the strengths of your style and appeals to a significant number of your Color group. This is not a comprehensive list, but it will show underlying patterns of preference. If unlisted careers offer similar patterns, your chances of success increase. Text in parentheses at the end of each section highlights the Color style characteristics that create success in that broad area.

According to our research, jobs italicized in the lists below are predicted to benefit from an above-average growth rate over the next several years. This information is based on the continuously revised data provided by the U.S. Department of Labor and Bureau of Labor Statistics on their websites O*NET OnLine (www.onetonline.org) and http://www.bls.gov/CAREEROUTLOOK/. There you will find in-depth information about job requirements and salary ranges.

There are successful people of all Color styles in all occupations. In non-ideal jobs, you can still shine by creating your own niche.

BUSINESS/FINANCE

accountant ▸ *auditor* ▸ bank officer (all types) ▸ budget/financial analyst ▸ credit analyst ▸ *financial advisor* ▸ *financial examiner* ▸ investment banker

▶ sales—high end (fewer contacts, more needs analysis) ▶ *stockbroker* ▶ treas-urer/chief financial officer ▶ venture capitalist (efficiency, observant of details, moral certitude and appropriateness, low tolerance for unconventionality)

BUSINESS/MANAGEMENT/INSURANCE/MANUFACTURING

actuary ▶ *administrative services manager* ▶ *chief information officer* ▶ compen-sation and benefits manager ▶ executive ▶ *executive assistant* ▶ *human resources specialist* ▶ *insurance claims examiner/underwriter* ▶ *management analyst* ▶ *man-agement consultant* ▶ *managers of all types* (construction, database, factory, financial institution, hospital, hotel, industrial production, office, sales) ▶ proj-ect manager ▶ *property manager* ▶ purchasing manager/agent ▶ real estate agent/appraiser ▶ *statistician* ▶ *technical writer* (accurate memory of details, bottom-line and cost oriented, well-developed administrative skills, need for order, give clear directions)

DIGITAL/HIGH TECH

computer programmer ▶ *computer systems analyst* ▶ *database administrator* ▶ *information security analyst* ▶ *information system manager* ▶ network systems administrator ▶ *software quality assurance engineer and tester* ▶ *web/software developer* (good memory for details, efficient, solid administrative skills, keep things orderly and on track)

EDUCATION

athletic coach/trainer ▶ *librarian* ▶ *professor* ▶ school principal/administrator ▶ university president ▶ vocational teacher (administrative skills, respect for "the system," common sense, thoughtfulness, practical experience)

HEALTH SCIENCE

dentist/dental hygienist ▶ *dermatologist* ▶ *gynecologist* ▶ *medical and health services manager/technician* ▶ *medical records technician* ▶ *optometrist* ▶ *phar-macist* ▶ *primary care physician* ▶ *public health officer* ▶ *radiologic technician* ▶ *surgeon/surgical technologist* ▶ *veterinarian/veterinary technologist* (accu-racy, keen observation of details, practical and measurable work, organi-zational skills)

LAW/LAW ENFORCEMENT/GOVERNMENT

compliance officer ▶ *corrections officer* ▶ division manager ▶ firefighter ▶ *inves-tigator* ▶ IRS agent ▶ judge/magistrate ▶ lawyer (particularly administrative, antitrust, bankruptcy, real estate, securities, taxation, transportation) ▶ military officer ▸ pilot ▸ *police officer* ▸ security consultant/guard (respect for rules and procedures, good administrative skills, observant of details, fact oriented, boldness, ability to make tough decisions)

SCIENCE RESEARCH/ENGINEERING/MATHEMATICS

cartographer ▸ engineer (civil, chemical, *environmental*, flight, health and safety, *industrial*, mechanical, nuclear) ▸ geologist ▸ meteorologist (good memory for details, efficient, ability to work with tangible things and projects, keep things orderly and on track)

OTHER

carpenter ▸ electrician ▸ general contractor ▸ mechanic ▸ plumber ▸ surveyor

---

CASE STUDY FOUR

When a Career Isn't Working

Brad Gunter was fed up, and the good money he was making wasn't enough compensation for the daily aggravations. Worse yet, he felt trapped. His uncle, Phil, who was a partner in a major Los Angeles advertising firm, had gotten him this high-paying job as an account executive. Brad desperately wanted to quit, but he could not let the family down.

Even weaving his way through L.A. traffic in his new Porsche Carrera wasn't cheering him up as it once had. The day had been especially grueling when it should have been triumphant. Brad had just landed a major airline account. Today, it seemed as if his private office had been stormed by everyone in the firm. The creative department wanted ideas and brainstorming, which Brad hated. The back office needed lots of hand-holding as it established an account larger than any it had ever seen. Brad was assigned to three new teams, and working on teams was something he dreaded. All he had wanted to do was sift through demographic information about potential airline customers and memo the right people. Instead, his reference materials had gone untouched all day, and Brad was suffering from the serious Introvert's overexposure to people.

Finally, a pleasant thought entered his crowded mind: Michelle, the lovely young woman he had just met. They had had a wonderful lunch conversation several days ago about her work as a real estate appraiser. Convinced at first that he would be bored out of his skull, Brad had been surprised by how interested he was in Michelle's work. The factual data gathering, the comparisons to similar properties, the long hours alone with papers to be interpreted—right now, Michelle's job seemed like heaven to Brad. It certainly was a job for which Gold/Blue Introvert Brad felt well suited.

Fast forward two years. Brad finally found the courage to give up his stressful account executive position despite family opposition. Using the money he made from his commissions (which ran well into six figures), Brad supported himself while studying to become a real estate appraiser. When Brad married Michelle, she quit her job so the two of them could form their own appraisal firm. Energized daily, Brad loves his new career and is about to hire several people.

Your Personality's Challenges

Gold/Blue Introverts have a unique set of potential work-related blind spots. Some listed below you have, others you don't. No one has them all. Tone down a blind spot by focusing on it, then choose more productive actions and make them habits. (Suggestions for doing so are in parentheses below.) You:

- May prematurely dismiss new ideas. (Dismiss nothing until you know the who, what, where, when, why, and cost of a new idea.)

- May focus too much on the flaws in the efforts of others and not give credit where credit is due. (Make a discipline of giving some sort of affirmation to a colleague after listing flaws. Acknowledge those who deserve it; say when the flaws are outweighed by the good work.)

- Stress immediate results and overlook long-range implications. (Invest some time in long-range planning and get more comfortable with it as a tool. Ask a willing Blue to help.)

- Are fixed in supporting established ways of doing things. (The tried-and-true contribute much to efficiency. But they won't keep your company alive when the market is moving or changing. Also, established ways can be improved. Focus on the who, what, where, when, why, and cost of changing a procedure so you can take some of the credit.)

- Are rigid about how others should perform their responsibilities. (This book reveals the strengths of other Colors, strengths you may be lacking. Results are the priority, not necessarily the efficiencies of getting there. Grant the wisdom of others some benefit of the doubt while awaiting proven results. If their way proves better than yours, you don't want to look stupid.)

Your Job Search—the Good, the Bad, and the Ugly

Gold/Blue Introverts need to process information. With some interviewers, particularly Golds and Blues, you will feel a comfortable rapport. But with other Colors, you need to prepare and rehearse responses outside your comfort zone. Many human resources people are Greens; study how to communicate effectively with this Color group before your first interviews.

Your natural strengths easily allow you to:

▶ Set realistic goals and time lines

▶ Adequately research prospective employees

▶ Be well prepared for interviews and come across as hardworking and competent

▶ Logically consider pros and cons of every offer

▶ Be patient with delays and obstacles

▶ Show confidence in your ability to deal with bottom-line issues

In order to tone down your blind spots, you need to:

▶ Go beyond your friends to expand your networking circle

▶ Prepare questions to ask interviewers

▶ Do some brainstorming with a willing Blue or Green to consider alternative careers

▶ Be more assertive about selling yourself

▶ Do some thinking about a prospective company's future direction (ask a willing Blue to help)

▶ Resist the urge to be overly cautious about change

▶ Step back to reflect for a day or two about a job's impact on you and your family when tempted to make a snap decision

The Gold/Blue Introvert's Interviewing Style

With an interviewer whose Color is close to your own, you will feel immediate rapport. However, if your interviewer seems to have a significantly different style (and it's statistically likely that many will have a Green component), use the suggestions in parentheses.

In following your natural style, you:

- Are calm and composed. (This can look like disinterest—most interviewers expect a certain amount of nervousness. Make sure to speak more than you normally do, especially at first.)

- Document your experience well, in an easy-to-follow manner.

- Prefer written communications before face-to-face meetings. (Practice interview questions before the meeting. This will boost your confidence.)

- Share few feelings with people. (A Green interviewer relies on his or her emotional response to you as a big part of the decision-making process. If your interviewer asks you questions like, "How did you get along with previous coworkers?" he or she may be Green. Prioritize building a personal rapport with such an interviewer by answering emotion-based questions at length. Role play with a willing Green.)

- Focus on the present. (Especially if interviewing for a senior-level position, you will need to prepare a position on future planning. Take a Blue colleague to lunch and run a few ideas by him or her before an interview. At least research public statements about the company's future direction prior to an interview.)

- Follow through with all details; respect deadlines and commitments. (Interviewers respect that you send requested items, call to follow up, show up on time, and send thank-you notes.)

Okay, go do something purposeful now. Later, check out chapter 14, "Blues Overall," then carefully read chapter 24, "Before I Do Something Stupid: Adjusting to Other Styles," to learn about the strengths of other Colors. Like all Colors, you need the strengths of others. You can put them to work for you if you know where to look and how to ask. If you invest time learning how to recognize the Colors who can best assist you, it will make everyone more effective and productive. You can do this by quickly reading the Blue, Red, and Green "Overall" chapters.

If you are actively engaging in a job search, jot notes in the Roadmap in chapter 27. Recording your strengths and strategies is a concrete and results-oriented way to navigate the minefields of a job search.

CHAPTER 22

Gold/Green Extroverts

YOU'RE NOT ONLY a Gold, you also have strong secondary characteristics of the Green personality. And you have tested as a Color Q Extrovert, which means you recharge your batteries by being with people rather than being alone. Your Color group values efficiency, accuracy, predictability, tradition, and social responsibility. Affirming others is a strong inner drive. These core tendencies should ring true with you, since they've been researched worldwide for well over half a century. (If not, return to your self assessment and follow the directions for reevaluating yourself.) It's important that you read the exact right profile, since you can significantly enhance your professional and personal relationships as well as your job search with the information that follows.

You Overall

Ensuring the welfare of those around you, whether family or colleagues, is the focus of your energy and has been since you were a child. You affirm others and put them at ease. People in your Color group have continuous curiosity about people and keen observational skills.

Testing new ideas makes you uncomfortable; you favor working with real things and sticking with what you've experienced. Since few details escape your notice, you may feel you've "seen it all." Preferring the here and now, you shun change and minimize future thinking.

One of your best qualities is your highly developed work ethic. Commitments and obligations are undertaken with utmost seriousness. Your follow-through is unwavering, and you easily mobilize others when help is needed. Strengths of your group include anticipating what needs to be done, getting involved in details, and organizing resources and procedures. Along the way you create harmony and stability, always aware of how you might serve both people and goals. You are a consummate volunteer or service career worker.

Straightforward yet diplomatically is how you prefer to communicate with others. The people who irritate you most are those who do not share your personal warmth and work ethic: the discourteous, the unreliable, and the unprepared.

Here's how all these qualities combine in a real-life Gold/Green Extrovert.

CASE STUDY ONE

Corporate Event Planning Executive

Upon meeting Frankie Lucostic, the first impression is of a wiry, fun-loving, gregarious man. He is a natural in his position as head of events, Americas, for a line of business at a leading New York global financial services firm.

"The focus is on creating an experience and how to overwhelm with service," Frankie says. "That's a natural for me." He plans and executes events start to finish, from initial strategy "to the really granular details when on-site. That is really rewarding," he says.

Event planners frequently are open to, and pursue, many different interests. Frankie's childhood dream was to become a plastic surgeon. But he majored in government and minored in marketing with the goal of attending law school. He was accepted, but decided it wasn't for him. "I took my first job based on company culture and my attachment to their work, and found an events role by chance," he explains. "Along the way I did stints in account management, internal corporate communications, and recruiting, but always came back to events," he says. "I couldn't keep away."

His Green secondary personality and Extroversion are energized by contact with clients, both internal and external. Becoming more strategic about events (a natural for Blues) is a harder discipline for detail-focused Golds. It took Frankie some time to learn how to manage outcomes. "Because I'm in the business of details," he says, "it can be hard for me to move on or let things go." But ensuring the welfare of attendees and coworkers is

Gold/Green Frankie's focus. "As much as you plan, there's always something unexpected," he says. "Keeps it fresh!"

His Gold primary has propelled him upward into management and administration. "In my previous job, I progressed to being a lead, where I still planned and executed but also managed a small team," he says. "I was promoted into a leadership role after that, taking on parts of the business/operations, and finally into head of the whole team. It 'takes a village' to do events, so a strong team is a must."

Frankie now leads a team of eight event professionals who produce over 200 live and regional events for over 100,000 senior executives. "These events are much higher 'touch,'" he says. A Gold/Green Extrovert's strength is motivating others to cooperate in achieving goals.

Although this hardworking leader doesn't plan to slow down anytime soon, he does know that creating a healthier work/life balance will be part of his future. But first, he says, "I always ask myself, in any role, what's my legacy?" Golds are very oriented to making a positive and lasting impact on the world. With Frankie's Extroverted talent for interacting with people and fostering interaction among so many others, that will not be hard.

You on the Job

AS A LEADER

Getting the right things to the right people, in the right amounts, to the right place at the right time—that is the crux of your talent. Outstanding logistical skills are the hallmark of Gold/Green Extroverts in leadership roles. Providing clear guidelines and instructions, you build productive teams on which all are kept well informed.

You welcome responsibility as a tool for instituting sensible rules and procedures. You feel accountable for proper use of all resources and are vigilant to prevent their misuse.

You are suspicious of the agendas of those who question authority, believing they are slackers or troublemakers. You are loyal and expect loyalty in return. The personal attention you give your people gains you not only loyalty but also goodwill.

AS A TEAM PLAYER

You encourage your teammates to share viewpoints and ideas. But when goals have been set, you're the one who provides clear and practical ideas to achieve them. Getting things accomplished on time and on budget is the only accept-able way. You keep the agreed agenda on track, keep progress records for everyone, get the needed resources, and respect rules and procedures.

While other team members may not realize what resource they need until they need it, you've already anticipated and supplied it. Your contribution to the team is immense. However, you may irritate others by talking too much. If nobody else has said anything for a while, solicit opinions. You also may ham-per your efforts by sulking over disagreements you tend to take too personally.

Look at figure 22–1 for a list of your natural work-related strengths.

FIGURE 22–1 *Natural Work-Related Strengths*

Approximately 80 percent of these attributes will apply to you. Check off those that do, and use them in your resume and interviews. This will set you apart from the canned responses of others. You:

- ○ Have a strong need to be of service to others
- ○ Acknowledge and respect the chain of command
- ○ Can easily repeat and sequence tasks
- ○ Deal well with details
- ○ Apply common sense
- ○ Motivate others to cooperate in achieving goals
- ○ Stay with the job until it's done
- ○ Get things done on time and under budget

Here is another Gold/Green Extrovert using her strengths in a very different way.

CASE STUDY TWO

Philanthropist, Historical Documents Preservationist

On many hot days of an earlier era, two little girls played in the gardens of the Ibrahim Palace, an architectural jewel set on the outskirts of Cairo, Egypt. One was a Hungarian who had escaped her native land several years before; the other was Princess Fazilé Ibrahim, a member of the Egyptian royal family and great-granddaughter of the last Turkish sultan.

Then, on what is still known today as "Black Saturday," political turmoil struck. Thousands of religious fundamentalists, communists, and radical students began gathering in the streets. Within twenty-four hours, many of the symbols that had given Cairo its glamor had been burned down. Guests were thrown out of their windows at the Shepherd Hotel. We could see the mobs pulling people out of their cars and stoning them to death. It is a memory that will remain forever, for this is the author's story as well.

The two families fled rapidly—one going to the United States and the other settling in France. It was thirty years before we met again.

Today Princess Fazilé is president of the Ibrahim Pasha of Egypt Fund, affiliated with the London-based Royal Asiatic Society. The organization is dedicated to encouraging the development of Ottoman studies internationally by publishing Ottoman documents and manuscripts of historical importance from the classical period up to 1839. A true Extrovert, she is an active, hands-on executive, traveling to elevate awareness of her fund's mission and encourage submission of manuscripts. "I was clear about the fact that I intended to involve myself in all the proceedings in order to reach the precise goal of my foundation," she said. Her focus and determination are very much Gold/Green characteristics.

Making scholars familiar with the work of the fund is a not a quick process, but Princess Fazilé continues the quest to find important Ottoman-era documents that will underpin historical research. "The fund is small, not well-known for the present, and nothing compels people to come to us," she says. "We have to smile and encourage . . . and be patient." She has traveled to Turkey to meet with historians at two major universities and has visited the Centre of Istanbul Archives.

When manuscripts of great historical importance do come to her notice, "then it is a blessed moment for me, when I no longer question the validity of my project," she says. She finds these discoveries most energizing. Golds have a reverence for history and its preservation.

The princess defines success as "doing something I care for and that some other people care for, too." When pushed about her strengths, she reluctantly says, "Maybe I am very stubborn; the fact is that I never got anything I wanted without giving a fierce fight." She claims she is not a businesswoman, but these Gold/Green Extroverted characteristics serve her well.

Ideal Work Environment

A stable, organized institution with a predictable future is where Gold/Green Extroverts feel most at home. When a job offer is made, leverage as much as you can from the list in figure 22–2.

FIGURE 22-2 *The Ideal Gold/Green Extrovert Work Environment*

Compare your current work environment to the descriptions below. Check all that ring true for you. If these descriptions seem obvious, that confirms you've tested your individual Color correctly. Other Colors, especially Blues, would find this environment uncomfortable and unproductive. The optimal Gold/Green Extrovert work environment:

○ Is a stable, well-recognized entity with a solid reputation in your community. You gravitate to established organizations; startups don't appeal to you.

○ Involves concrete and practical projects and products. Intangible services are tough for you to quantify and measure. Stick with the things you can touch and see.

○ Has clear rules, reporting lines, and expectations. Valuable time is wasted trying to make up rules as you go along. You don't want to be bothered by this.

○ Allows you to work within a group or team. You need people to stay energized.

○ Contains trustworthy coworkers. You take an interest in the well-being of colleagues and clients, and prefer that it's reciprocated.

○ Is service oriented. You are by nature service oriented and want to work in a place that honors those values.

○ Rewards reliable people. It's rare that you fail to meet your deadlines.

○ Provides financial security. You take pride in being competent and expect to be compensated appropriately.

○ Makes you feel like part of a big family. You thrive in collegial places.

○ Allows you to factor in the needs of your family. Since you make sure goals are achieved at work, you expect to be able to take time for significant family needs.

A corporate culture integrating the above elements is fertile soil for your career advancement.

The worst type of work culture for a Gold/Green Extrovert is impersonal and highly competitive. Constant change makes you feel that your great administrative and organizational strengths are valueless. You need rules, stability, and positive personal interactions in order to feel comfortable at work.

When Extroverted Gold/Greens work in nonideal corporate cultures, productivity is stunted and career achievements become an uphill climb.

The Extroverted Gold/Green's Ideal Boss

Even a great job can be frustrating under the wrong boss; a mediocre job under a wonderful boss is pretty hard to leave. Gold/Greens get along especially well with other Golds. But bosses of other Color types who possess the characteristics in figure 22–3 also can be good mentors.

FIGURE 22–3 **The Gold/Green Extrovert's Ideal Boss**

Check off if your boss:

○ Shows appropriate personal concern for each staff member

○ States clearly what needs to be done

○ Sets achievable goals

○ Is reliable about providing needed resources

○ Holds to firm completion dates

Careers That Attract Gold/Green Extroverts

Gold/Green Extroverts like Princess Fazilé Ibrahim and Frankie Lucostic cluster in fields that provide professional respect, require high levels of competence, and contribute in a meaningful way to society (especially in well-known institutions). You need predictability and stability to be at your best. Upon reaching a high level of responsibility, you assemble a competent and loyal staff.

Please note that not all the following careers will appeal to you, but recognize that each, in some way, draws on the strengths of your style and appeals to a significant number of your Color group. This is not a comprehensive list, but it will show underlying patterns of preference. If unlisted careers offer similar patterns, your chances of success increase. Text in parentheses at the end of each section highlights the Color style characteristics that create success in that broad area.

According to our research, jobs italicized in the lists below are predicted to benefit from an above-average growth rate over the next several years. This information is based on the continuously revised data provided by the U.S. Department of Labor and Bureau of Labor Statistics on their websites O*NET OnLine (www.onetonline.org) and http://www.bls.gov/CAREEROUTLOOK/. There you will find in-depth information about job requirements and salary ranges.

There are successful people of all Color styles in all occupations. In non-ideal jobs, you can still shine by creating your own niche.

BUSINESS/MANAGEMENT/PROMOTION/SALES

compensation and benefits manager ▶ *convention and event planner* ▶ *corporate trainer* ▶ *customer service representative* ▶ *energy efficiency expert/executive* ▶ *human resources manager/specialist* ▶ insurance underwriter/agent ▶ *labor relations specialist* ▶ lobbyist ▶ *marketing executive* (radio, television) ▶ office manager ▶ *performing arts administrator* ▶ *personal financial advisor* ▶ *public relations manager/specialist* ▶ real estate agent/*manager/appraiser* ▶ salesperson (tangible products) ▶ service sales representatives ▶ urban and regional planner (human interaction, organizational skills, straightforward and diplomatic communication, service career orientation)

DIGITAL/HIGH TECH

customer relations manager ▶ human resources recruiter for high-tech staff ▶ *social media manager* (excel at connecting technology people with staff and clients)

EDUCATION

athletic coach/trainer ▶ *principal* ▶ *school administrator* ▶ teacher (preschool, elementary, middle school, home economics, special education) (meaningful contribution to society, respect for rules, professional respect, service career orientation)

HEALTH SCIENCE/PSYCHOLOGY

biomedical technologist ▶ *chiropractor* ▶ *dental hygienist* ▶ *dentist* ▶ dietitian ▶ *exercise physiologist* ▶ *healthcare administrator* ▶ *hospice nurse* ▶ *hospital administrator* ▶ *nurse*/nursing instructor ▶ *optometrist* ▶ *pediatrician* ▶ *pharmaceutical sales rep* ▶ *pharmacist* ▶ *primary care/family physician/physician assistant* ▶ *public health educator* ▶ *radiological technologist* ▶ *speech pathologist* ▶ *therapists of all types (occupational, physical, radiation, respiratory, speech)* ▶ *veterinarian/vet assistant/technologist* (high levels of competence, professional respect, service career orientation, observant of details, curious about people, put people at ease, ensuring welfare of others)

HUMAN SERVICES

child care center director ▶ counselor (career, *child welfare, employee assistance, family, substance abuse*) ▶ *fund-raiser* ▶ historical documents curator/preservationist ▶ philanthropist ▶ religious leader (clergy, rabbi, religious educator) ▶ *social and community service manager* ▶ social worker (service career orientation, human interaction, affirming of others, help stabilize others, professional respect, contribute meaningfully to society, respect for tradition)

LAW/HOSPITALITY/SMALL BUSINESS

hotel/restaurant manager ▶ innkeeper ▶ lawyer (limited interest in law except fields that include children, consumer affairs, domestic, and healthcare) ▶ retail owner/manager (service career orientation, interaction with people, diplomatic, observant of details, ensuring welfare of others)

OTHER

caterer ▶ *cosmetologist* ▶ court reporter ▶ fashion designer ▶ flight attendant ▶ *hairdresser* ▶ interior designer ▶ landscape designer ▶ museum conservator ▶ *paralegal* ▶ personal trainer/exercise instructor (service career orientation, eye for detail, interaction with people, affirming of others, keen aesthetic sense)

CASE STUDY THREE

Energy Efficiency Executive

Laura Van Wie McGrory is deeply immersed in providing for the world's energy needs. She is vice president, international policy, for the Alliance to Save Energy, a nonprofit organization founded in 1977 by U.S. Senators Charles Percy and Hubert Humphrey. This organization focuses on American energy policy and improving global energy efficiency.

Laura manages energy efficiency projects in Asia, Africa, southeastern Europe, and Latin America. These include international energy productivity, policy and regulatory reform, green building certification, building code implementation, utility demand-side management capacity building, financing municipal efficiency programs, energy-efficient transportation efforts, and water supply projects. Efficiency and social responsibility are two key drivers for this Color group.

She came to her current position with an impressive resume, starting with a master of international affairs degree focusing on international environmental policy from Columbia University's School of International and Public Affairs.

She began developing research reports for the World Bank, the U.S. Environmental Protection Agency, and the Intergovernmental Panel on Climate Change. She gained more international exposure as head of the Washington, DC, office of the Lawrence Berkeley National Laboratory. This brought her into contact with the U.S. Department of Energy, where she helped draft rule makings for U.S. energy efficiency appliance standards. She also provided technical support to the Asia-Pacific Partnership on Clean Development and Climate and the Asia-Pacific Economic Corporation.

Her work appeals to her Green side. "Most engaging is finding synergies and collaborating with policymakers from other countries," she says. But being a primary Gold, she focuses on facts rather than visions. "Some of my best successes are combining information from many experts into a coherent and useful report," she says. "I don't come with the big, new, breakthrough ideas. I engage others, then follow through and make sure projects are carried out properly and with high quality."

But when offered a well-earned governmental dream job in Washington, Laura turned it down. "The decision," she recalls, "revolved around whether we would move to this charming small town two hours from DC, or stay so I could take the job. Then my son Ian asked me, 'Will you be home after school? I want to see you more!'" Laura chose the small town. "Life is a juggling act."

Your Personality's Challenges

Gold/Green Extroverts have a unique set of potential work-related blind spots. Some listed below you have, others you don't. No one has them all. Tone down a blind spot by focusing on it, then choose more productive actions and make them habits. (Suggestions for doing so are in parentheses below.) You:

▸ Get too involved with details, ignore the big picture. (Find a willing Blue and lunch with that person twice a month. Occasionally emulate his or her long-term strategic thinking so it's a tool when you need it, but it will never feel natural.)

▸ Need significant praise and appreciation and get dispirited when there is none. (Not all Colors verbalize appreciation. It's there, but not evident. Either ask, "How am I doing?" or give yourself a pep talk. You know how you're doing, and you're usually doing very well.)

▸ Don't handle competitive situations well. (When you cannot turn the tide to cooperation, or calm things down, step back and disengage. Refuse to play the game. Most of the time, this is the only way to defuse the pressure.)

▸ Tend to stick to what has worked in the past. (There are many paths to the same place. All have their strengths and advantages. Yes, your way is the right way—one of many. Ignore your discomfort once or twice a year and examine the advantages of another way.)

▸ Do not naturally see new possibilities. (If your experience isn't addressing a new situation well, you get discouraged and hopeless, sometimes giving up. Get help—talk to someone, preferably a Blue or Red, to see beyond the now. Resist insisting on procedures just for their comfort value.)

▸ Make up your mind too quickly. (Even if you receive new information, it's difficult for you to reverse a position. Often in life you have felt stuck with a position not in your best interest in order to get something done. Throw a cog in the machine when you feel the need [especially if you have doubts about a marriage or having a child]. Believe it or not, it will be good for everyone.)

Your Job Search—the Good, the Bad, and the Ugly

Gold/Green Extroverts are better than most Colors at drumming up informational interviews and getting referrals to job leads. Your strengths and blind spots below apply equally to both informational and formal interviews.

With some interviewers, particularly Golds and Greens, you will feel a comfortable rapport. But with those of other Colors, you need to prepare and rehearse responses outside your comfort zone. Many human resources people are Greens; make a study of how to communicate effectively with this Color group before your first interviews.

Your natural strengths easily allow you to:

> Have a clear action plan for your search and proceed in an orderly fashion

> Have measurable, realistic, and well-defined goals and meet them

> Be patient with job application rules and procedures

> Have a wide network of friends and colleagues upon which to draw for job leads

> Adequately research a company before the interview

> Follow through on details of a job search, like writing appropriate thank-you notes

> Create time lines, daily status reports, and budgets that reduce stress on you and the family

In order to tone down your blind spots, you need to:

> Balance networking and research

> Be willing to consider less-obvious career opportunities and ways to get interviews

> Resist getting depressed and gloomy about turndowns; they're not personal rejections

> Plan a think-through session; reflect for a day or two about long-term implications of a job for both you and your family before deciding

The Gold/Green Extrovert's Interviewing Style

With an interviewer whose Color is close to your own, you will feel immediate rapport. However, if your interviewer seems to have a significantly different style, use the suggestions in parentheses. Mercilessly exploit these natural abilities of yours and get more job offers.

In following your natural style, you:

> Have an accurate and well-presented resume. (Accurate may not mean intriguing. Write descriptions that invite the interviewer to delve deeper; ask a willing Green for assistance.)

▶ Focus on the present. (Especially if interviewing for a senior-level position, you will need to prepare a position on future planning. Take a Blue colleague to lunch and run a few ideas by him or her before an interview. At least read public statements about company direction.)

▶ Come across as stable, hardworking, warm, and with solid past accomplishments. (Good foot in the door, but not enough. Awareness of bottom-line considerations is just as important. Adjust some of your language to address cost management if applicable.)

▶ Demonstrate enthusiasm for the job. (This becomes a negative if you "gush." Keep sentences short, body language under control, hand gestures below the neck.)

▶ May not think outside the box. (Your orderly mind knows what your next career step should be but tends to close off other potentials. You prefer established fields, but there are always those you haven't considered that may allow you to move higher and faster than your planned career path.)

Take a break now to socialize. Later, read chapter 4, "Greens Overall," then carefully read chapter 24, "Before I Do Something Stupid: Adjusting to Other Styles," to learn about the strengths of other Colors. In certain key areas, you need their strengths. You can put them to work for you if you know where to look and how to ask. If you invest the time, you'll learn how to recognize the Colors who can best assist you. This will make you more effective and productive.

If you are actively engaging in a job search, jot notes in the Roadmap in chapter 27. Recording your strengths and strategies is a concrete and results-oriented way to navigate through the discouraging parts of a job search. It also will help capture what you learn on informational interviews and remember whom to thank when you land your new job.

CHAPTER 23

Gold/Green Introverts

YOU'RE NOT ONLY a Gold, you also have strong secondary characteristics of the Green personality. And you have tested as a Color Q Introvert, which means you recharge your batteries by being alone rather than being with people. Your Color group has gentle and supportive people who value tradition and have strong follow-through skills. It's helpful to know your strengths so you can maximize them and your weaknesses so you can delegate or ask for help with them. Suggestions follow for all of this.

You Overall

You are quiet and reflective, and the focus of your energy is to ensure the welfare of those under your care. This core tendency surfaces early in your life. Very few people get to see your rich inner world because you always are more focused on the needs of others.

At work this translates to a highly developed work ethic where commitments and obligations are undertaken with seriousness and given top priority. A practical, detail-oriented, and thorough person, you can always see and address what needs to be done at each phase of a project.

Your warmth, sense of responsibility, and desire to create stability and harmony lead you to service careers and volunteer activities. But you don't last long in hectic and ambiguous environments; stable organizations that provide ample private time to plan will better support your ambitions.

Authority, history, and tradition are things you respect. So is the conservation of any kind of resource, natural or man-made. You find change, abstract concepts, and untested theories irritating. When you start imagining things, it's usually worst-case scenarios that fill you with doom, gloom, and self-doubt. Pulling yourself back to the real world makes you feel better, and you prefer staying there. Imagination is not your friend, and the vivid imaginations of Greens in particular make you uncomfortable.

If you have coworkers who are discourteous, unreliable, noisy, or unprepared, it drives you crazy. Conflicts are problematic for you and avoided wherever possible, allowing bad behaviors to continue unchecked.

At cocktail parties or business functions, you just enjoy blending in. Controlling the attention or taking a dominant role isn't something you want or need. You leave the starring roles to others. One on one is the way you prefer to communicate, and you listen attentively. Putting others at ease is a talent you've acquired through your natural curiosity about people and your keen powers of observation.

CASE STUDY ONE

Obstetrician/Gynecologist and Military Veteran

Gold/Greens make very reassuring obstetricians and gynecologists. They are thorough, knowledgeable, and warmly personable. That describes Elizabeth Lucal, M.D., FACOG.

"I felt obstetrics/gynecology has always been the right career path," Elizabeth says. "I feel that it chose me more than I chose it. My strengths are being meticulous, detailed, persistent, and outspoken. I also think some of my strengths are good degrees of compassion and empathy for other people's situations."

The young girl who wanted to be a veterinarian became a young woman who committed herself to four years of medical training at Michigan State University, College of Human Medicine, and four years of OB/GYN residency at Tripler Army Medical Center in Hawaii. Today, Elizabeth is affiliated with Health Quest Medical Practice seeing patients in their New York offices in Fishkill and Poughkeepsie.

"The element that is most engaging is teaching," she says. "First, I believe in order to have physicians with good ethics, morals, and respectful patient interactions, residents must be taught and provided with good examples of this behavior. Second, teaching forces me to stay current with medical information and standards. Third, I enjoy the interaction of teaching; and fourth, I learn more than I teach in this role of faculty."

Although she enjoys writing and dictating notes about her patients' appointments, she does not enjoy the grind of updating the electronic medical records. "Sadly, I cannot delegate this," she says.

Elizabeth is proudest of her abilities to make the medical system accessible to patients without money or insurance. She is also proud when she can pick up on details missed by others. "Some of my best successes," she recalls, "have been early diagnosis of medical problems that were overlooked by other providers."

Elizabeth is a dedicated physician who has not taken a vacation in over three years. "To recharge my batteries, I read, I run, I practice yoga," she says. And, typical of a Gold, "I try to spend a lot of time with my family."

You on the Job

AS A LEADER

Getting the right things to the right people, in the right amounts, to the right place at the right time—that is the crux of your talent. Outstanding logistical skills are the hallmark of Gold/Green Introverts in leadership roles. You supply clearly defined guidelines and instructions for your staff, and you often jump in and share the work.

You see your role as providing for the organization's practical needs, to which you attend as if providing for a family. You welcome responsibility, feel keenly accountable, and prevent misuse of key resources. Everyone is kept informed, which reaps goodwill and productivity.

When making important decisions, you go step by step, avoiding all foreseeable risks. You absorb and assess as much factual information as possible and are uncomfortable going with your gut.

AS A TEAM PLAYER

You rarely seek to lead but encourage others to express their ideas, provide positive feedback, and usually are modest about your own contributions. When a team needs a practical reality check, you're the one to provide it. Dependable and reliable, you do thorough work, meet deadlines, respect rules and procedures, and don't understand the motivations of others who behave differently.

If you speak up about the less productive actions of team members and they argue with you, you are apt to take it too personally.

Look at figure 23–1 for a list of your natural work-related strengths.

FIGURE 23–1 **Natural Work-Related Strengths**

Approximately 80 percent of these attributes will apply to you. Check off those that do, and use them in your resume and interviews. This will set you apart from the canned responses of others. You:

- ○ Can organize people to accomplish well-defined goals
- ○ Observe the needs of others and supply them whenever you can
- ○ Are practical about what needs to be done and how to do it
- ○ Support and encourage others
- ○ Work well on a team
- ○ Are not ego driven
- ○ Follow the rules

Now see how one Gold/Green Introvert uses these strengths in a different field.

CASE STUDY TWO

Tax Lawyer

Those with a Green personality component switch careers more easily than other personality types. Yours is a unique adaptability—you sense the lay of the land almost immediately and are able to respond appropriately and creatively. Martha Miller, a Gold/Green tax lawyer for forty-two years, is an excellent example.

Martha was an economics major in college at a time when that was a daring choice for a woman. "I wanted to get an MBA, but in 1966, women weren't welcome in MBA programs. This made me mad, so I went to law school instead. The only course I really did well in was tax law. When I graduated, I was encouraged by the law firms to take a job as a secretary—at the time, women made $7,500 a year as an attorney, $7,800 as a secretary. (Male attorneys made $13,800.) So I got mad again, and acted professionally for about eight years, playing sadomasochist nuns and psychotic school teachers. To even out my income I worked for H&R Block, preparing taxes, teaching the tax course, and managing offices. Between acting and Block, I always made more money than I would have practicing law in a big firm.

"My performance career culminated as a tax and finance feature reporter for two years for NBC News in New York. I got fired as part of a budget shortfall, so I opened Miller Tax Law, LLC, in New York City. Later I moved to Connecticut, taking my tax clients with me."

Lawyer, tax preparer, actress, television news reporter—Martha's Green adaptability is perfectly balanced by her Gold primary personality in the tax-law field. Her Gold side minds the details while her Green secondary handles the long-term thinking and emotional hand-holding this job requires. "Many people come to me in abject fear, totally absorbed by what they think is an unsolvable tax problem," Martha says. "Within an hour, I can usually convince them that they are going to be all right. They often cry at the beginning of the interview, whether man or woman. By the end, they are laughing and smiling."

However, her Green side suffers under the filing and document-tracking demands. "Giant piles of paper are the burden of any law office," she says, sighing.

Martha pursues physical activities during her free time, often working on her stunning Victorian home in the foothills of the Berkshires. "Because my work is so conceptual, I find I need to do physical work to effectively relax," she says.

Gold/Greens are more likely than most to fulfill their dreams rather than put them on hold. Martha is no exception. "I don't even have a bucket list," she says.

Ideal Work Environment

You, like Dr. Elizabeth Lucal, gravitate to stable, recognized entities with solid reputations in the community. When a job offer is made, leverage as much as you can from the list in figure 23–2.

FIGURE 23-2 *The Ideal Gold/Green Introvert Work Environment*

Compare your current work environment to the descriptions below. If these descriptions seem obvious, that confirms you've tested your individual color correctly. Other Colors, especially Reds, would find this environment uncomfortable and unproductive. The optimal Gold/Green Introvert work environment:

○ Is a stable and well-respected institution with a predictable future. You work hard and want to be rewarded with money and respect. New or distressed companies can't offer this. You are a quintessential corporate worker and you want to ally yourself with a firm that stands behind its people and products.

○ Involves concrete and practical projects and products. Intangible services are tough for you to quantify and measure. Stick with the things you can touch, see, and immediately evaluate.

○ Is oriented to serving customers and staff. You have a deeply rooted principle of serving others. If your company disregards that, you will not work there long.

○ Values and returns loyalty and commitment. These are a deep and natural part of the core of who you are. In today's workplace, few companies can afford to offer their employees the loyalty they once did. Today, you are better off choosing to place your loyalty with a mentor rather than a company; but there are still a few good firms around.

○ Has a work/life balance program that respects the family needs of staff. Family is your first priority, and you are too good a worker not to be allowed time for family needs.

○ Is quiet, orderly, and calm. The one situation you are weakest at coping with is chaos.

○ Allows for private space. As an Introvert, your batteries get drained when dealing with people, even if your people skills are superb. You recharge your batteries by being alone. If you have to share your work space with others, you will feel a lot more fatigue at the end of the day. You think and perform better in a private space where you can reflect in depth on projects; insist on one as a condition of employment if possible.

A corporate culture integrating the above elements is fertile soil for your career advancement.

The worst type of work culture for an Introverted Gold/Green is highly competitive and rewards intuition over factual accuracy. Environments of constant change, like startup or distressed companies, can stress you to the point of physical illness.

When Introverted Gold/Greens work in nonideal corporate cultures, productivity is stunted and career achievements become an uphill climb.

The Introverted Gold/Green's Ideal Boss

Even a great job can be frustrating under the wrong boss; a mediocre job under a wonderful boss is pretty hard to leave. Gold/Greens get along especially well with other Golds. But bosses of other Color types who possess the characteristics in figure 23–3 also can be good mentors.

FIGURE 23-3 *The Gold/Green Introvert's Ideal Boss*

Check off if your boss:

○ Is organized and sets clear objectives

○ Is reliable and trustworthy

○ Takes a personal interest in each employee

○ Is loyal

○ Provides needed resources

Careers That Attract Gold/Green Introverts

The company you'll call home is one where you can work in a secure career path for many years under the guidance of clear rules, procedures, and expectations. Predictability and stability bring out your best work. You particularly need to be rewarded for your abilities to be accurate and get things done, like tax lawyer Martha Miller. Financially well-managed companies are what you instinctively prefer.

Please note that not all the following careers will appeal to you, but recognize that each, in some way, draws on the strengths of your style and appeals to a significant number of your Color group. This is not a comprehensive list, but it will show underlying patterns of preference. If unlisted careers offer similar patterns, your chances of success increase. Text in parentheses at the end of each section highlights the Color style characteristics that create success in that broad area.

According to our research, jobs italicized in the lists below are predicted to benefit from an above-average growth rate over the next several years. This information is based on the continuously revised data provided by the U.S. Department of Labor and Bureau of Labor Statistics on their websites O*NET OnLine (www.onetonline.org) and http://www.bls.gov/CAREEROUTLOOK/. There you will find in-depth information about job requirements and salary ranges.

There are successful people of all Color styles in all occupations. In non-ideal jobs, you can still shine by creating your own niche.

BUSINESS/MANAGEMENT/PROMOTION/SALES

administrative assistant ▶ bookkeeper ▶ *convention and event planner* ▶ *customer service representative* ▶ *human resources specialist* ▶ insurance underwriter/agent ▶ lobbyist ▶ *marketing executive* ▶ performing arts administrator ▶ *personal financial advisor* ▶ *public relations specialist* ▶ real estate agent/appraiser ▶ salesperson (tangible products) ▶ service sales representative ▶ small business owner ▶ staff coordinator (human interaction, organizational skills, straightforward and diplomatic communication, service career orientation)

CREATIVE/OTHER SERVICES

antique dealer ▶ artist ▶ caterer ▶ *cosmetologist* ▶ court reporter ▶ fashion designer ▶ flight attendant ▶ genealogist ▶ hairdresser ▶ interior designer ▶ jeweler ▶ landscape architect ▶ librarian ▶ museum curator ▶ *paralegal* ▶ personal trainer/exercise instructor ▶ researcher (service career orientation, eye for detail, interaction with people, affirming of others, keen aesthetic sense)

DIGITAL/HIGH TECH

human resources recruiter for high-tech staff ▶ *social media manager* ▶ *tech support specialist*

EDUCATION

guidance counselor ▶ *school administrator* ▶ teacher (elementary, middle school, preschool, special education) (meaningful contribution to society, respect for rules, professional respect, service career orientation)

HEALTH SCIENCE

anesthesiologist ▶ *audiologist* ▶ biologist ▶ *biomedical technologist* ▶ *chiropractor* ▶ *dental hygienist/lab technician* ▶ dentist ▶ *dietician/nutritionist* ▶ elder care specialist ▶ *exercise physiologist* ▶ *healthcare administrator* ▶ *home health aide* ▶ hospice worker ▶ *hospital administrator* ▶ *medical records technician* ▶ medical researcher ▸ *nurse*/nursing instructor ▸ obstetrician/gynecologist ▸ *optometrist* ▸ *pediatrician* ▸ *pharmacist* ▸ *primary care/family physician/physician assistant* ▸ public health educator ▸ *radiological/surgical technologist* ▸ *speech pathologist* ▸ *therapists of all types (occupational, physical, radiation, respiratory, speech, substance abuse)* ▸ *veterinarian/vet assistant* (high levels of competence, professional respect, service career orientation, observant of details, curious about people, put people at ease, ensuring welfare of others)

HUMAN SERVICES
child care center director ▸ counselor (career, child welfare, employee assistance, family, substance abuse) ▸ *fund-raiser/grant coordinator* ▸ religious leader (clergy, rabbi, religious educator) ▸ *social and community service manager* ▸ *social worker* (service career orientation, human interaction, affirming of others, help stabilize others, professional respect, contribute meaningfully to society, respect for tradition)

LAW/HOSPITALITY/SMALL BUSINESS
innkeeper/lodging manager ▸ lawyer (limited interest in most legal fields except those that focus on children, consumer affairs, domestic, healthcare, tax) ▸ *retail owner/manager* (service career orientation, interaction with people, diplomatic, observant of details, ensuring welfare of others)

CASE STUDY THREE
When a Career Isn't Working

Bertie Feldman learned a lot by doing his cousin Tom a favor. Tom decided to run for state treasurer and asked Bertie to manage his campaign. Bertie was deeply flattered; his cousin complimented him on his superior abilities to tune in to people's needs, handle details, and complete follow-through tasks. "Bertie," his cousin said, "no one is better at these things than you!"

It probably helped that Bertie recently had been laid off from his middle management job with a big enough severance package to see him through the four-month campaign. But Bertie also knew it wouldn't just be his cousin getting exposure. Introverted Bertie was determined to use the experience to get his resume around and meet people with whom he would never otherwise come into contact.

The cramped campaign quarters did not allow Bertie a private office. Over time, this became a major fatigue factor, with volunteers dropping in to ask questions or talking too loudly on their phones. Gold/Green Bertie much preferred the stability and predictability of his old job; by contrast, the campaign was uncomfortably fluid, with candidate plans changing constantly. Concrete-thinking Bertie was at a loss during strategy sessions, when, as campaign manager, he should have been leading the discussion. But strategies and theories stymied Bertie's factually oriented Gold/Green character.

He was great, however, at managing the volunteer staff. No task ever lacked a competent person, and even the media noted how well his cousin's campaign was organized. Tom won the election, and Bertie knew what he wanted to do and where.

Two weeks after the elections, Bertie was offered the job of his dreams: managing the volunteer staff at the National Historical Museum two towns away from his home. Half of his time would be spent doing research in a private (hallelujah!) office. The salary was identical to the one at his old job, with superior benefits. Bertie's family was especially happy when he came home revved up at the end of each day.

Your Personality's Challenges

Gold/Green Introverts have a unique set of potential work-related blind spots. Some listed below you have, others you don't. No one has them all. Tone down a blind spot by focusing on it, then choose more productive actions and make them habits. (Suggestions for doing so are in parentheses below.) You:

▸ Don't see the forest for the trees. (Details, rather than the big picture, are your preferred focus. Without an overview, your detail decisions may be flawed. Keep in mind the end result and the details become clearer.)

▸ Need approval and get dispirited if it's not expressed. (Myth: If they don't express it, they don't feel it. Fact: More than one Color feels appreciation without expressing it. Sometimes, you just have to reward yourself.)

▸ Overreact to competition and infighting. (When you can't avoid conflict, you become cold, snappy, and overly negative. Be proactive; nipping it in the bud will drain you less. You'll beat competitors with your tireless follow-through; don't be afraid of them. They have something to prove; you don't.)

▸ May be overly cautious about new ways. (Focus on whether the new is practical; that's your strength. Support pilot projects and trial periods before saying no.)

▶ Can be less assertive and direct than needed. (You prefer to blend in; but occasionally you have to step up and share your knowledge. This is what it takes sometimes to get the job done. Do it without reservation.)

Your Job Search—the Good, the Bad, and the Ugly

Gold/Green Introverts have the advantage of being best one on one. With some interviewers, particularly Golds and Greens, you will feel a comfortable rapport. But with those of other Colors, you need to rehearse responses outside your comfort zone.

Your natural strengths easily allow you to:

▶ Assemble a close and supportive network

▶ Construct an accurate and compelling resume

▶ Create a clear action plan

▶ Have measurable and well-defined short- and long-term goals

▶ Research and collect facts on prospective employers

▶ Proceed through the interview process in an orderly way

▶ Come across as hardworking, warm, and prepared

▶ Be patient with what needs to be done and job application rules

▶ Follow through on all details of the search and are decisive when the right opportunity turns up

In order to tone down your blind spots, you need to:

▶ Not take delays and obstacles as rejections

▶ Prevent stress by organizing time lines, status reports, and a job-search budget to track how well you are meeting your goals

▶ Stretch yourself socially to broaden your network

▶ Drill down to bottom-line implications and be tough when focusing on that aspect of a job

▶ Role play uncomfortable salary negotiations (get a willing Blue or Red to assist)

▶ Refuse to give in to depression after being turned down

The Gold/Green Introvert's Interviewing Style

With an interviewer whose Color is close to your own, you will feel immediate rapport. However, if your interviewer seems to have a significantly different style, use the suggestions in parentheses.

In following your natural style, you:

▶ Listen more than you speak. (This can look like disinterest. Make sure to speak more than you normally do, especially at first.)

▶ Prefer written communications before face-to-face meetings. (Read several back issues of pertinent trade journals if necessary. Gather facts from all sources: Internet, library, annual reports. Such preparation will boost your confidence.)

▶ Prefer to talk about specific details, schedules, and deadlines. (A Green interviewer relies on his or her emotional response to you as a big part of the decision-making process. If your interviewer asks you questions like, "How did you get along with previous coworkers?" he or she may be Green. Prioritize building a personal rapport with such an interviewer. Role play with a willing Green.)

▶ Focus on the present. (Especially if interviewing for a senior-level position, you will need to prepare a position on future planning. Take a Blue or Green colleague to lunch and run a few ideas by him or her before an interview. At least read public statements about the company's future direction prior to an interview.)

Okay, go do something valuable to your community now. Later, check out chapter 4, "Greens Overall," then carefully read chapter 24, "Before I Do Something Stupid: Adjusting to Other Styles," to learn about the strengths of other Colors. Like all Colors, you need the strengths of others. You can put them to work for you if you know where to look and how to ask. If you invest time learning how to recognize the Colors who can best assist you by reading figure 1 in each of the "Overall" Color chapters, it will make everyone more effective and productive.

If you are actively engaging in a job search, jot notes in the Roadmap in chapter 27. Recording your strengths and strategies is a concrete and results-oriented way to assess the progress of your job search.

PART 6

GETTING THE JOB

Before I Do Something Stupid
Adjusting to Other Styles

PEOPLE LEAVE JOBS because they dislike other people more often than because they dislike their tasks: "If it weren't for my boss, I'd really love my job." "If Mary would just stay out of my hair, I'd be able to complete my projects on time." Certain Color Q personalities clash with others because they don't recognize each other's strengths. Believe it or not, your boss and your coworker Mary can actually make your work easier if you learn their strengths. In this chapter, you'll learn how to do this using Color Q. Start by identifying the Colors of others (see figure 1 in each of the "Overall" Color chapters) and then determine what they can do for you. Finally, there are tips on how to speak their languages.

Giving someone the self assessment in chapter 2 often is not feasible. So here's how to do Color Q detective work. Follow the steps in figure 24–1 to assess someone else's Color. (These tips work outside the office, too; for example, on dates or when trying to improve relations with your spouse or parents.)

FIGURE 24–1 **Assessing Someone Else's Color**

Figuring out someone's Color is not easy. It takes time and close observation to figure out someone's full Color type. But if you can assess any part of their Color makeup, it will go a long way toward improving communications.

Everyone has a Gold or Red component, and a Blue or Green component. In this section, we will concentrate on identifying these components. If you can recognize these pieces, whether they are primary or backup, you're ahead of the game. In addition, everyone is either an Extrovert or an Introvert.

There are three steps to revealing these components:

1. First, look at the person's work space. Try to look at it in the morning, at noon, and after they have gone home for the day.

They're a Gold if: The desk is usually uncluttered, has no piles, and everything is neatly filed. Golds begin and end projects before starting new ones. Other clues: Golds tend to be serious and formal and always on time.

They're a Red if: The desk is a mess of files, papers, and piles. Usually everything is a work in progress. Other clues: Reds are loose and relaxed (may even have their feet up on the desk) and often time pressured or late.

2. The second piece of this detective work is the Blue/Green component. Start a conversation and talk about any comfortable subject, but notice:

Green versus Blue: How much do they personalize the relationship with you? Greens will, Blues won't.

They're a Green if: There's a lot of small talk, an effort to personalize the relationship even if it is business focused, an effort to put you at ease.

They're a Blue if: There is limited chitchat, a sense of distance, a desire to keep the relationship on a professional basis; if they are brief and terse, gets to the point, imparts a sense that they are appraising you.

3. Finally, everyone is either an Introvert or an Extrovert. Both may have good people skills, but they express themselves in different ways.

Extroverts are more talkative, speak in a louder voice, and gesticulate more. They may even speak before thinking and later change their mind.

Introverts listen more, tend to have more subdued energy, and gesticulate less. They think before answering and will rarely change their minds.

You can observe people's style while they are speaking and adjust your behavior accordingly. The benefit is that all will be more comfortable in your presence and listen to what you have to say.

Once you have an idea about someone's personality Color, you can begin to change the tone of your interactions. Two things will happen: You will get more help from your adversaries, and they will respect you more. You will come to appreciate their strengths, too (perhaps to the point of even liking them, a little).

Getting Along with the Other Colors at Work

Whether you are managing, selling to, motivating, or working with others, Color Q helps hone your approach. Use the tips below to change the tone of your communications with troublesome bosses and coworkers, and note the results. If you've accurately assessed their primary Color, the effects will be significant.

COMMUNICATING SMOOTHLY WITH GOLDS

When managing a Gold, give precise expectations, and then provide a stable environment with clear channels of communication and authority. You need to come across as decisive and organized, emphasizing firm procedures and deadlines. Then get out of the way and respect the Gold's unique ability to get things done.

When selling to, persuading, or working with a Gold, make sure you first have you own act together and any presentation or meeting will run smoothly. Be reliable enough to arrive at your meeting on time. At all costs, avoid vague information and abstract theories; stick with being factual, accurate, precise, and down to earth. Make your points sequentially. Avoid words like *feel* and *believe*. Use words like *tradition*, *respected*, and *proven*. Follow whatever procedures the Gold has requested. Respect the hierarchy of the Gold's department or company; if one says you have to talk to somebody else, he or she means it and is not blowing you off.

COMMUNICATING SMOOTHLY WITH BLUES

When managing a Blue, you need to be visionary in order to capture his or her interest. Explain how what you're doing will have an impact in the future—even have global consequences. Establish demanding goals or Blues will get bored and distracted. Debate with the Blue and don't take challenges personally; it's a sign you've got Blue's interest. Be open to making changes based on his or her insights and analytical skills. Above all, provide Blues an autonomous environment with minimal guidelines. They won't disappoint you.

When selling to, persuading, or working with a Blue, it is imperative to come across as competent or he or she will not respect you or your message. Present the "big picture" first and limit the facts, which dampen their interest. Show the long-term potential of new solutions. Don't become personally offended by anything Blues say. Respond with ingenuity and logic. Avoid words like *feel* and *believe*; use words like *think* and *know*.

COMMUNICATING SMOOTHLY WITH REDS

When managing a Red, face to face is always better. Memos and emails do not engage Reds. They need stimulation, fun, freedom, and independence to be on top of their game, so provide them with the most flexible and self-paced environment possible. Reds not only enjoy crises, they will create them if they are bored; so avoid meetings, rules, and memos where possible. Use a Red to solve problems and crises, and allow him or her to follow instincts. Reds are difficult to control and impossible to micromanage, but they will not disappoint you if you provide them the above conditions.

When selling to, persuading, or working with a Red, be brief and use action verbs like *stimulate, liven up, challenge, enjoy,* and *confront.* Hands-on demonstrations are way better than computer slideshows. For Reds, timing is everything, so don't continue if they're distracted. Acknowledge the distraction and ask to meet again later that day. Get to the point, avoid theories and frameworks, and stress the immediacy of your solutions. Be very flexible, open ended, and ready for fly-by-the-seat-of-your-pants decisions and fast closes.

COMMUNICATING SMOOTHLY WITH GREENS

When managing a Green, provide him or her with a harmonious environment and stress opportunities for personal growth. Greens become troubled and distracted by undue competition and personal conflict; minimize this among coworkers. Personalize your working relationship—ask about their families and pets in appropriate ways.

Be inspiring and positive. Work with them to establish a mutually accepted vision and allow them creative freedom to address it. Give frequent feedback, but keep it diplomatic; they are turned off by harsh criticism or fear tactics. They prefer to work collaboratively, so imposing strict hierarchies on Greens reduces productivity rather than increasing it, as with Golds.

When selling to, persuading, or working with a Green, above all personalize the relationship. Ask what he or she needs, then listen empathetically to the answer. Expect the Green's discussion to be nonsequential, but know that he or she will return to the original point. When presenting your product or solution, give the big picture and limit support facts, unless they communicate the impact on people. Use words like *feel, believe, value,* and *like.* Be insightful and idea driven, and stress innovative and future-driven solutions.

INTROVERT VERSUS EXTROVERT

Often you will be communicating with someone who is your opposite. If you find conversations getting cut short, this may be the reason. If you are an Extrovert speaking with an Introvert, just bring your energy level down a notch. Never jump in to fill an Introvert's silence, no matter how uncomfortable it makes you. One time, I let an Introvert think silently for seven minutes on the phone; he had constructed an entire conference panel for me with topic, speakers, and copy.

If you are an Introvert speaking with an Extrovert, raise your energy level a little, make eye contact, and ask questions to keep the dialogue going.

TAKING CONTROL OF YOUR WORK ENVIRONMENT

If you have assessed correctly the primary Color of your boss or coworker, you will see a dramatic and immediate improvement in your communications using these Color Q guidelines. Relationships will improve, tasks will be accomplished more smoothly, and teams will get less bogged down in conflict.

If following these tips does not produce much result, you need to reassess that person's primary Color or avoid behaviors typical of your own Color that create communication irritants. (One example: Trying to force a sequential conversation on a nonsequential-thinking Color.) The "Overall" Color chapters can assist.

Before you quit your job, try changing your approach to those who irritate you at work. At least you will add to your people skills. You may even get a promotion, salary increase, or find you already have the job of your dreams.

CHAPTER 25

Would I Make a Good Entrepreneur?

THERE ARE THREE answers to the question, "Would I make a good entrepreneur?"

1. All Colors can be entrepreneurs.

2. All Colors need the help of other Colors to succeed in their new venture.

3. Some Colors make better natural entrepreneurs than others (see figure 25–1).

The reason you need the other Colors on your entrepreneurial team is that natural entrepreneurs have their weaknesses and less-natural entrepreneurs have their strengths. So it's not where you start as an individual—it's the team you assemble that ultimately will make or break your venture.

FIGURE 25–1 *Colors as Entrepreneurs*

Colors that make the best entrepreneurs, starting with the most naturally gifted:

Reds

Blues

Golds

Greens

Remember, all Colors can be entrepreneurs because all need the help of the other Colors to succeed. Golds and Greens should partner with Reds and Blues to provide a balance of talent.

Here are the innate entrepreneurial styles of the four primary Colors. You also will have some of the strengths of your backup Color as well.

The Gold Entrepreneurial Style

HOW GOLDS SET GOALS

You are one of the best of all Colors at setting goals and making plans to achieve them. You prioritize, follow through, and evaluate progress effortlessly. What you are not good at is modifying your well-laid plans to adapt to changing circumstances.

Before casting your business plan in stone, run it by people you respect who are of other personality Colors. Ask them what additional options to consider, especially involving a work team or your family. Don't rush into it, even if you are excited and energized.

Then, schedule reevaluations at specific points along the way. Mark your calendar to sit back and reflect whether your goals are being met or you need to readjust them. You may be tempted to avoid this uncomfortable task; inviting a Blue or Green to help prevents procrastination. This one exercise could spell the difference between success and failure.

GOLDS AT THE START OF THE VENTURE

You are not one of the world's dreamers and schemers, but many Golds have come up with brilliant business ideas and gotten rich from them. At your core, you are driven to be a responsible overseer of people and resources, and this makes you a cautious risk taker. In your favor, you are not likely to be diverted by other opportunities, as Reds and Blues often are. You will rely on tried-and-true methodology to move predictably from one milestone to the next. Once in business, your first priority is establishing order. Systems and procedures are in place virtually from day one. The sooner you can create predictability in your business, whether in sales, manufactured inventory, or cash flow, the more comfortable you are.

Foreseeing and responding to changes in the marketplace will never be your forte, and handling unexpected crises is downright stressful to you. Make sure you have a Blue or Green on board to identify future trends that might impact your business. Get a Red to buffer you from the normal crises to which all young firms are subjected.

CASE STUDY ONE

The Rooneys—Father and Daughter Entrepreneur Team

Trisha Rooney Alden is president of R4 Services, LLC, a leading records-management company she formed over two decades ago. She always wanted to be an entrepreneur and has let little get in her way. This includes marriage, having two babies, and joining her husband in another city while keeping her business headquartered in Chicago. Shuttling between clients and family in some fifty trips a year utilized all her Gold organizational skills. She needed help.

Enter her father, Phil, former CEO of a public company who, of late, had been enjoying a stress-free life managing his investments. Today he comes into R4 Services at 5:30 every morning without getting paid. Why so early? "That's when the day starts operationally," he explains. "By 8 am clients have urgent needs and we need to respond to them in a timely fashion."

For Golds, family is key, and Phil truly enjoys the opportunity of helping his daughter fulfill her dreams (even in the early hours of dawn). Of course, he is quick to point out that she makes all the decisions. "R4 Services was a multi-million-dollar business when I came aboard," he stresses. "I just provide support and advice where needed."

Trish and Phil are both Gold backup Greens, and the firm's culture reflects this. For instance, Trish has a small cubicle rather than a large corner office. "I love it that way," she says. "I am out of the office a lot with clients; this way I get to hear everything that is going on," she adds, reflecting the Green need for connectivity.

In order to succeed in a business that handles intricate records management and destruction issues for some 600 clients, collaboration between father and daughter is key. So is listening to, and cultivating the opinions of, the service and warehouse staff. Phil picks up donuts each morning to ensure that the early arriving staff has something to eat.

Both father and daughter take great pride in the low turnover of their staff, noting 60 percent have been with the company for over ten years. They say one of their goals is to help employees have good lives and a great place to work. This is a classic example of how Gold/Greens attend to the practical needs of others.

Trish sees her top strengths as working well with people, listening deeply to clients to discover needs, communicating clearly, and always delivering what has been promised. All these strengths express her Gold/Green components. Clients are highly energizing to her. "I like to organize them," she says, "and to call them often to talk about present and future needs. They are my passion!"

What about stress areas? Pricing services and having clients negotiate downward are stressful, as are doing budgets and focusing on the financials of the business. These reflect her Green side, which dislikes confrontation and excessive work in the area of numbers. Here she relies on her father's thirty-plus years of business experience.

As two Gold/Greens, father and daughter have established an easy work relationship. He oversees operations, she focuses on new business development. The mutual respect is evident and contributes to the firm's steady growth.

Meanwhile, they are also actively involved in a wide range of philanthropic organizations involving children, museums, universities, and hospitals. In true Gold fashion, they welcome opportunities to take care of their community.

The Red Entrepreneurial Style

CASE STUDY TWO

Serial Entrepreneur: Jewelry to Toiletries to Home Textiles

The Red personality makes a good entrepreneur. Reds are very present-centered, able to see opportunities immediately. Red/Green Extroverts like Dianne Morris create linear career paths from seemingly less-than-linear opportunities.

In 1966, English major Dianne's law school plans were derailed by family economics. Undaunted, she found a special internship program at NASA. She spent the next half-decade as a contract specialist at NASA and the Jet Propulsion Laboratory.

She came to realize that legal work did not hold her interest. (The details of law can pose a problem for Reds, who need spontaneity and new challenges daily.) She did know she wanted the challenge of starting her own company.

She enrolled in design classes and started creating jewelry pieces using many unusual materials. "I think department stores were especially open to new designers and innovations in the 1970s," says Dianne.

She managed this company through a divorce and a move from Los Angeles to New York City. There she met John Chapman, who was importing soap from Spain and looking to distribute to hotels. As partners they created Miraflores Designs. In the 1980s, they designed, manufactured, and distributed coordinated lines of toiletries for Sheraton, Hyatt, and many other hotel chains.

In 1986, they sold Miraflores to an emerging public company, leaving Dianne the means to fund an "I Have a Dream" program for inner-city school children. In 1990, it also allowed her to buy Charles Bay, Inc., which sold flannel sheets to catalogs. "This was a rather low margin business. I evolved it into Bay Linens, Inc., which produced higher-end top-of-the-bed ensembles," Dianne says. Customers included Bloomingdale's, Horchow's, and Dillard's department stores.

Not every opportunity a Red identifies is a good fit, however. "I also acquired China Seas, a fabric company creating high-end fabrics for interior decorators," she says. "This proved to be too different and complex a market, so I sold it at a loss."

But collegial Reds value more than money. "I kept the license with a Japanese department store, which was a very enjoyable connection for many years," she says.

In a changing 2008 market, she licensed out the Bay Linens brand with an agreement for consulting to the new licensee. "In 2010, I started to investigate the idea of a website for women over 50. This became www.ZestNow.com, which publishes writers with information and inspiration."

Dianne's college English major interests emerged in editing and writing for the website. It's ideal for both her spontaneous Red and people-oriented Green personality traits. "This work can be done anywhere, anytime," she says. "I love the energy of new trends. Women over 50 and 60 form a new force, with lots of exciting activities and relevant ideas."

HOW REDS SET GOALS

Reds don't plan, they evolve. Planning is an ongoing process of flexible decisions. You set goals by instinct, always ready to turn on a dime. The ability to change direction based on market needs is a very real strength. But setting real goals that others must work on is a challenge. Set short-term targets; your people will have a clearer direction, and immediate successes energize you.

REDS AT THE START OF A VENTURE

Reds are the born entrepreneurs of the world but need the right circumstances to thrive. You are natural risk takers, negotiators, and crisis managers, skills that are critical in the startup phase of a venture. You excel as long as what you are doing is in demand and business is brisk. When a venture ceases to be fun and stimulating, your attention wanders. However, in crisis mode you excel, coolly managing the situation long after others have caved in.

Reds are impatient with formal education and prefer practical knowledge. These street smarts serve you well in new ventures. When interested, you become a real specialist in your field, with or without formal training. You see rules and procedures as guidelines only and never feel particularly bound by them (to the chagrin of any Gold partners).

Your freedom of thought lets you surf the marketplace with fresh ideas and new ways of responding to customer desires. A Green will help you market those terrific ideas and get your promotional tasks done quickly. Conventional ways are the last thing on your mind when beginning a new project. Strategic thinking and organizational skills ultimately are needed, however. Bring a Blue on board to help with strategy and a Gold to organize your office.

The Blue Entrepreneurial Style

HOW BLUES SET GOALS

You're a natural at strategizing, creating plans, and refining them along the way. Too much complexity is your goal-setting blind spot. Be sure to add practical details and concrete steps to your business plan. You won't enjoy it, but it will help keep you realistic about your plans.

CASE STUDY THREE

Bagels for Everybody

Nordahl "Nord" Brue is the founder of the Bruegger's Bagel chain. Like many Blues, he excels at combining passion, good ideas, and financial business acumen into single entrepreneurial ideas. Others see him as both intense and playful. "He is a deep thinker," says Chris Dutton, former CEO of Green Mountain Power, "who can analyze issues on several different fronts."

Recognizing the many skills required to run a successful venture, Nord always partners with someone whose talents enhance his own. Always a few steps ahead of national trends, in the early 1980s he saw the potential of turning bagels—then a niche, urban product—into a "quick service" food concept that would appeal to a national audience. Brue's strategy was to start in secondary and suburban markets, far away from metropolitan centers like New York, Philadelphia, and Chicago where bagels were well known, in order to test the economic feasibility while educating his customers' tastes.

Brue was right. By the mid-1990s, Bruegger's had grown into almost 500 stores throughout the country and ushered in the first "healthy alternative" quick-food concept. He sold the company in 1996 for a stock trade worth $123 million, rebought the company for $45 million a year later, and resold it again for an undisclosed amount in 2000.[1]

Brue has since chaired Franklin Foods, a soft, unripened-cheese manufacturer. While excited about its potential, he's not wedded to it, or any company he builds. "If Kraft says we have to have it, if it's worth more to them than to me, then I'll do a new thing," he told *Vermont Business Magazine* in January 2004.[2] Brue, at the time of our interview, was also chairman of four boards, which he thoroughly enjoys. "I am always better at dealing with the big picture," he says, "which is another way of saying I am not great at the details. My mission is to get these companies to articulate a vision that will take them to the next level—I find that very exciting," he says, in typical Blue fashion.

BLUES AT THE START OF A VENTURE

Many a Blue has launched a successful business off limited information or a hunch. It's the ideas that excite you, and you're at the peak of your talents when creating and refining them. You understand and accept that risks are part of the deal, and you are well able to cope with them.

Daily routine makes you restless; your style is to handle many projects at once. Seeing new trends in the marketplace is an entrepreneurial strength. But it can be a weakness in attempting to actually get things done.

Fortunately, Blues delegate freely and rely on other Colors instinctively. You're the idea person, and you want others to handle the people, procedures, and controls. Make sure you get a Green on board to tap substantial people and promotional skills, a Red to move things along, and a Gold to set up those needed procedures.

The Green Entrepreneurial Style

HOW GREENS SET GOALS

For you, goals and plans are changeable, depending on whatever is exciting to you at the moment. Prioritizing is problematic for you, especially when two or more exciting things compete for your attention. The process and the people you meet along the way are more important to you than final outcomes.

You will stick to a goal if it helps you find your deepest possible satisfaction. If you can stick to a (relatively) permanent core goal, especially one that reflects your personal values, underlying goals will be more achievable and less of a distraction.

Other Colors will criticize and pressure you into making rigid, financially oriented plans "to keep your business on the right track." You will not complete these plans and will frustrate those who depend on you to set direction. You must have the ability to make legitimate detours while keeping sight of the ultimate destination. More than any other Color, you need to partner with a friend, preferably a Gold or Red, who can ground you in the present when needed. You do best when collaborating with other Colors.

CASE STUDY FOUR

Restaurant Owner

You are an entrepreneur at heart if you have tons of ideas for improving every company that hires you. During Sasha Fitzroy's twenty-eight-year career as an event planner, one fact bothered her: customer service was rarely prioritized.

"Customers were expected to accept mediocre food, materials, even venues," she recalls. "Where were the new customers coming from when disillusioned ones stopped coming? An extra $10 upgrade in food or service would produce hundreds or thousands of dollars in repeat business; but the bean counters couldn't track it, so they ignored it."

Sasha dealt with these front-line complaints directly and yearned to start a business where she could test her customer-service theories. She got her chance in her fifties, when she and her husband opened a Connecticut breakfast and lunch café on a sleepy, small-town Main Street with not much chance of walk-in trade.

"I knew we would have to create a destination business," she says. "What better way to do that than to implement my long-held customer-service values?"

Sasha set out to call all her customers by name instead of number, quickly learning the names of regulars. She brought food to the table instead of requiring customers to pick it up, surveying their further needs as she did so. She made personal connections wherever she saw an appropriate opportunity.

"My mission statement became, 'I want each customer to walk out the door happier than when they came in,'" she says. "People yearn for true welcome, acceptance, and hospitality; to be treated as special."

It worked. Almost 60 percent of independent restaurants fail or are sold after three years.[3] "Next year will be our fifteenth anniversary," this people-oriented Green states proudly. Sasha now passes her customer-service values on to her four new employees.

GREENS AT THE START OF A VENTURE

Greens are less motivated by material gain than other Colors. You prefer to provide value and express your creative energies in whatever business situation stimulates you. Sometimes that will be an entrepreneurial venture, most often prompted by a change in employment status, a disagreement with the practices of an employer, or the need for a family-oriented work schedule.

The ability to create value is both your strength and your blind spot. You will build an extremely loyal clientele, but often think little of sacrificing profit margin to achieve a certain quality of product or service. This loyal clientele, however, is the heart of your business success. High customer loyalty and low staff turnover often get a Green enterprise through rough times when other companies fail.

Your superior abilities to promote and market get you noticed quickly. A Green company often takes off fast but then needs the tough negotiating skills of Reds and the business systems implemented by Golds to survive in the fast lane. You also have the added frustration that your considerable people and communications skills are underestimated by other Colors, who want you to focus on the balance sheet rather than the customer base.

CHAPTER 26

Money and Compensation

FOR ALL COLOR Q personalities, money itself is either a mirror of self-worth or a means to an end. But how we negotiate our salaries, manage our budgets, and save for important goals is very much driven by our primary and secondary Color Q personalities. Each Color has a different and unique competence when handling this all-important aspect of life. Your natural Color Q salary negotiating and investment styles have been researched by author Shoya Zichy for over a decade with close to 4,000 people. Some of her proprietary results are being made available here now, and only in this book.

Greens and Money

Given a choice, Greens prefer to deal with other things in life. When supporting just yourself, you see money as a tool to further your own personal development and create aesthetic surroundings. The rabid pursuit of riches usually turns you off. If you are the breadwinner, however, your attitude and involvement change rapidly. People you care about depend on you, and you will learn what it takes to provide for them.

Greens approach money in one of two predictable ways: you are either focused or spontaneous. Focused Green/Golds take a disciplined approach to saving for significant life goals like retirement. Spontaneous Green/Reds are sporadic savers and planners at best and innately high-risk takers when investing. While Green/Reds seem unlikely to ever accumulate enough to retire, you are supported by your almost psychic ability to predict investment trends.

Both types of Greens develop warm, trusting relationships with advisors or financial planners, serving as excellent sources of referrals.

You want to hear how a company impacts people more than about its analytics before investing in its stock. Social investments are of particular interest to you.

GREEN/GOLDS

Compensation When negotiating a compensation package, usually you do not push hard enough. If you like the job and the people, and a reasonable number is offered, you'll take it. This often means you have folded too early in the negotiation. You may even accept a salary lower than you want just to get the job.

Tips Don't be so nice. Research what you are worth and practice negotiating, preferably with a Red friend. You have a right to expect reasonable compensation for the value you provide. The other side expects you to play the game, and you'll leave money on the table if you don't. It will never feel natural, but you can learn the game and play it well.

GREEN/REDS

Compensation The money a job pays is not your top priority. Does the job help you grow? Does it allow you to express your creativity? Then lucky you, you've hit the jackpot, and whatever it pays you is icing on the cake. You expect people to notice your good work and increase your salary accordingly. Of all the Colors, you need the most practice before walking into a salary negotiation because you truly hate to argue, especially about money.

Tips As with the Green/Golds above, practice with a tough-minded friend how to play the chess game of salary negotiations. Don't accept the first amount offered. Have a well-researched counteroffer in mind. **This is the one time in your life when it's okay not to be nice.** Make a list of things you could buy with the extra money you negotiate; this will provide incentive. If the salary remains low, suggest extra time off, a company vehicle, a private office, or free health insurance for your family instead. Use phrases like, "With my qualifications, I am expecting X." You deserve to be compensated in a way that means something to you for the value you provide.

Reds and Money

Reds are the risk takers of the investment world, especially when you feel you have sufficient knowledge and disposable income. As in other areas of life, you like to operate by your own rules. You can become quite adept at dealing in the stock (and other) markets.

Your strength is picking up investment cues others miss. You'll benefit from your acute powers of observation and the broad storehouse of practical knowledge you've accumulated since birth. These, combined with your above-average flexibility, create opportunities you pounce on with good timing.

More than other Colors, you prefer to invest in individual stocks rather than mutual funds unless handling family money. Advisors to you are a source of research, execution, and record keeping. Detailed planning just gets in the way of plunging into interesting investments.

Your savings account, if it exists, is likely to be starved for attention. You tend not to save. You simply don't obsess about money and figure it will be earned as needed.

RED/BLUES

Compensation For you, tomorrow is another day to earn another dollar. It's likely you have been through both rich and lean times. Your aggressive negotiating style works well in compensation discussions. In fact, other Colors come to you for advice before walking into salary negotiations.

RED/GREENS

Compensation You are a good negotiator, but your style is more relaxed than that of Red/Blues. You also feel tomorrow is another day to earn another dollar, and you can live on a lot of money or a little. You won't, however, leave any money or benefits on the table during salary negotiations.

Blues and Money

Blues use money as proof of competence. The higher your salary, the more competent the world sees you. More than other Colors, you understand money in the abstract as a flow rather than a stagnant resource. But Blue/Golds and Blue/Reds differ in their approaches to money. Where Blue/Golds are disciplined savers, Blue/Reds typically are not.

In your favor, you are intrigued by complex asset-allocation strategies that determine how much to invest in stocks, bonds, and other vehicles. You will benefit in real returns from this ability. Against you is your overconfidence.

Because you are more likely than most to research and understand all the components of your portfolio, you forget that markets are not always rational.

BLUE/GOLDS

Compensation You know exactly how much you are worth before you walk in the door to interview. You will drive compensation negotiations to their highest possible level, leaving no money or benefit issue unexplored. Other Colors come to you for advice before their salary negotiations.

BLUE/REDS

Compensation You know what you're worth, what's available, and how to get it. You relax into the process and enjoy the give-and-take of it. Often the people with whom you've negotiated give you far more than they were intending and come away feeling good about it. You are perhaps the smoothest negotiator of all the Colors, leaving nothing on the table, and agreeably removing the chairs as well.

Golds and Money

There's a reason your group was named the Golds. Money is extremely important to your sense of security. You are highly focused on saving and long-term planning and fully in control of your cash flow at all times. You abhor the misuse of money and rarely go into debt or squander the assets you have.

Your investments have to be well-researched, backed by a solid track record, and fully documented with concrete facts. As long as investments meet these criteria, you'll invest directly in the market; but mutual funds are a popular option for Golds. You want your portfolio to be your passport to a worry-free future, and you are likely to achieve this goal early in life.

You have a limited tolerance for risk and volatility, favoring time-tested strategies. Fixed-income instruments like bonds and Guaranteed Investment Contracts make you comfortable in a portfolio balanced with blue-chip stocks.

Financially, you are a meticulous record keeper. You can reconcile the accuracy of your accounts without the assistance of intermediaries. You prefer working with well-established firms, insisting upon advisors who are organized and consistent and produce predictable results.

GOLD/BLUES

Compensation You are a focused and tough negotiator, having researched what you're worth well in advance. Gold/Blues can be prone to bag-person syndrome, the fear you will wind up penniless on the streets. Because you feel your security is on the line, you accept nothing less than everything there is to get.

GOLD/GREENS

Compensation Although you, too, have the bag-person syndrome suffered by your Gold/Blue cousins, it doesn't drive your negotiation process as strongly. Typically, you won't push the envelope as hard at salary negotiations. Consequently, you may leave the bargaining table with a sinking feeling that you will not be making the money you deserve, unable to allay the lurking bag person in your mind.

Tip You are organized enough to have researched what the market pays for your skills but are likely to accept a lesser amount after one counteroffer. Role play with a willing Gold/Blue, or any Red, to help you find strategies and phrases with which you are comfortable. A Red/Green is particularly likely to have a style you can emulate.

PART 7

CREATING
A CUSTOMIZED
ROADMAP FOR YOUR
PROFESSIONAL LIFE

CHAPTER 27

A Roadmap for Putting It All Together

THIS IS A DIARY area for those who want to record notes on the material provided in this book. You can collect the ideas you want to revisit here, so you don't have to go looking through the chapters again. It's an excellent place to centralize the information collected during a job search.

List your top three work-related strengths here (choose from figure 1 in your personality's chapter).

1.

2.

3.

List your top three ideal work environment conditions (choose from figure 2 in your personality's chapter).

1.

2.

3.

List your top three characteristics of an ideal boss (choose from figure 3 in your personality's chapter).

1.

2.

3.

List five careers that you would like to research. (If you are already in the workforce, include at least one that is different than what you are doing now. If you are a student, choose one that is out of the pattern of your proposed career path. Eliminate all careers you feel you *ought* to pursue and include only those you'd *enjoy* pursuing.)

1.

2.

3.

4.

5.

For each of the five careers you chose above, do the following steps:

1. Look up that career on the government's website https://www.onet - online.org.

2. Print out the activities and skills required for that career.

3. Compare these activities and skills against your profile's description of the ideal job. How well do they match?

4. Determine if you are you an Introvert or an Extrovert. Does the level of people contact seem energizing or draining to you?

5. Research the educational requirements. Do you need more schooling?

6. Look at the bottom of the web page for the salary. Could you live comfortably on it?

7. Identify several companies you'd like to work for, listing pros and cons.

8. Make a contact list—call or ask people you know for the name and number of the right person to contact at your preferred companies, and if possible research job openings before inquiring. Usually within six random inquiries you will find someone who can make an introduction.

Review your desire to be an entrepreneur:

1. List your top three entrepreneurial strengths as defined in your primary Color section of chapter 25, "Would I Make a Good Entrepreneur?"

2. List your top three concerns about being an entrepreneur. Do a reality check. Talk to several entrepreneurs in your community and ask how they addressed these concerns. Most will be happy to talk with you.

3. List the skills you don't have to be an entrepreneur. Next to each, make notes on how you would get help with these. List the Colors with whom you would need to partner (check your Entrepreneurial Style).

If you don't have a clue what you want to do:

Think of a time you had a peak experience. What were you doing and why were you successful?

What topics of conversation do you find fascinating?

To what kinds of magazines and articles are you drawn?

What recreational activities/hobbies do you enjoy most or have you thought about starting?

Where are you on the stability versus change and risk scale? Place an X at the appropriate point on the scale.

Want/Need Security //_____0_____ // Will Take Risks

Choose three careers that incorporate these interests and skills. (If you're good at something, like acting, don't think you just have to be an actor. Presenting skills and high ability to focus are skills used in such areas as teaching, sales, and corporate training.)

Job-search highlights.

Networking notes.

People to thank/acknowledge.

Company research notes.

Resume reality check.

   1. Run your resume by friends or family of different Color groups.

   2. Go to the Resource section at the back of this book for helpful websites.

List your top five interviewing strengths and read before your appointment for encouragement (select from the "Interviewing Style" section of your personality's chapter).

List your top three interviewing weaknesses and ideas for addressing them (select from the "Interviewing Style" section of your personality's chapter).

Compensation research notes.

Compensation negotiation strategies to employ (read before your appointment).

And finally, ways to have fun while job hunting. Creative strategies for getting attention, rewards for doing something difficult, contacting old friends—make your personal list and do it all.

We leave you with the Ladder of Success; use Color Q to help you climb to the top.

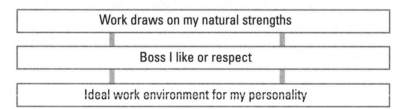

| Work draws on my natural strengths |
| Boss I like or respect |
| Ideal work environment for my personality |

Having the above will make you successful. Later, if you can tap into your passion or compelling interest as well, you will be truly outstanding. Enjoy your journey.

| My primary passion or compelling interest |

NOTES

CHAPTER 3

1. N. S. Gill, "Four Humors/Hippocratic Method and the Four Humors in Medicine," updated July 2016, accessed Dec. 8, 2016, www.ancienthistory.about.com/cs/hippocrates/a/hippocraticmeds.htm?rd=1.

2. Norman Winski, *Understanding Jung* (Los Angeles: Sherbourne Press, 1971), 10, 329.

3. Myers-Briggs Type Indicator® and MBTI® are trademarks of the Myers-Briggs Type Indicator Trust in the United States and other countries.

CHAPTER 4

1. Sumit Agarwal, Souphala Chomsisengphet, Neale Mahoney, and Johannes Stroebel, "The Impact of Consumer Financial Regulation Evidence from the Card Act," *Microeconomic Insights*, updated Dec. 15, 2015, accessed Dec. 9, 2016, http://microeconomicinsights.org/the-impact-of-consumer-financial-regulation-evidence-from-the-card-act/#note-274-2.

2. Megan Bungeroth, "East Sider of the Year," *Our Town*, Mar. 29, 2012, 20.

3. Mary Milliken, "Angelina Jolie Receives Humanitarian Award from Academy," *Cyclical Consumer Goods*, Nov. 17, 2013.

4. Joyce Chen, "Angelina Jolie References Her Kids as She Visits Refugee Camp in Jordan: 'It Breaks My Heart,'" *USWeekly online*, Sept. 9, 2016, www.usmagazine.com/celebrity-news/news/angelina-jolie-references-her-kids-on-visit-to-jordan-refugee-camp-w438980.

CHAPTER 5

1. "Top Women in Wealth Management, 2009–2015," *Wealth Manager Magazine*.

2. "Top Women-Owned Businesses, 2013–2014," *Crain's New York.*

3. "Fastest 50 Growing Businesses," *Crain's, New York,* Oct. 2013.

CHAPTER 9

1. Donald Trump and Tony Schwartz, *Trump: The Art of the Deal* (New York: Random House, 1987), p 1, and paperback edition from Ballantine Books, 2015.

2. Ibid., p 40 in 1987 Random House hardback edition, and p 63 in the Ballantine Books paperback edition.

3. David Von Drehle, "The Making of President Donald Trump," *Time,* Nov. 9, 2016, http://time.com/4564440/donald-trump-wins-2/.

4. Ibid.

5. Charlotte Triggs. Available on https://www.scribd.com/article/330831225/Donald-J-Trump-Victory-Against-The-Odds"

6. Ibid.

7. Ibid.

8. Patricia Beard, *Growing Up Republican* (New York: HarperCollins, 1996), 196–197.

CHAPTER 11

1. Bunny Williams, *An Affair with a House* (New York: Stewart, Tabori and Chang, 2005); *Bunny Williams' Point of View* (New York: Stewart, Tabori and Chang, 2007); *Bunny Williams' Scrapbook for Living* (New York: Stewart, Tabori and Chang, 2010); *Bunny Williams on Garden Style* (New York: Stewart, Tabori and Chang, 2015); Bunny Williams, with Christian Brechneff, Page Dickey, Jane Garney, Schafer Gil, Roxana Robinson, and Angus Wilkie, *A House by the Sea* (New York: Abrams, 2016).

CHAPTER 14

1. Evan Thomas, "Bill and Hillary's Long, Hot Summer," *Newsweek,* Oct. 19, 1998, 38.

2. Ibid., 41.

3. Lucinda Franks, "The Intimate Hillary," *Talk,* Sept. 1999, 174.

4. David Keirsey and Ray Choiniere, *Presidential Temperament* (Del Mar, CA: Prometheus Nemesis, 1999), appendix.

5. James Bennett, "The Next Clinton," *New York Times,* May 30, 1999, 26.

6. "The Wealthiest in America," Forbes 400: The Wealthiest In America/2016 Ranking, www.forbes.com/profile/elon-musk/.

7. Ibid.

8. Charles Schwab Corporation website, Press section, Resources, The Charles Schwab Corporation, Corporate Fact Sheet, Oct. 31, 2016, www.aboutschwab.com/about.

9. Terence P. Pare, *Fortune*, June 1, 1992, accessed Feb. 20, 2006, www.highbeam.com.

10. Betsy Morris, "Charles Schwab's Big Challenge," *Fortune*, May 2005, accessed Feb. 20, 2006, www.highbeam.com.

11. Ibid.

12. Ibid.

13. Rebecca McReynolds, "Doing It the Schwab Way," *U.S. Banker*, July 1, 1998, accessed Dec. 12, 2016, www.highbeam.com/doc/1G1-20940228.html.

14. "Charles and Helen Schwab Foundation," accessed Dec. 12, 2016, www.schwabfoundation.org.

CHAPTER 20

1. Robert Kurson, "Mellody Hobson, Thirty-Three, Is a Financier with a Big Dream: To Teach the Poor How to Be Rich, One Classroom at a Time," (The Benefactor)," *Esquire Magazine*, Dec. 1, 2001, accessed Dec. 21, 2005, www.highbeam.com.

2. Noah Jackson, "The New Breed," *Time*, Dec. 20, 2004, accessed Dec. 21, 2005, www.highbeam.com.

CHAPTER 25

1. Joyce Marcel, "Profiles in Business," *Vermont Business Magazine*, Jan. 2004, 17.

2. Ibid., 23.

3. Randy White, "The Truth About Restaurant Failure Rates," Randy White's Blog, White Hutchinson Leisure and Learning Group, Feb. 24, 2011, accessed Dec. 12, 2016, www.whitehutchinson.com/blog/2011/02/the-truth-about-restaurant-failure-rates/.

BIBLIOGRAPHY AND RESOURCES

Bibliography

BOOKS: GENERAL

Beard, Patricia. *Growing Up Republican*. New York: HarperCollins, 1996.

Trump, Donald, and Schwartz. *Trump: The Art of the Deal*. New York: Random House, 1987.

Winski, Norman. *Understanding Jung*. Los Angeles: Sherbourne Press, 1971.

BOOKS ON CAREER DEVELOPMENT

Ancowitz, Nancy. *Self-Promotion for Introverts®: The Quiet Guide to Getting Ahead*. New York: McGraw-Hill, 2010.

Bolles, Richard. *What Color Is Your Parachute? 2016: A Practical Manual for Job-Hunters and Career-Changers*. New York: Ten Speed Press, 2015.

Davidds, Yasmin, with Ann Bidou. *Your Own Terms: A Woman's Guide to Taking Charge of Any Negotiation*. New York: AMACOM, 2015.

Markel, Adam. *Pivot: The Art and Science of Reinventing Your Career and Life*. New York: Atria Books, 2016.

BOOKS ON THE MYERS-BRIGGS TYPE INDICATOR AND TEMPERAMENT PERSONALITY MODELS

Berens, Linda V. *Understanding Yourself and Others: An Introduction to the 4 Temperaments*. Huntington Beach, CA: Telos Publications, 2010.

Demarest, L. *Looking at Type in the Workplace*. Gainesville, FL: Center for Applications of Psychological Type, 1997.

Dunning, Donna. *What's Your Type of Career?* Boston: Nicholas Brealey, 2010.

Hammer, Allen. *Introduction to Type and Careers, Career Management and Counseling*. 2nd ed. Mountain View, CA: CPP, Inc., 1994.

Hirsh, Sandra, and Jean Kummerow. *Introduction to Type in Organizations.* Palo Alto, CA: CPP, Inc., 1998.

Keirsey, David. *Please Understand Me 2.* Del Mar, CA: Prometheus Nemesis, 1998.

Kroeger, Otto, Janet Thuesen, and Hile Rutledge. *Type Talk: Type Talk at Work.* New York: Delta, 2002.

Martin, Charles R. *Quick Guide to the 16 Personality Types and Career Mastery.* Huntington Beach, CA: Telos Publications, 2003.

Myers, Isabel Briggs, with Peter Myers. *Gifts Differing.* Palo Alto, CA: CPP, Inc., 1980, 1995.

Myers, Katharine D., and Linda K. Kirby. *Introduction to Type: Introduction to Type Dynamics and Development.* Palo Alto, CA: CPP, Inc., 1987, 1994.

Quenk, Naomi. *Was That Really Me?* Palo Alto, CA: CPP, Inc., 2002.

Tieger, Paul D., Barbara Barron, and Kelly Tieger. *Do What You Are.* New York: Little, Brown, 2014.

Zichy, Shoya, with Ann Bidou. *Personality Power.* New York: AMACOM, 2013.

ADDITIONAL BOOKS AND RESOURCES ON THE MBTI AND TEMPERAMENTS

American Management Association *www.amanet.org*
Offers Myers-Briggs Type Indicator (MBTI) certification training.

Center for Applications of Psychological Type *www.capt.org*
Provides training and consulting services for professionals and the public. Also publishes type-related materials, compiles research to advance the understanding of type, and maintains the Isabel Briggs Myers Memorial Library.

**Consulting Psychologist Press, Inc. (CPP)
and Davies-Black® Publishing** *www.cpp.com*
The publisher and distributor of the MBTI instrument and related materials. CPP also publishes business and career books and provides training and consulting services for organizations.

Keirsey Temperament Theory *www.keirsey.com*
Publishes and represents the work of David Keirsey and others specializing in temperament theory.

OKA (formerly Otto Kroeger Associates) *www.oka-online.com*
Management consulting firm that offers a variety of training programs, seminars, materials, and books based on the MBTI, temperament theory, and psychological type.

Psychometrics Canada Ltd. *www.psychometrics.com*
Offers assessments, seminars, and ongoing research for organizational development.

Type Resources *www.type-resources.com*
Provides workshops, training, and consulting on the MBTI for leadership and team development.

Resources

ASSESSMENTS, GENERAL COUNSELING, AND INFORMATION CENTERS

www.ColorQPersonalities.com
Provides access to the author's resources.

The U.S. Department of Labor and the National O*NET Consortium
online.onetcenter.org.
Provide information on an extensive range of careers, including job functions, required skills, related subfields, median salary, projected growth rate, and more.

www.careercc.org. Career Counselors Consortium is an organization of professional career counselors who work with clients on job search, resume development, assessment, career change, and performance coaching. Nationwide consultations are by phone or in person in the New York tri-state area.

www.acpinternational.org. The Association of Career Professionals International is a global nonprofit organization with members in over thirty chapters in the United States and abroad who provide lifelong career coaching related services.

www.jocrf.org. The Johnson O'Connor Research Foundation is a nonprofit scientific research and educational organization that administers a proprietary battery of tests to measure people's natural aptitudes in eleven areas to help them make decisions about school and work. These measured traits are highly stable over long-term periods. For information about locations in eleven cities, check the website.

COLLEGE/FIRST JOB ENTRY-LEVEL SITES

www.campuscareercenter.com

www.experience.com

GENERAL JOB BANKS

www.bestjobsusa.com. A comprehensive site.

www.careerbuilder.com. Recruitment center for over thirty-five U.S. newspapers.

www.hotjobs.com. Central resume database where companies search.

www.interbiznet.com/hunt/companies. Useful when checking the job-site pages of individual companies.

www.jobbankusa.com

www.monster.com. The largest job/resume bank.

www.nationjob.com

www.nydailynews.com. New York Daily News want ads.

www.nytimes.com/yr/mo/day/jobmarket. New York Times want ads.

www.truecareers.com. Includes a contest that wipes away your student loan.

OVERALL CAREER ADVICE AND JOB SEARCH

academy.justjobs.com/careers/

www.careeronestop.org/Toolkit/ACINet.aspx

www.careerchangecentralLLC.com

www.indeed.com

www.themuse.com

www.mynextmove.org

www.evilhrlady.org

www.vault.com

SPECIFIC NICHE JOB SITES

Advertising, public relations, and graphic arts: *www.creativehotlist.com; www.prweek.net*

Home employment: *www.homejobstop.com*

Engineering: *www.engineerjobs.com*

Freelance professional services: *www.freelance.com*

Human resources: *www.HR.com*; *www.evilhrlady.org*

Legal: *www.legalstaff.com*

Nonprofit: *www.idealist.com*

Pharmaceuticals: *www.RXcareerCenter.com*

Older workers: *www.aarp.org*; *www.seniorjobbank.com*

Sales professional: *www.jobs4sales.com*; *www.NASP.com*

Teaching: *www.higherEdjobs.com*

Women only: *www.careerwomen.com*

INDUSTRY/COMPANY RESEARCH
www.downside.com. Direct access to latest company financials.

www.vault.com. Well-presented reports on different sectors.

www.wetfeet.com. Industry profiles plus much more.

SALARY INFORMATION
www.salary.com

CAREER SEARCH TOOLS AND STRATEGIES
www.bls.gov/ooh. U.S. Labor Department occupational outlook handbook.

www.myreferences.com. Will check your references for you.

www.nycareerzone.org. Supported by New York State Department of Labor.

www.oalj.dol.gov/libdot.htm. Dictionary of Occupational Titles.

www.rileyguide.com/jobs.html. Should visit at least once for advice on job search.

RESUME PREPARATION
www.jobstar.org/tools/resume/index.htm

www.pongoresume.com

www.winway.com

OTHER RESOURCES
www.volunteermatch.org. Find out about volunteer opportunities; could jump-start your next career.

INDEX

ABOUT THE AUTHORS

Shoya Zichy has made five career changes within the wealth-management, journalism, and training industries in order to find the work that draws on her most natural skills. She finds that by following your passion, you create a unique brand that, in turn, effortlessly attracts the attention of others. Her work has been featured in *Fortune, Barron's, Newsday,* the *Chicago Sun-Times, US 1,* and the *Washington Post,* and on CNN, among other media outlets. She is a frequent speaker and seminar leader, and her client list includes Bank of America, Deloitte & Touche, Merrill Lynch, Northern Trust, Prudential, UBS, and the U.S. Treasury. She lives in Pennsylvania and is the author of *Women and the Leadership Q* and *Personality Power.* Her books are available in Arabic, Chinese, Korean, and Vietnamese.

For more information, visit her website at www.ColorQPersonalities.com.

Ann Bidou has published hundreds of articles and written regularly for publications such as the *Chicago Tribune.* She also coauthored *Personality Power* with Shoya Zichy in 2013 and *Your Own Terms* with Yasmin Davidds, Psy.D., in 2015, both for AMACOM. She has long been a student of Zichy's Color Q system, and it has changed her life from Wall Street executive to award-winning author and small business owner in the Berkshires. She lives in Falls Village, Connecticut.